A Cultural Approach to Discourse

Also by Shi-xu

CULTURAL REPRESENTATIONS

READ THE CULTURAL OTHER
(coedited with M. Kienpointner and J. Servaes)

Journal edited by Shi-xu

JOURNAL OF MULTICULTURAL DISCOURSES

A Cultural Approach to Discourse

Shi-xu
Professor of Discourse and Cultural Studies
Zhejiang University, China

First published 2005 by
PALGRAVE MACMILLAN
Houndmills, Basingstoke, Hampshire RG21 6XS and 175 Fifth Avenue, New York, N.Y. 10010
Companies and representatives throughout the world

PALGRAVE MACMILLAN is the global academic imprint of the Palgrave Macmillan division of St. Martin's Press, LLC and of Palgrave Macmillan Ltd. Macmillan® is a registered trademark in the United States, United Kingdom and other countries. Palgrave is a registered trademark in the European Union and other countries.

ISBN 1–4039–4334–6

This book is printed on paper suitable for recycling and made from fully managed and sustained forest sources.

A catalogue record for this book is available from the British Library.

Library of Congress Cataloging-in-Publication Data
Shi-xu
    A cultural approach to discourse / Shi-xu.
       p.   cm.
    Includes bibliographical references and index.
    ISBN 1–4039–4334–6 (cloth)
    1. Discourse analysis – Social aspects.   2. Language and culture.
I. Title.

P302.84.S538 2004
306.44 – dc22

2004054294

10 9 8 7 6 5 4 3 2 1
14 13 12 11 10 09 08 07 06 05

Printed and bound in Great Britain by
Antony Rowe Ltd, Chippenham and Eastbourne

To Sander
and
your future cultural life

National
College of
Ireland

IFSC
Mayor Street
Dublin 1
Ireland
international@ncirl.ie
International Office

Contents

Preface and Acknowledgements   ix

Introduction   1

Part I   Theory and Methodology

1 Discourse and Reality   13
  Introduction   13
  Representationalism   14
  A reality-constitutive view of discourse   18
  Meaning and context   33
  Conclusion   40

2 Discourse and Culture   42
  Introduction   42
  The universalist discourse   44
  Critical studies of culture   51
  Theorizing from in-between cultures   57
  A pluralist account of discourse   59
  The goals of CAD   67
  Conclusion   68

3 Political Ethnography   71
  Introduction   71
  Foundationalism versus interpretivism   74
  An in-between cultural stance   86
  Discourse research strategies   90
  Conclusion   100

Part II Practical Studies

4 Deconstructing the Other Place   105
  Introduction   105
  The construction of the Other Place and contradiction   107
  Imperialist pleasure and prejudice   111
  Conclusion   129

5 **Reading Non-Western Discourses**   132
   Introduction   132
   Discourse and reading cultural others   133
   Contextualizing research on non-Western discourse   139
   Making sense out of the Other's accounts   144
   Conclusion   162

6 **Fanning the Sparks of Hope from History**   165
   Introduction   165
   Identity: a historical-comparative approach   167
   The reconstitution of historical data   173
   Analysing discourses of identity   175
   Conclusion   196

7 **Promoting New Discourses of the Other**   199
   Introduction   199
   Intercultural studies   200
   Power in intercultural communication   202
   Formulating and warranting new discourses of cultural others   204
   Conclusion   210

Notes   212

References   216

Author Index   228

Subject Index   231

Preface and Acknowledgements

I have intended this book first of all for students and teachers in discourse studies (including discourse analysis, speech communication and media studies). For them, I have tried, among other things, to advocate a culturally pluralist, in particular in-between-cultural, approach to language, communication and discourse. Moreover, I have meant this book for researchers and scholars in the other social sciences, particularly cultural studies. For them, I have tried to introduce a more language-oriented approach to their subject matter, be it social, cultural or psychological. Finally, I hope that the contemporary culturalist endeavour will provide stimulation for opening up new cultural research to those individuals who sense the profound importance of interacting with worldviews, theories, methods, issues, topics and data other than those of their own cultures.

I would like to express my gratitude to Lee Cherleng and Manfred Kienpointner for supplying some of the analytical data used in Chapter 5, and to David Pettigrew and Niall Burns at the University of Ulster for providing information support. I must also acknowledge the gracious assistance of my students in the Netherlands, Singapore and the United Kingdom in collecting some of the data for this book. I gratefully acknowledge that parts of chapters 5 and 7 have appeared in my papers published in the *Journal of International Communication* (co-author, 2003, 9:2) and *Journal of Intercultural Studies* (2001, 22:3) respectively. But these chapters are much expanded and revised versions.

In writing this book I have benefited literally from people all over the world, in particular those from the Netherlands, Singapore and the United Kingdom where I have lived and researched for the past 15 years. Their influence manifests in the book in more ways than they might even realize. Going back to the details here would probably embarrass them. I can only mention a few of my friends, mentors and colleagues here: (from the Netherlands) Teun van Dijk, Frans van Eemeren, Robert Maier, Els Weijiers, Gerrit van Vegel, Jan ten Thije, Veronica Ribalaygua, Tessa van Ham, Laura Vening, Wei-hua Chi, John Neubauer; (from Singapore) Desmond Allison, Peter Tan, Zhu Hui, Bao Zhiming, Anthony Guneratne, Terence Dawson; (from the UK) Kim Wooller, Emi Canclini, Martin Kraemer, Alice Tomic, Charles Antaki, Michael Billig, Darck Galazinski, Deborah and James Ryan, Heather Walker, Nicola

Schmidt-Remfree, Owen Hargie, John Wilson; and (in the world at large) Jaan Valsiner, Manfred Kienpointner, Galey Modan, Lawrence Wong, Kwokkan Tam, Monica Heller, Susan Erhlich, David Irwin, Robert Arundale, Shen Dan, Jan Blommaert, Michael Meeuwis, Marie-Thérèse Claes and Ahmed Sahlane. To my editor, Jill Lake, I feel a special indebtedness, for taking up this project and for working through it with me. I must also thank my extended family for their love and for putting up with my absent-mindedness. I dedicate this book to my son, Sander, with concern and hope for whose future cultural world I say these words.

SHI-XU

Introduction

In this book I shall present a cultural approach to discourse. That is, I shall treat discourse as neither objectively given nor universally organized. Instead, I shall argue for a notion of discourse as culturally saturated forms of verbal communication, or, in other words, as a set of diversified and competing constructions of meaning associated with particular groups of people. Further, I shall suggest ways in which discourse research can be rendered to achieve a particular kind of cultural politics. The cultural politics here consists specifically in facilitating cultural cohesion and common progress by deconstructing discourses of cultural repression on the one hand and promoting new discourses of cultural solidarity and prosperity on the other. To show the range of research tasks that the present approach can be applied to, moreover, I shall provide a number of empirical, practical studies dealing with pressing cultural issues.

It may be useful at the outset to define what I mean by 'discourse' and 'culture', respectively. In this book I use the term 'discourse' to refer to linguistic communication in social, cultural, historical and political contexts. As such, discourse is neither merely text and talk reducible to linguistic forms, as is the case in some language-oriented disciplines, nor just a unit of meaning independent of the forms of realization, as often occurs in the other social sciences. Rather, discourse is conceived of as construction of meaning – representing and acting upon reality – through linguistic means in concrete situations. It is thus a unity of both form and meaning. And it is not merely a form of talking or writing, but also a way of thinking. And such thought and talk have consequences on states of affairs. In everyday parlance, the closest equivalent for 'discourse' would be 'ways of speaking'. The phenomenon of thinking and talking of the Third World countries amongst western businessmen as 'cheap labour', for example, is the sort of way of speaking, or discourse, that I am referring to here. In the present account, discourse is seen as infiltrated by culture. By 'culture' I do not mean any essentialized, pure or homogeneous identity of a group or community, as is often assumed in some quarters and distinguished accordingly on the basis of language, geographical location or historical epoch. Rather, from a cultural studies perspective (which I shall sketch out in Chapter 2), I understand culture as a diversity of competing practices of meaning construction, or forms of life, of particular groups of people. Such symbolic practices are not in equal relation with each other, but in contest or opposition. Such intercultural tension occurs, at the present time, typically on the borders of 'race', nation, class and gender. Since culture permeates all human symbolic practice, discourse, the quintessential and pervasive form of symbolic practice, is cultural through and through. Consequently, discourse can be seen as a set of divergent and mutually opposing 'language games'. Thus, the discourse of the Third World countries as 'cheap labour' is not a universally agreeable or 'understandable' way of talking. Rather, it is an instantiation of a particular, in this case western, (business) culture, in opposition to other, culturally different, ways of speaking and understanding, potential or real.

Before specifying the cultural approach to discourse, I should also like to say a few words about the context surrounding it. The present project has been motivated by two major concerns, which involve both the ordinary world and the academic circle. On the one hand, the contemporary, everyday world is becoming at once increasingly interconnected and antagonistic, such that the paradoxical international (dis)order threatens our common cultural existence. On the other hand, rather than helping to reduce such cultural imbalance and conflict, mainstream scholarship on language, communication and discourse, it seems to me, is striving precisely to maintain, consolidate and expand that very order. Let me spell these out a little bit.

I begin with the broader social world, because this is the context in which academia is embedded. As we move into the new millennium, the world's nations, institutions, regions, populations and communities are becoming more and more interconnected and interdependent, through border-crossing, human migration, trade and commerce, international travel, the mass media, the World Wide Web and so on. What people say or do 'here' can directly affect lives 'there'. 'Our' well-being also depends on 'their' states of affairs. And yet, difference and division between these international organizations and populations are also being deepened and intensified at the same time. Witness the widening gulf between the richest and poorest countries, the ethnic cleansing in the former Yugoslavia, the circles of violence between Palestine and Israel and, of course, the literally daily talk of war in the American and British western media ever since 11 September 2001. A news story carried in the British *Sunday Telegraph* (15 December 2002) epitomizes this new condition of at once accelerating interconnection and heightening confrontation:

> North Korea, singled out by America as part of the world's 'axis of evil', yesterday launched a vitriolic attack on Britain's favourite secret agent, accusing him of 'insulting the Korean nation'. In a statement, the Communist country's Secretariat of the Committee for the Peaceful Reunification of the Fatherland condemned the new Bond film *Die Another Day*, which shows 007 being tortured in a North Korean jail, as a smear and called for it to be removed from cinema screens worldwide. 'It is a dirty and cursed burlesque aimed to slander North Korea and insult the Korean nation,' the statement said. 'It clearly proves that the United States is the root cause of all disasters and misfortune of the Korean nation and is an empire of evil.'

The media report here links up North Korea and the whole Korean nation with the United States and Great Britain. In an important sense the publication in the English medium also interconnects the audience the world over. The international circulation of the film that is behind the journalism, too, functions to establish links between the world's population. At the same time, however, the text, together with the quotations of the North Korean source in it and the film behind it, fills the international media recipients and thereby intercultural relations with misgivings, animosity and demonization. Such international communication does not bring the already divided world any closer, but, on the contrary, only alienates the world's different cultures even further.

The scholarly community, on the other hand, is much more subtle and indirect about such matters, of course. I am thinking especially of my own field, discourse studies, including discourse analysis, linguistic semiotics, speech communication and media communication and such like. Here much of theory and research seems to continue to operate under the self-assured discourses of 'objectivity' and 'universality'. That is, on the one hand, language is often portrayed as something objectively given and universally organized. On the other hand, the scientific discourse on language is usually presented as neutral, impersonal and relevant and applicable across all cultures. Questions about the constitution of reality and knowledge, however, are rarely asked and the possibility of the cultural nature of scientific discourse seldom discussed. As a result, worldviews, theories, methodologies, methods, topics, issues, data and such like from different, especially non-Western, cultures are usually excluded or marginalized. To crown it all, the powerful globalized marketing of the discourses of objectivity and universality, through the hypermedia, international travel and academic communication, consolidate this totalizing trend.

Were we to pause to trace where the discourse studies practitioners' philosophies, theories and methods come from, whose data they analyse and how they market their intellectual products globally, then we may realize, however, that this objectivist and universalist confidence might be misplaced. Indeed, it seems to me that it is still largely Anglo-American/European Western outlooks, concepts, procedures, issues and data that dominate the field of language, communication and discourse, albeit in differential and varied ways. It has already been shown, for example, that the current dominant theories of language and communication can be traced to a set of distinctly Western values, desires and ideas (for example, Bellah *et al.* 1985; Cameron 1992; Carey 1992; McQuail 2000). The very concept of human language in linguistic science is constructed through the use of preferred metaphors of Western science to achieve particular disciplinary and professional purposes (Shi-xu 2000a). Indeed, the shaky foundationalism and universalism and the cultural imperialist ideology operating in the discipline need to be replaced with a radical cultural turn that will open the door to vast, unfamiliar and culturally diverse intellectual traditions, perspectives, materials and concerns.

Let me make clear that the present approach is not merely a body of theory, or a set of methods, or a series of empirical studies alone, but spans an entire research system. Thus, it has its own specific epistemological, theoretical and methodological standpoints and practical empirical orientations (in terms of specific topics, issues and objectives). I shall call this interrelated research system a cultural approach to discourse (CAD).

Epistemologically, the cultural approach to discourse does not take knowledge to be a copy of reality or universal truth, as if it can be independent of the knowing individual, cultural patterns of thinking, the modes and means of representation, the context of the use of knowledge, and so on. Rather, it takes knowledge to be socially oriented, culturally organized and symbolically mediated (Foucault 1980; Rorty

1991). Accordingly, the present work produces its academic knowledge, whether in the form of theory, method, analysis or conclusion, not as dispassionate and universal descriptions, explanations or truths, but as ways of thinking and speaking which are motivated by an explicit, consciously chosen cultural politics, as mentioned above.

Theoretically, the present approach does not subscribe to any of the established models as the only, correct or standard one. Instead, it proceeds from between cultures and consequently from a global-and-local position and views discourse as a diversity of 'language games' in competition with each other. It has taken up this position because of two principal observations. On the one hand, the current theory of language, communication and discourse at an international level is largely western in perspective, whereby relevant concepts from non-western and Third World countries are virtually excluded. On the other hand, there has been a long intellectual tradition that treats language as varying in form and function from culture to culture (for example, Sapir 1949; von Humboldt 1988; Whorf 1956). For instance, in western cultures, language is often used as an expression of valued individual reason and self-identity (Bellah *et al.* 1985; Carbaugh 1993; Carey 1992). But in eastern cultures, speech communication is generally held as a tool for maintaining relationship and harmony (Chen 1998, 2002; Liu 1996; Young 1994). When we see discourse as a set of culturally infiltrated and contested 'games', we become equipped to deconstruct discourses of imperialist truths by highlighting culturally different perspectives, for example. We shall then also be able to study the relation between discourses in terms of power. In addition, we can help transform cultural realities and relationships by advocating new ways of speaking.

If there is no such thing as a unified or completely shared form of discourse, then universally applicable methods or forms of analysis become impossible. Methodological imperialism will only strip phenomena, concerns, issues and topics of their local, cultural relevance. At worst it will reproduce ethnocentrism and engender cultural antagonism. Thus, methodologically, the present approach sets great store by ethnographically appropriate, globally eclectic and politically engaged principles of identifying problems and making sense of data, beyond acultural descriptions, explanations or interpretations. This means that analysis of discourse will depend on not just textual properties but also local and global contexts. In that connection, it will pay special attention to the voices or understandings of the subordinated groups whom the researcher chooses to help. Furthermore, it will draw on a researcher's personal–cultural and, if possible, diasporic knowledge and experience as critical interpretative resources.

Empirically, the present approach is not interested in just any sort of discourse or just any problem constituted through discourse, but particularly those discourses where urgent cultural issues, especially questions of cultural relationship in the contemporary world, for example domination, exclusion, rebuilding or transformation, are at stake. Moreover, it does not merely analyse past and present discourses, but also, as an actively transformative mode of research, imagines and advocates possible future discourses in pursuit of cultural equality and emancipation. Thus, the present approach will pay critical attention to culturally repressive discourses as a topic and object of interest. It will also study the hitherto culturally marginalized discourses as a way of widening and enriching human communication. In addition, it will attempt to formulate and warrant new discourses of cultural reality and relationship that may discourage culturally repressive discourses and stimulate further communication conducive to cultural freedom.

I do not wish to be misunderstood. I am not claiming that CAD is a unique or superior approach in relation to existing ones in discourse studies. This field is broad and growing rapidly, especially in America, Europe and Australia. Listing even many excellent examples from which the present work has benefited may still discriminate against others.[1] Aside from the complications that the influential traditions are not themselves unified traditions and that there is overlapping among them, it may be said that the present work shares an interest in discourse and also in the notion of discourse as having a creative and transformative role in constructing and changing reality. More importantly, it shares a political commitment to resisting discursively produced power and domination through critical research. But the present approach lays more emphasis on a cultural or, more specifically, in-between cultural, perspective on knowledge, discourse theory and research and, moreover, puts a premium on a creative and transformative mode of research with regard to issues of cultural relationship. To schematize:

- In contrast to universal knowledge, CAD emphasizes the cultural and so power-saturated nature of knowledge and chooses to practise an in-between cultural, pragmatic form of reflexivity in favour of cultural coexistence and progress.
- In opposition to a totalizing theory of discourse, CAD stresses a cultural and in particular post-colonial perspective on discourse, as

differing, competing and critical-conscious ways of making meaning and capable of cultural transformation.

- Rather than *a priori*, universal methods, CAD advocates political–ethnographic strategies that are designed to undermine culturally repressive discourses on the one hand and to help rearticulate discourses in favour of cultural coexistence and progress on the other.
- Beyond 'ordinary', 'neutral' and 'familiar' data, topics, issues and objectives, CAD pursues a new and flexible mode of discourse research that changes its object of enquiry according to the cultural political priorities of the moment: for example, Western colonialist discourses of its cultural 'others', marginalized discourses from non-western cultures, questions of how to raise hope in 'troubled' societies, or questions of how to formulate and warrant new discourses of cultural coexistence and freedom.

Finally, let me briefly describe the contents of the book. The first two chapters outline the theoretical framework of CAD, with special reference to the relation between discourse and reality and the relation between discourse and culture, respectively. In Chapter 1, I argue for a reality-constitutive perspective on discourse. Here I begin with a critique of representationalism in linguistic communication theory and research. I show that the notion of linguistic communication as a mirror of reality not only encourages the monopoly of truth but also fails to take note of the capacity of language to create, maintain and transform reality. Consequently, I offer an alternative, broader, concept of linguistic communication, in terms of discourse. I argue that discourse, defined as situated ways of speaking of and acting upon reality, is thoroughly reality-constitutive: reality, whether internal or external, personal or cultural, linguistic or otherwise, consists primarily in discourses. And I suggest why this view of discourse can motivate scholars and students of discourse to actively engage with the real world. In addition, the chapter discusses a set of issues and debates closely associated with discourse: description/action, self/other, tradition/change and meaning/context.

Can there truly be a universal and, for that matter, comprehensive, integrated form of discourse analysis? Building upon Chapter 1, I argue in Chapter 2 for a cultural perspective on discourse and consider its implications for cultural political research. I start by critiquing universalism in discourse studies by analysing its cultural origins, the whiteness of the discipline and the theoretical and political consequences of its practice. Then, drawing on cultural studies' notion of culture and its projects of post-colonialism and diasporicism, I propose an in-between-cultural strategy for reconceptualizing discourse. Accordingly, I outline a culturally pluralist notion of discourse as diversified, competing and dynamic ways of constructing and acting upon reality that saturate the whole ways of life of human groups. Finally, given the culturally saturated (dis)order of human discourses, I lay out the cultural political objectives, or cultural politics, for the present discourse research project: to assist in subverting culturally repressive ways of thinking and speaking on the one hand and on the other hand advocating new ways helpful to groups who are already dominated, excluded or discriminated against.

Now that the theoretical perspective and the cultural political objectives are set out, I move on in Chapter 3 to outlining the methodology of CAD. First I critically examine the foundationalist view of social science and its alternative, interpretivism. Then, drawing on the insights from the latter, I argue that, to overcome methodological imperialism, a more radical principle is needed: to generate knowledge from in between cultures. Proceeding from this conceptual framework of social science, instead of prescribing fixed, universal methods, I offer two strands of suggestive, experimental and open-ended discourse research strategies that are oriented to local cultural circumstances. These are in nature 'deconstructive' (that is, subverting discourses of cultural repression) and 'transformative' (that is, formulating and warranting new discourses of cultural cohesion and progress), respectively.

The project of CAD is meant to be a form of intellectual activism that communicates with students and scholars not merely through theory, but also through empirical research. Thus, the rest of the book presents a set of practical studies, illustrating the kinds of concerns, initiatives and strategies in the cultural turn being advocated here.

Chapter 4 directs attention to Western popular discourses of its cultural 'others'. Whilst theoretical and analytical work on the Western colonialist discourse of the Other has singled out the stereotype as its central, constitutive strategy, this chapter points to a relatively marginalized area: contradiction. The study is based on a set of everyday, mass-mediated Western data – an American socio-political and cultural analysis of Singapore, Dutch travel literature on China and Western media reports on the Hong Kong transition. It argues that the discourse of contradiction is a powerful apparatus of pleasure and prejudice, of differentiation and discrimination, especially with respect to cultural-other places (the Other Place), and hence sets out to examine forms and meanings of the strategy of contradiction across different genres and through quantities of data. Based on the empirical analysis, further, I outline and defend subversive, alternative and creative discourses conducive to cultural coexistence and common progress. Thus, it will be seen, for example, that the Other Place often consists in contrasts, incongruities, inconsistencies, paradoxes, oppositions or discrepancies; in terms of the underlying principle, the cultural Other Place may be constructed as self-contradictory, regionally contradictory, globally contradictory, temporally contradictory or socio-economically contradictory. It will be revealed too, however, that such 'contradictions' are not so much objective facts and certainly not in the Other's terms, but rendered present and real through universalized Western theorems, Western modernist metaphors and Western definitions of the Other's situation.

Chapter 5 turns to non-Western discourse with a view to giving the cultural 'Other' a voice in the Western discourse community and thereby encouraging a new level of understanding of the Western 'Self' and a new level of East–West intercultural communication. I begin by discussing what constitutes non-western discourse, why the western community, lay and professional, should 'read' it routinely and how it should do so. Then, to take these propositions seriously, I go on to study the concrete case of China's and Hong Kong's media discourses on Hong Kong's historic transition in 1997. Here a cultural-contrastive approach is adopted, that is, identifying and making sense of a culture's discourse against the backdrop of what has been repressed and marginalized in a corresponding cultural discourse. Consequently, new, subversive and complex discourses of China and Hong Kong unfamiliar to the West are highlighted. For example, there are important discourses on the cause and the significance of Hong Kong's return. Moreover, instead of self, identity and boundary, Hong Kong's and China's media are centrally concerned with relationship-building, not only between themselves but with the rest of the world as well.

Chapter 6 focuses on the discourse of 'troubled' communities and aims to identify moral progress in their identity discourses. Proceeding from the view that a discourse community may have the critical consciousness to transform itself, I adopt a historical-comparative approach and set out to identify and characterize changes of collective identity in the media discourses in (Northern) Ireland over the past hundred or so years. Then, I compare and evaluate the different historical identity discourses in terms of an explicit, chosen criterion: the degree of antagonism with its Other. Consequently, the chapter claims that there have been steady, large moral leaps in the historical identity discourse. The earlier intergroup animosity gives way to subsequent intergroup cooperation as the discourse of militant nationalism is replaced, successively, by the discourse of majority/minority, the discourse of neighbours and the discourse of equal partnership. In conclusion, it is suggested that there is more hope in Northern Ireland than might have been realized and, further, that the historically achieved discursive transformations will set new speech conditions for its future discursive and cultural advancement.

Finally, Chapter 7 shows how to make discourse research play a creative, transformative role in the ordinary and academic world as part of the CAD programme. Here I focus on the professional domain of intercultural contact and communication, broadly defined (that is, in business, education, the media, multicultural society and international relations), which poses a major challenge for contemporary societies, eastern and western alike. I first identify, among other things, the neglect of power and domination as the fundamental theoretical and practical problem, an ideological discourse only reinforced by mainstream professional thinking and practice in intercultural communication and relations. Then, I argue that, in order to overcome the repressive power of intercultural communication, new communicative norms, in the form of socially accepted ways of speaking or discourses, have to be created and sustained. In this process, discourse researchers can play an active professional role, namely to formulate, justify and promote new discourses for culturally common existence and progress, in dialogue with local cultural communities. As illustrative examples, I sketch out the theses of diversity, equality, common goals and moral rationality, as well as supporting arguments for these theses.

Some terms used in this book deserve mention. I do not consider the 'West', the 'non-Western Other', 'Western discourse' and such like as essentially given entities. They are neither internally homogeneous nor externally discrete; their meanings are unstable and constructed for specific purposes. For this reason, I have generally used these terms in lower case. However, in this book I also advocate the cultural politics of employing strategic realism or 'Marxism without guarantees' (Hall 1996c) or 'contingent foundationalism' (Butler 1992) as a way of highlighting 'real' difference in cultural power and hence conditions of cultural domination, exploitation and exclusion. In this case I use capitals for emphasis, as in the 'West' or 'non-Western Other'. In a similar vein I have used the phrase the 'Third World'. This has been criticized for possible negative assumptions. But, for want of a better alternative and because of its common usage, I have retained it here and refer especially to the three continents of Asia, Africa and Latin America as a legacy of European colonialism and American neocolonialist, imperialist expansion.[2]

Part I
Theory and Methodology

1
Discourse and Reality

Introduction

Any theory of language, communication or discourse will carry with it some underlying assumption about how it is related to the world. In philosophical terms, it will take a certain epistemological stance. It is hard to imagine a theory of human speech that does not have some assumption about how the world, hence knowledge of it, is accessed and how the access is related to language. So I will begin this book with an epistemologically oriented account of linguistic communication. The specific view that I will develop in this chapter is, put simply, that linguistic communication or discourse is not separable from the world or reality, but can be seen as thoroughly constitutive of it. I shall call this perspective the reality-constitutive view.

I need to discuss this basic view of language also because it is in opposition to what seems to be the dominant epistemological position in the field of language studies. The latter position, by the way, is also deeply rooted and widespread in western culture, at both professional and popular levels. It is namely the idea that language is a sort of mirror of reality, or a window on to the world, and so detachable from the objects that it describes. Thus, for example, a functional approach normally assumes language to be a reflection or at least refraction of external social context; a formal approach, similarly, a reflection or refraction of the mind. Ultimately, there is a possible, neutral, scientific language to describe an independently given reality, whether social, psychological or linguistic. I shall call this kind of epistemological stance the representationalist view.

In the following, I shall first critically examine the representationalist model of language and communication, with special reference to its disciplinary and political consequences. Then, I shall argue for an alternative, the reality-constitutive view, and consider its advantages for discourse studies. In addition, I shall discuss other concepts central to the study of discourse, including those of meaning and context. (In Chapter 2, I shall take a step further and argue for a *cultural* perspective on discourse, in opposition to universalism in the field of linguistic communication.)

Representationalism

It may be observed that within mainstream scholarship on language and communication there is a dominant, though often implicit, epistemological stance that speaking and writing are a more or less accurate description of things, events and people. This is particularly so with regard to the understanding about the language scholar's own academic, professional or scientific language. This view has been variously characterized as the 'conduit view', 'mapping view', 'mirror view', 'picture theory' or 'transmission model' (Carey 1992; Gergen 1999: 19–21; Grace 1987; Hall 1981; Reddy 1993). Grace (1987: 6) characterizes the mapping view thus: 'there is a common world out there and our languages are analogous to maps of this world'. Similarly, Carey (1992: 15) states, 'The transmission view of communication is the commonest in our culture – perhaps in all industrial cultures . . . communication is a process whereby messages are transmitted and distributed in space for the control of distance and people'.

The representationalist conception of language and communication seems to underlie much of linguistic communication scholarship as well as of other social scientific disciplines working with linguistic data (here I am thinking especially of psychology, sociology, history and so on). This may be seen, for instance, in the fact that research often fails to pay sufficient attention to context, including that of the researcher, and to the role that language itself plays in the constitution of knowledge and facts. This can also be seen in the two major perspectives in modern western linguistics, universalism and relativism. The former position holds that mankind shares the basic mental concepts and that, as a result, particular languages represent the world in basically the same way. The latter position holds that individual languages constrain different worldviews and therefore represent the world slightly differently. In either variant, language is taken to be a picture of the world and, so far as the picture is concerned, the difference is merely a matter of degree (Montgomery 1995: 224–5).

With regard to the last point, it may be added that a distinction can be made between a stronger and weaker version of representationalism (see also Grace 1987 for consequences of this difference). A stronger version insists on direct access to the world, whereas a weaker one does not. But, again, both acknowledge that there is a given world independent of experience and so also of linguistic communication.

The representationalist view involves several interrelated assumptions. Let me tease them out; this will make the subsequent critical analysis clearer. A first assumption is that there is a real, commonly shared world that is objectively given, 'out there'. It can be accessed by human senses, even though imperfectly; hence there are slight differences in the ways in which different languages represent it. Or at least, in some 'dialectic' or dualistic conception of language and social structure, the material world constrains human ways of experiencing and expressing it. Further, the world is of a different matter, or different order of things, altogether from linguistic communication, which would then require other forms of analysis than linguistic and textual.

Second, the thing named linguistic communication is thought to be essentially arbitrary and transparent. Free of norms and values, it has no meaning in itself; it is merely a sort of mirror of reality. 'Real' meaning lies outside language. For this reason, linguistic communication is often conceptualized as an empty 'system' of 'levels', 'categories', 'rules' and 'structures'. Its function is solely and universally to refer to, represent, reflect, or at least refract, reality, whether it is the inner experience or the external world or whatever (I shall take up the issue of universalism in Chapter 2).

Finally, the relation of linguistic communication to the world is conceived to be that of reference and representation: it neither casts its own image on to the world nor changes it, for example. A statement is considered to be a kind of stand-in or surrogate for states of affairs in the world. Consequently, 'meaning' (or content or message or information) is something that is *contained* in the linguistic sign (or code). From another perspective, the process of linguistic communication is that of encoding by the producer and decoding by the recipient.

To schematize:

Linguistic communication

- Linguistic communication is a container, or vehicle, in which information (or content or message) is stored and through which information is exchanged between individuals or groups.

- Linguistic communication, as a container of information, is itself transparent and arbitrary with respect to the information contained. So it is separable from the latter.
- The function of linguistic communication to pass information is universal.

The world

- There is one independent world common to all human beings.
- The world can be known more or less directly (so objectively).
- Due to yet imperfect perception, the world may be divided up slightly differently by different languages.

The relation between linguistic communication and the world

- Linguistic communication is a more or less accurate description of the world.
- Since there is only one common world and since linguistic communication, as description, corresponds to that world, content is fixed and inter-translatable across languages.
- Linguistic communication is different in kind and separable from the world; so the two are irrelevant to each other.

My contention is that the representationalist view is inadequate for both discourse research and human cultural survival. The problems here are interrelated, but for the sake of exposition I shall treat them separately. To start with, we may realize on closer inspection that representationalism as just described is neither natural nor neutral; holding it as the only way to understand human discourse excludes other alternative and potentially useful ways. The idea of linguistic representation can be traced through the spread of religion and science back to Plato in western history and culture (Carey 1992; Gergen 1999: 19–21). Further, as Reddy (1993) has shown, this view has been mediated by particular western forms of discourse, such as common metaphors in the English language (as in, for example, 'The story gives a clear picture of what happened'). In addition, the discipline's scramble for science has contributed to the portrayal of linguistic communication as a neutral means of representation (Grace 1987). The cultural nature of language models and its ramifications will be discussed further in the next chapter; but here let me stress that the dominance of the representationalist notion may suppress other cultural perspectives.

Next, the representationalist notion itself fails to recognize that linguistic communication is characterized by human motivation and meaning creation (Grace 1987: 8–9; Kress 1991). Consequently, it ignores the active role of language in the mediation and creation of reality. A moment's reflection will reveal that linguistic forms impose meaning (hence cultural norms and values) on the things, people or events they 'represent' (see Lee 1992) and manipulate perception (Fowler *et al.* 1979). Observe, for example, the semantic difference of the passive voice in 'Twenty people were shot dead' as opposed to the active voice in 'The solders shot dead twenty people'. Observe, too, the apparently innocuous categorization of 'people' as opposed to, say, 'women', 'children' and the 'elderly'.

Further, because the representationalist notion fails to take into account the context with which linguistic communication is inalienably linked, it tends to be logocentric, that is, to take meaning to be encapsulated in the word. Structuralism in linguistics and post-structuralism in literary criticism focus attention on the linguistic system ('grammar' of various kinds) and written texts (including 'text grammar'), respectively. Here text/grammar is taken as the locus of meaning (for example, 'metafunctions' in Halliday's functional linguistics). Consequently, historical, cultural and institutional conditions and circumstances are left out of the picture (Hall 1981). Observe, for example, the lack of ethnographic and institutional research in certain forms of discourse analysis (see Billig 1999 for a critique of conversation analysis on this score). Notice also the tendency to disregard the context (for example, social and institutional positions) of speaking actors in favour of their words.

Moreover, by portraying language as merely descriptive, representationalism often fails to take note of the performative, or action, aspect of language. Benjamin (1968), Foucault (1970, 1980) and Wittgenstein (1968) have in various ways critically examined the notion of language as the mirror of the mind and of reality in favour of a notion of language as action. Mey (2001: 93), following speech act theory (Austin 1962; Searle 1969), describes the problem accurately when he says:

> Many linguistic theories take their premises in some rather simple-minded assumptions about human language: that it is nothing but a combination of 'sound and meaning' (thus in most descriptive grammars), or that language can be defined as a set of correct sentences (thus in most generative transformational thinking). The basic flaw in such thinking is that it does not pay attention to language as an activity which produces *speech acts*.

In addition, and more seriously for linguistic communication research, the mirror view renders it impossible to research into the dynamic relation that linguistic communication may have with the world, or, for that matter, individual experience and cultural development. Since the relation of language to the world is assumed to be merely referential, it would make little sense for the language scholar not only to study how language creates reality as I pointed out above, but also to ask how language might constitute the world. Because the world itself is understood as a different order of things, how the world, and the peoples and cultures in it, might exist in and depend on the mode of speaking is simply out of the question.

This brings me to my point about the consequences for human cultural development. It will be realized that, since the representationalist view holds that the world is separable from the way that we talk about it, there is no way that individuals and groups can use language and communication to (re)create or transform themselves and the world(s). Thus, it renders language research helpless against the 'external' human cultural conditions themselves and, for that matter, the world's trade and finance, war and peace, and indeed the struggle against global hegemony, capitalism, sexism, racism, sectarianism and so on. Thus, representationalism is a rather pessimistic view of language and communication with respect to their role in human cultural life. Moreover, whilst the stronger version of the representationalist presumption makes possible the monopoly of truths and suppression of dissenting voices in everyday as well as academic life, the weaker version encourages relativism in thinking and talking of human cultural affairs, protecting repressive forms of discourse. In both ways, they hinder argumentation for better or more useful ways of speaking. In addition, since representationalism presumes just one shared world and hence fixed content, there is no need or benefit to retain unfamiliar and smaller languages, or more broadly to listen to and to read culturally different discourses. Consequently, the existing human horizons of reality and experience could be narrowed and impoverished if and when the endangered languages die and marginalized discourses are silenced.

A reality-constitutive view of discourse

In this section, drawing on critical insights from a range of social sciences, I shall outline an alternative, thoroughly reality-constitutive, perspective on linguistic communication. Because the conventional notion of linguistic communication is too narrow, as I suggested above, I shall start by suggesting a broader definition, under the term 'discourse'. Since the current reconceptualization of the relation between discourse and reality has implications for other, commonly debated discursive relations – those between discourse and description, discourse and Self/Other and discourse and history – I shall also discuss them following the description of the reality-constitutive view.

Defining discourse

Interest in discourse studies has been proliferating especially since the 1990s. And yet the definition of the field is a contentious business. There is, in fact, little consensus as to how discourse should be defined. For one thing, neither the term 'discourse', nor the concept I have in mind here, is in common, everyday usage in the English-speaking world. For another, in the social sciences, there has seemed to be a general tendency to take discourse as purely ideas, notions, theories or meanings, as if they were independent of particular symbolic forms of realization. Consequently, the term can refer to just anything, ranging from historical documents or fashion to architecture. To make matters worse, the term has been used in a number of different senses in the social and linguistic sciences, referring to such things as particular ideas, written or spoken texts, cognitive structures, or patterns of cultural symbolic practice. Still a further barrier is the cultural perspective in the definition. Discourse is not universal, hence the impossibility of a universal definition – a topic I shall discuss at length in Chapter 2.

In the Introduction, I offered a preliminary definition of discourse, as 'linguistic communication in a cultural context'. That characterization, given the 'cultural context', is a broader notion than 'linguistic communication' as studied in a representationalist model. However, it is not specific enough: 'linguistic communication' can mean various things, for example. In what follows, drawing on different strands of work on discourse (for example, Barker and Galasinski 2001; Chouliaraki and Fairclough 1999; Foucault 1970, 1972, 1980, 1986; Laclau and Mouffe 1985; Potter and Wetherell 1987; Renkema 1993; Schiffrin 1994; van Dijk 1985, 1997; Wodak 1996), I shall give some further specifications to the definition. (Other respecifications will be given in Chapter 2.)

To begin with, I would like to redefine 'linguistic communication in a cultural context' as *construction of meaning through the use of (primarily) linguistic symbols in a concrete cultural context*. For this I shall use the term 'discourse'; it also has the advantage of avoiding the traditional assumptions associated with 'language', 'communication' or 'linguistic communication'. To the term 'discourse', the nearest equivalents in everyday parlance would be 'versions of events' and 'ways of speaking'. Thus, speaking of the Third World as 'cheap labour' in the western business circle, for instance, is a discourse worthy of our attention. Other examples of discourse may be talk of women as 'less rational and capable' in patriarchal societies, the proposition in industrialized civilizations that 'the interest of man is above that of nature', or 'the individual self is the locus of reason' as a discourse rooted in western culture. To clarify the current definition, let me highlight a few points.

A first point is that discourse is not a shared, merely linguistically constituted, written or spoken text. Rather, it should be seen as composed of both text and context, text being inextricably linked with context (Mey 2001; van Dijk 1985, 1997; Verschueren 1999). In this case, context is an inalienable part of discourse. As I shall discuss later in the chapter, context can be a useful resource for making sense of data under study. Therefore, to study a text, the researcher should take into account such extra-textual factors as personal, institutional and cultural circumstances, as appropriate.

Second, in close relation with the above point, discourse can be executed through a number of, often interlocking, symbolic systems, for example speaking/writing, genre, gesture and posture, singing, the media (Hodge and Kress 1988). Thus, discourse may be in a written, or spoken, modality (further, modalities can be intermingled, say, written to be spoken, or spoken to be written). Written or spoken discourse may also be carried through conventional or new media: for example, the press, the radio, television, the telephone and the World Wide Web with visual and audio facilities. Mediated written or spoken discourse is further couched in some specific genre, which may range from casual conversation, public speech, literature or journalism to a legal document. Each of such symbolic systems, it should be realized, has its own significance; an email message has a different effect from a *tête-à-tête* talk, for example.

Third, it should be reflected that the kind of thing I call discourse is not peripheral but central to our individual, social and cultural life (Shotter 1993). Further, it is at least ancillary to the other modes of our symbolic life, say music, dance, art, film, sport or museums (Hodge and Kress 1988). It is a familiar but important fact that we spend our day speaking, listening, reading, or writing to each other. Even in private (meditation), we think and feel largely in verbal terms (Harré and Gillett 1994). Even ballet, symphonies, photography, paintings or gymnastics would lose much of their meaning – or not be there in the first place – had there not been the discourses preceding, surrounding or partaking of them. For instance, what ballet is has to do with the way it is talked of and written about in society, for example, as a form of 'high art', 'aesthetic enjoyment' and so on. Architecture, real as it is, cannot be separated from the way it has been historically documented, interpreted and distributed. Narratives of architecture mediate the way it is defined and the way that future architecture will evolve. Thus, discourse is a primary, prevalent and prevailing part of our cultural symbolic life. (It is for this reason that the term 'primarily' is used in the definition.)

Fourth, it should be pointed out that the phrase 'construction of meaning' refers not only to a particular way of describing or representing the world, but also to the accompanying action upon it. In linguistic, semiotic and cultural studies, emphasis is frequently placed on 'construction' or 'representation' and, for that matter, images and versions of events. But language and communication do not merely provide descriptions of reality: they also perform actions at the same time, which bring about changes to states of affairs. In other words, discourse is not merely what people say, but also what they do by saying something. This also implies that discourse is a form of social practice that has specific goals or purposes and consequences. Think of 'Hi!', 'Would you please pass me the salt?', 'Shut up!' or 'I love you!' Identity is claimed, obligation imposed, command made, relationship maintained or changed thereby. In a speech act perspective (Austin 1962), all representations perform social action (I shall return to this dimension later in the chapter).

Fifth, it should be noted that discourse is always about some topic or issue – be it an object, people, an event, imagination or whatever – with respect to which a particular statement or theme or proposition is made. This implies that the choice of discourse to study is hardly neutral but reflects the interest of the researcher. Often, in (textbooks on) discourse analysis, there is a pressure to offer universal, context-free or at least generally applicable 'methods of analysis', 'templates', or 'toolkits'. But an obvious consequence of this would be the abstraction of communicative activity from the local, practical concerns. The present approach, therefore, does not purport to be interested in and describe just any discourse but will try to choose those discourses whose topics or concerns reflect culturally pressing issues, say racism, sexism, capitalism, imperialism or cultural unity and diversity (I will explain this choice in Chapter 2).

Finally, the present approach is interested in discourse not so much as unique, individual practice and experience as patterns of speaking or writing of a group, community or institution and individual interactions with them. In the west, the way that the Muslim world is talked about is not merely a matter of scattered, singular creations by some particular individuals. Rather, it is connected with or follows a broader European tradition of colonialism (Pennycook 1998). Because of the issue-oriented and patterned character of discourse, I shall also use the term as a count noun, in addition to the mass noun referring to the diverse phenomenon as a whole: for example, the discourse of democracy in China, the discourses of self, racist discourse or the Western discourse of the Third World countries.

In sum, discourse is an organic combination of meaning and (primarily) linguistic form that concerns particular topics (or a particular construction of reality and action upon it) in specific types of cultural context. Such will be the object of theoretical analysis, methodological deliberation and practical, cultural political engagement in the rest of the book.

Discourse/reality

Now that we have redefined language and communication more broadly as discourse, the first question we must consider is the relationship between discourse and reality, as I suggested at the very beginning. What I want to argue below is that discourse is not separable from, but constitutive of what is conventionally perceived as a neutral, independent object world – or experience and reality, external to discourse. To show this, let me begin with a real life example.

Consider Bin Laden, whom the United States has accused of masterminding the terrorist attacks in New York on 11 September 2001. Can we separate the person from all the accounts that are produced of him? To start with, that Bin Laden becomes an object of talk, or an 'interesting' topic, is a phenomenon that is inextricably bound up with other, previous stories about him. The talk of Bin Laden will derive its meaning in part from these texts. Further, what Bin Laden is inseparable from is the use of talk: speaking (of him) in certain ways under certain conditions can achieve certain desired results. Thus, from the US government, we hear for example that he is an 'evil'; in this way, military action to destroy him becomes justified. From the groups that are hostile to that government, we hear that he is a 'hero'; in that way opposition is expressed and achieved. Indeed, it seems that there is no definitive way of determining what kind of person Bin Laden is other than an endless variety of ways of talking about him. Someone might, however, object to all that and want to form their own opinion about the person. He is a misled fanatic, or a result of imperialism or a man with a strong conviction, one might say. But such a judgement, it would be realized, cannot be born out of individual, unspeakable rationality, but has to be formulated in relation to existing discourses, including culture-specific vocabulary. The judgement itself thus constitutes a piece of discourse and, moreover, a denial, dismissal or alternative to other existing or potential discourses about Bin Laden. It should be noted, too, at this juncture that the judgement is subject to reformulation, or further versioning, through time and space, for example when new revelations are made. Someone might even give up all such second opinions and go to the mountains to find Bin Laden and observe him in order to get first-hand knowledge. But again, such knowledge will have to derive from and be form(ulat)ed on the basis of interview talk and/or casual conversations and one's own cultural discourses. So, while there is no denying the existence of Bin Laden, the person, my point is that that person (including his weapons) is inseparable from culturally situated texts or talk about him.

More generally, it may be appreciated that a silent world is unthinkable. Speech plays a pivotal role in the construction of reality and there is no way to separate 'reality' and our language about it. Reality, be it society, culture, history, self, mind, people and things around us, thoughts and feelings inside us – the lived experience or lifeworld – is not just a neutral, independent given, 'out there'. Rather, it involves human cultural perception, categorization, characterization, evaluation and so on. As Shweder (1990) has argued, our world is an 'intentional' one: it is saturated with our own concepts, interests and desires as the persons who experience it, such that the person and culture 'interpenetrate' each other. Objects or phenomena of enquiry presuppose the researcher's own concepts, classification and theory. More centrally for the present argument, the representational processes involved, or the experienced realities, entail the use of language, hence the discursive construction of reality (Berger and Luckmann 1967; Burr 1995; Potter 1996). Thoughts and experiences can only become shared through language; thoughts and experiences would be vague, unless and until they become verbalized (Kress and Hodge 1979: 5). Bin Laden, to some, is an 'evil'; to others, he is a 'hero'. But 'evil' and 'hero' are not natural categories; they come from cultural vocabularies. From another perspective, our social cultural reality is primarily and predominantly a *discursive* one, with individuals, groups and institutions speaking, writing, reading and listening to each other, accomplishing various practical tasks. According to Shotter (1993), all we have is 'conversational realities'. Without language, life simply cannot go on. I will elaborate this point in Chapter 2 when I consider the nature of culture.

On the other hand, discourse does not simply describe the world 'as it is'. Nature or reality 'as it is' would not otherwise require discourse. We use discourse to offer a particular, ideologically motivated point of view on, or conception of, reality (Fowler *et al.* 1979; Vološinov 1986). And discourse imposes context-specific structure, definition, conception, interpretation, evaluation and so on upon it. (The cultural configuration of reality through discourse will be discussed in Chapter 2.) To call Bin Laden 'evil', a 'hero' or whatever are neither natural nor neutral ways of describing the person, but constructions of reality that are derived from culture-specific vocabularies and expressions and oriented towards particular situations and specific purposes.

Further, it may be added that reality is also interconnected with discourses, real or potential, in the relevant context. That is, the way that things, people or events are formulated has to do, at least in part, with other ways of speaking by other people, at other times and in other places. Surrounding texts thus produced can, for example, penetrate or help shape the way that reality itself is constructed. Consequently, reality and contextual (or intertextual) discourses may not have clear demarcation lines between them but are fused together, so to speak. (In essence, they are of the same order of things: both are cultural interpretative phenomena.) Think of the fact that very few people in the west have had actual contact with the Chinese and yet most seem to have a fairly clear idea of what they are and what they do. Such a 'reality' is possible only because there has been a body of background discourse(s) about them or prior discourse(s) behind them and it is such discourses that help delimit and define, and so make present, that reality.

I am not saying, of course, that there are no thoughts and feelings, or that Bin Laden does not exist, or that the American bombs over Afghanistan and Iraq are not real. Rather, my point is that reality, real as it is, cannot be independent of social symbolic practice in and through which it (also) becomes relevant, significant and consequential in our life, as object, means or reason for action. More particularly, I want to stress that reality does not exist outside of especially *discursive* practice in and through which it becomes a relevant or significant topic, resource for talking, or object for action. As Laclau and Mouffe (1985: 108) clearly explain:

> The fact that every object is constituted as an object of discourse has *nothing to do* with whether there is a world external to thought, or with the realism/idealism opposition. An earthquake or the falling of

a brick is an event that certainly exists . . . But whether their specificity as objects is constructed in terms of 'natural phenomena' or 'expression of the wrath of God' depends upon the structure of a discursive field. What is denied is not that such objects exist externally to thought, but the rather different assertion that they would constitute themselves as objects outside any discursive condition of emergence.

In a similar vein, Potter suggests (1996: 7) that 'constructionist arguments are not aimed at denying the existence of tables . . . but at exploring the various ways in which their reality is constructed and undermined'. Because, on these accounts, no reality escapes discursive construction, or connections with it, I call the present perspective *thoroughly* reality-constitutive.

The notion that discourse has a central role to play in the constitution of people, objects and events actually has a long intellectual history (for example, Berger and Luckmann 1967) and is a cornerstone in social constructionism (Gergen 1999). Currently, it is getting increasingly wider acceptance, as in history (White 1973, 1990), anthropology (Clifford 1986, 1997), psychology (Gergen 1994; Potter and Wetherell 1987) and literary criticism (Said 1978, 1993). In language studies itself, the view that linguistic communication makes up reality as we know it can be traced to de Saussure's (1966) structuralism, in which a sign is composed of an arbitrary combination of the signifier ('sound image') and the signified ('meaning'), and to Whorf (1956), for whom language *is* thought and culture. In a more recent formulation, Grace (1987: 3) argues:

It has been said that sciences create their own objects of study . . . this creation of their objects by the sciences is only one aspect of the more general phenomenon which has been referred to as 'the social construction of reality'. Those who speak of our reality as socially constructed are emphasizing the part played by cultural constructs in our effective environment . . . The human species – and no other – possesses the one essential tool which makes a social construction of reality possible. That tool is language. Not only is language the means by which this kind of reality construction is accomplished, it is also the means by which the realities, once constructed, are preserved and transmitted from person to person and from generation to generation. Hence it is entirely appropriate to refer more specifically to the *linguistic* construction of reality.

(Emphasis original)

However, the notion that there is somehow an external (subjective or objective) world dies hard. Sometimes, to avoid the anti-structuralist, anti-essentialist critique, a compromising model of 'both action and structure' or 'both discourse and society' is posited. Implicitly it is assumed that both are independently given objects and therefore can be objectively described. In such a 'dialectic' strategy, the idea of a separate, object world, whether in the form of social, psychological, economic or cultural factors, creeps back in. Further, it might be realized that the binary model, which is committed to both interpretivism and foundationalism, is self-contradictory: if discourse both creates and is constrained by society, then the term 'society' cannot refer to the same thing. For, the two processes (that is, creating and being constrained) cannot occur at the same time but only in tandem with each other. More particularly, the model still begs the question of how it is that discourse/action is 'constrained' or 'influenced' by 'structure' or 'society' and the question of how the latter are known in the first place. Are 'structure' and 'society' and their 'causal force' themselves not cultural constructions? I have suggested discourse as *thoroughly* constitutive of reality precisely to emphasize the fact that 'structures', such as 'society', 'cognition', 'culture', and the presumed causality are themselves cultural constructions, too, just like the texts we study (for a critique see also Barker and Galasinski 2001: 46–7).

Now, why is a thoroughly reality-constitutive view, such as the present one, a good thing to believe in? There are a number of disciplinary and political reasons. First, to understand human cultural reality, be it sociological, psychological, historical, or whatever, we can study discourse as a legitimate topic of enquiry – the ways that reality is discursively formed, maintained, utilized or changed. This will also give us an opportunity to detail and highlight the role that discourse plays in the construction of reality. The discipline of cultural studies has not, as Barker and Galasinski (2001: 1, 62) rightly point out, paid sufficient attention to the detailed ways cultures are reproduced and a prominently discursive perspective will come in handy. Second, shifting attention away from the conventional topics in the social sciences to the discourses in which social cultural reality is constructed can help undermine authoritarian claims of truth, by, for example, revealing the discursive, hence rhetorical, bases and origins of the 'truths'. In this way, we can become more critical of the taken-for-granted foundations of reality (see, for example, Chapter 4). This leads to my third point. Since the thoroughly reality-constitutive view recognizes the researcher's own professional activity as a form of discursive construction, too, it requires the researcher to guard against truth-claiming and to reflect on the social and cultural consequence and so responsibility of their work. Finally, and more importantly perhaps, if reality does not exist outside of social discursive practice, then it becomes possible for us to engage in more active, interventionalist forms of research. For example, we can research into new forms of discourses and grounds to advocate them in society so that hegemonic realities can be changed and new realities helpful to the already disadvantaged groups created (see, for example, Chapter 7). I shall explore such methodological implications in more detail in Chapter 3.

Given the reality-constitutive account of discourse, some of the conventionally understood relations in discourse will need to be reconsidered as well. These include those between discourse and description, discourse and self and discourse and tradition. In the critical process, I shall highlight the often neglected relations of discourse with action, with social others and with critical and creative consciousness.

Description and action

Discourse often functions to describe. A lot of settings require descriptions, for instance the press, courts of law, science, and indeed various everyday situations. Consequently, as descriptive discourses, news reports, eyewitness accounts, research papers, ordinary stories and so on arise. And yet, because of the dominant assumption of the representationalist model, the descriptive function of linguistic communication is often taken to be the only, or primary, one, at the expense of the function of discourse as a form of social action. This happens typically in structuralist and post-structuralist theories of language where meanings are supposed to lie within the confines of the linguistic system or a set of texts.

A careful consideration of even the most mundane uses of language will reveal its crucial social action dimension. 'I'm concerned about your view' is not simply a description of the speaker's inner state, but can also mean a *criticism* of the addressee's point of view and/or a *warning* against possible actions following from that point of view. When I say to my son, 'I'll give you five pounds every weekend', that is not merely a description of a future action of mine: if I forget or fail to give him the money on time, he might protest and demand, 'A promise is a promise!' Why? My earlier statement has functioned also as an act of *promise*, which obliges me to a particular, subsequent course of action from which he expects benefit. When a declaration 'I love you' is made, tremendous change will take place in the relationship and in the subsequent interaction between the persons involved. During the recent political conflict in Northern Ireland, the Unionist Party says to the opposing political party Sinn Fein, 'No guns, no government'. The statement is not only a description of a future scenario (that is, if Sinn Fein fails to disarm the IRA, then it cannot hope to share government), but can also be taken as a challenge, a threat and an ultimatum.

Such implicit, socially consequential, meanings of language use Austin (1962) and Searle (1969) have called 'speech acts' in their speech act theory. That is, they are what people *do* by saying certain things; such 'doings' cause change in states of affairs. Whilst speech act theory deals merely with decontextualized sentences, the present perspective considers discourse as wholly and thoroughly performative: discourse performs social action at all social interactional levels (such as those actions taking place between individuals, institutions and communities). By 'social action', I mean in particular the activity that has particular purposes or goals (for example, to persuade customers to buy goods, to win over friendship, to impress one's boss or to threaten an opposing party) and particular consequences on people or states of affairs (for example, changing someone's perception, constraining somebody's freedom of action). Thus, if discourse offers a certain descriptive version of event or purports to tell the truth, it would be useful to examine what purposes that version of event or truth may be designed to achieve and what effect it may have on the recipient or the current situation.

This is a good point at which to draw attention to another important dimension of social action and so of discourse: power. Following Foucault (1980: 93), I take power to be constituted in social action and discursive practice in particular:

> in a society such as ours, but basically in any society, there are manifold relations of power which permeate, characterise and constitute the social body, and these relations of power cannot themselves be established, consolidated nor implemented without the production, accumulation, circulation and functioning of a discourse. There can be no possible exercise of power without a certain economy of discourses of truth which operates through and on the basis of this association.

Power can take at least two forms. One is the asymmetrical relation between individual, collective or institutional actors (for example, the relations between a boss and employee, a parent and a child, or West European and Third World countries); this consists in the *context* or background of action. Foucault (1980) has called it 'relations of forces'. Another is the purpose, or the effect, of getting others under control (for example, silencing, deception, ridicule, intimidation, domination, oppression, exclusion, discrimination or resistance). Discourse, as social action, does not occur in a power vacuum but more often than not in unequal power relations and, at the same time, discourse is often oriented towards power interests and has power consequences.

Further, it should be realized that discourses of power are often in disguise and that therefore they need special critical attention. That is, dominant speakers or writers may conceal or make natural power relations and power practices by, for example, appealing to objectivity, neutrality or authority. I shall call such discourses *ideological*. That is, ideological discourses are those ways of speaking that render unequal power relations and practices as if they were non-existent, natural or to be taken for granted. Thus, knowledge, power and discourse are inter-meshed (Foucault 1980).

When we understand discourse in terms of not simply description of the world but social action, hence power and ideology, then we shall become wary in encountering discourses that appear to describe or tell the truth. Such discourses need to be subjected to ideological critique, as Gergen (1999: 22) suggests:

> Virtually any authority – whether a scientist, scholar, supreme court judge, or religious leader – could be subjected to *ideological critique*, that is, critique aimed at revealing the interests, values, doctrines, or myths that underlie seemingly neutral claims to truth. As ideological critique suggests, their words are not pictures of the world; rather, their interests lead them to select certain accounts and not others. What has been left out, what descriptions are they suppressing? Further, given the distinct possibility of self-interest, we are encouraged to ask how the authorities gain by way of their particular accounts? Who is being silenced, exploited, or erased?

Self and relation

In a representationalist model where language is a mirror of the mind, an important part or function of linguistic communication is the expression of the self, self-consciousness or self-identity. For, in western culture, the individual person is valued as the source of reason and so truths. Consequently, the question of self-identity has been one of the central, perennial and persistent preoccupations on the language-oriented research agenda, and not just in popular discourses. The sheer deluge of papers, books and conferences on identity year in, year out attest to this overriding interest.

However, what seems to have been overlooked, or perhaps systematically excluded, is the question of relation-building through discourse – relation as not just a social product (for example, an enlarged or more inclusive self), but also a social process (for example, forging relationships of various kinds and thereby accomplishing other practical goals). In their everyday discursive and cultural practice, people are also concerned with relations, relations with other individuals, the family, groups, institutions, nations, cultural patterns and so on and so forth. Often, even what is said is of no importance, but the fact that something is said, in particular ways, may serve to establish or maintain a certain social bond. Think of greetings or exchange of pleasantries. As part of the process of speaking of and acting upon the world, speakers and listeners, writers and readers, may interrelate and interconnect each other and still others; they may be creating, maintaining or transforming relationships of various kinds. Consequently, participants in any discourse situation become intermingled: 'they' may turn out to be part of 'us', and 'we' part of 'them'.

In some non-western cultures, language and communication function not so much to assert individual self or identity as to seek to maintain and strengthen relationships, thereby achieving social and communal harmony (Chen 1998). In fact, the relational and relation-building nature of human communication has roots in western conceptions as well: for example, Malinowski's (1936) notion of 'phatic communion' and what Carey (1992) has called the 'ritual' view of communication. Only, this relational character has been overshadowed by the western preoccupation with the individual Self.

During the historic transition of Hong Kong in 1997, China's and Hong Kong's press produced many texts and speeches about the event. The mainstream communication and media studies pay a lot of attention to the unique identity of Hong Kong but tends to marginalize discourses of relation-building or otherwise dismiss them out of hand as either imperialistic ideology and submission to that ideology. But a more relation-minded perspective on language and communication would reveal that Hong Kong's and China's discourses are not merely concerned with the identities of either, but prominently oriented to (re)establishing and maintaining a bond between themselves and beyond. Thus, from mainland China's perspective, the inclusive relations of 'sovereignty', 'compatriots', 'fellow sufferers', 'family' and 'economic collaborators' are regularly formed and maintained through narratives, metaphors and arguments; from Hong Kong's perspective, similarly, the connections with China in terms of 'family', 'compatriots', 'bridge', 'economic partners', 'hinterland and frontier' and so on are established and sustained through the use of similar rhetorical means (see Chapter 5).

Thus, from the present reality-constitutive view, discourse is not just an utterance of self-identity, but to be understood as a way of forging, maintaining and transforming both Self and Other, both identity and relationship (see also Ang 2001). These can take different forms: individuals' and groups' identity or identities, self-consciousness, voices, perspectives, relationships, or different complexes of these. It may be noted, too, that they are often designed for accomplishing other practical purposes. So we should be speaking of discursive selves and Self/Other relations.[1]

Narration, description, argumentation, explanation or linguistic communication more generally construct the image, identity, voice and perspective not just of the writer or speaker, but are inextricably bound with those of others, individual or collective. What would be particularly important, then, is research into how such relations are, and can be, established, nurtured, transformed or, for that matter, broken, especially in the present time of social alienation, rising nationalism and international fragmentation.

Tradition and moral rationality

In the representationalist mode of thinking, the development or transformation of language and communication is usually taken as an epiphenomenon or even non-issue, for linguistic communication is regarded as either an immovable convention, or a passive reflection of external structural change. Little attention is paid then to the possible, self-reflexive character of discourse, and of the critical consciousness of the producer of discourse. Consequently, the intrinsic creativity of discourse and the potentials of discourse for human cultural progress are neglected.

Witness today's ways of speaking of women, blacks or Asians in the west. They are no longer the same as twenty years ago, thanks in large part to the feminist and anti-racist movements and critiques. How could it be possible for these movements and critiques to arise from within western discourse? How could they become accepted in western society and serve as norms that discourage cruder forms of sexist and racist talk? And how could the new discourses of women and ethnic groups of non-western origins be adopted in professional and everyday life? Or from another perspective, will the present-day hegemonic and hostile order of discourse remain forever? Is there no direction beyond domination and resistance or is discourse doomed? Questions such as these become all the more urgent and acute, especially for engaged discourse researchers, as the globalized and interdependent world seems to become increasingly more fragmented, divided and antagonistic.

It seems to me that discourse is not static or passive with respect to history. There is something dynamic beyond the repressive effects of linguistic tradition. More specifically, I am thinking of the critical consciousness with which discourse responds dynamically to old habits of thinking and speaking – what I shall term as moral rationality. By this, I mean the awareness, or motivational force, underlying discourse and hence the discourse producer to question continuously historical conditions, both as texts and contexts, and thereby to create culturally 'better' realities. The term 'rational' here emphasizes the fact that discourse is reflexive upon its historical context and, based upon this historical critical consciousness, oriented towards generating new and helpful realities. And yet, rationality does not favour just any transformation, but functions with an ethical principle. Thus, the term 'moral' here points to the fact that discursive rationality is guided towards 'truer', 'more justified' or 'freer' constructions of reality that are culturally specific.

In the study of linguistic communication, there is already the recognition of the role of social normative principles. Think of the cooperative principle of conversation of Grice (1975), the politeness theory of Brown and Levinson (1987) or the normative rationality of communication of Habermas (1976: ch. 2, 1984, 1987; see also Austin 1962). However, these are concerned with universal forms of rationality of human communication. Emphatically, here I do not mean that discourse (and the discourse producer) is determined by some universal system of norms and values. It is not. Rather, discourse is oriented towards culturally specific norms and values (see also Back 1996: 11). From another perspective, discursive moral rationality comes from historically specific discourses. Consequently, valued 'progress', 'development' and 'transformation' of historical discourse are 'positive' only from culture-specific and contemporary perspectives.

In Foucault's later works (1986, 1987), more attention is paid to and greater emphasis put on ethics and hence human, subjective agency as an account for change. For Foucault, ethics and agency are the possible subject positions that speakers can take and to exercise these is to take or create such subject positions. In the present perspective, moral rationality includes not just such possible speaking positions to take, but also the capacity to take any conceivable, new and culturally warranted position in discourse, more broadly speaking. Thus, just as 'habitus' has 'transformative capacity' (Bourdieu and Wacquant 1992; May 1996: 127), so discourse is equipped with the intrinsic capacity or spirit to free itself from its past towards a 'better' future. The present vision is thus based on a fundamental faith in human discourse and in the relevant speaking communities, that is, in their capacity to recreate a historically better reality and experience, for example freed from domination, repression, prejudice or exclusion. It may be cautioned that there may perhaps be setbacks somewhere and sometimes in discourse development, but it is hopeful in the long run. This is thus an optimistic vision.

Meaning and context

Discourse, as an object of enquiry, poses a central problem of meaning, and hence of interpretation, for the researcher. Discourse is essentially a *meaning*-making activity (recall the definition of discourse above). There is a sense, consequently, in which to study discourse is to study its meanings. So, in this section, I shall discuss some of the characteristics of meaning. And yet, the meaning of discourse cannot be understood without investigation into the context in which a text in question is embedded. So I shall examine the notion of context as well.

The dialogical construction of meaning

In a representationalist model, meaning is usually understood as content, or message, or information contained in a language, which corresponds to things in the world. Thus, meaning is static, fixed and given, just as the experienced reality is. The context of language use, including that of the researcher, is often considered unproblematic or explained away. Here structuralist forms of analysis, such as functional approaches or content analysis, come to mind. In such cases, the role of the speaker and researcher in creating meaning and the shifting of meaning through context are smoothed over.

In the reality-constitutive view, in contrast, meaning is defined as a property of discourse (that is, text and context) as a whole, so more holistically. This means, to begin with, that the discourse researcher is not interested in, say, the meaning of clouds in the sky as such, or the meaning of the economic reform in China, or the meaning of life, unless such meanings are rendered present and relevant to some specific situations through textual practice. Second and more particularly, it means that meaning is considered here as understandings produced in and through particular texts (for example, specific ways of speaking) and particular contexts (for example, particular persons' interpretations). In this case, both text and context are meaningful phenomena and they both need to be taken into account in sense-making (the relation of context to text will be discussed shortly).

In the present perspective, too, meaning is viewed as socially constructed in nature. A number of closely related dimensions of this conception may be highlighted here. First, meaning is not just a given, 'out there', but also a subjective production. In particular, meaning is interconnected with the reader and the researcher of the text, for example their knowledge of the situation, perspectives and interests in the matter (Gadamer 1989). Consequently, discourse can be polysemic. The UN resolution regarding weapons inspection in Iraq, for example, says that if Iraq fails to comply, then it will face 'serious consequences'. The meaning of 'serious consequences' is not definitive or determinate; it could mean condemnation or sanction, or it could mean military action. It depends on the circumstances in which the resolution was formulated and passed and is also determined by the people who interpret it. That the phrase 'serious consequences' is used may be due to a variety of considerations. It could be the case that the UN members who would favour military action were, however, prevented from specifying the consequences in military terms but were given the room to argue that military action is entailed in 'serious consequence'. Or it could be because those members who would not favour military action intended 'serious consequences' precisely to exclude the possibility of military action. Further, the fact that the meaning of 'serious consequences' is left as vague and ambiguous also gives rise subsequently to possibilities of different interpretation. Those who favour military action can argue in that direction but those who do not can refute that as well. In this case, it would be important not only to investigate the context of any speaking or writing but also to examine how people exploit the ambivalent nature of (the meaning of) discourse.

Second, meaning is neither the product of an individual or unique speaker nor the inherent property of a text. Meaning is a social, joint production (Bakhtin 1981; Shotter 1993), the participants here ranging from surrounding texts, others' voices and activities, cultural norms and so on. That is, the discourse that people produce always has a history behind it; further, they draw upon, appropriate, quote and respond to the discourses of other individuals, groups, institutions or communities. Just as discourse cannot be reduced to a piece of written or spoken text, so it cannot be understood as the product of an individual. The UN resolution as just discussed is a typical example of the multi-voiced nature of discourse meaning. The quote from Bakhtin above on the social interconnections of an author's discourse provides another case in point: the meaning of a novel is not that of the individual author alone but has to do with the wider context. Consequently, it would be useful to examine the intertextuality (Fairclough 1992) or dialogicality (Bakhtin 1981) in discourse.

Last but not least, meaning is neither static, nor fixed to a definitive situation. Rather, it varies across time and space (Heritage 1984; Schegloff 1981). Consequently, it can be vague and subject to further interpretation; hence Derrida's (1976) notion of *différance* (that is, difference and deferral). This can be due to a number of reasons or seen from a number of perspectives. For one thing, different people may interpret the 'same' text in different ways. For another, as the setting shifts (for example, when new contextual information is obtained), the same people can change their mind. Furthermore, through social interaction, argumentation and negotiation, people can reject or modify the meaning of discourse and generate new ones. In the above discussion of the UN resolution on Iraq, we have already seen that 'serious consequences' was interpreted in different ways. Thus, it makes good sense to speak of discourse meaning as linguistic–symbolic, dialogical and social construction (Bakhtin 1981).

Context as resource for interpretation

In the present perspective, whilst the text, the linguistic activity on a particular topic, is of central analytical focus, context is critically important, too, as an interpretative resource for the understanding of discourse. The properties of context analysed above suggest that discourse studies may become far-fetched or unintelligible unless it takes into account context, including the context of other texts and utterances, as well as possible, alternative interpretations of a text in question. In other words, context functions to make texts intelligible and to account for the purposes and effects of a text under study.

The example of 'No guns, no government' from Northern Ireland that I described earlier shows the crucial role of context in the understanding of discourse. Let us consider 'Mummy water' in child language, for another example. In terms of its form, the grammatical structure is not clear and can be variably interpreted, for example as underlying 'Mummy's water', 'Mummy give me water' or 'Mummy there is water on my neck'. The same can be said of its meanings: for example, it can mean, 'Give me water', 'I want water instead of orange juice', 'Wipe the water off my neck' or 'This is water'. A written or spoken text isolated from the context is vague in not just form but also meaning.

However, the notion of context is not a cut-and-dried one; the boundary between the text and context is fluid and porous (see below). To make matters worse, there are different kinds of conception of context in the field (for an overview see Schiffrin 1994: ch. 10; see also Duranti and Goodwin 1992; Hymes 1974; Mey 2001).

In the present study, context is defined as any background relevant to the discourse researcher's understanding of a text in question. This background can be the discourse participants' mutual knowledge, their interpersonal relations, the setting, and surrounding symbolic activities (I shall describe these shortly).

Put in these terms, context is also defined as relative to the text under study. Thus, the former is seen as the background to the latter, whilst the latter is the focal point of interest or in question, hence the foreground to the former. (This is, by the way, in keeping with the present view that textual practice constructs and acts upon reality.) In that connection, it should be noted, too, that it is relative to the researcher. Which piece of context is relevant and how it is relevant to the text in question has to do with the worldviews, perspective and aims of the discourse researcher. Because of this angle of approach, the context in which the text occurs will be studied to the extent that it is relevant (background) to the understanding of the text in question. From this relational perspective, context is to be used mainly as an interpretative resource, or frame (Goffman 1974), for making sense of the text in question (Duranti and Goodwin 1992: 2–3). The discourse researcher will not, generally speaking, investigate the 'context' in the way that an anthropologist would do, for example. How much contextual information is needed often depends on the aims and circumstances of the research(er). What is relevant context or not is limited by the researcher's personal knowledge and experience, for example. It is important to keep in mind, though, that, whilst the text is a special unit of analysis as foreground or figure, in order to make proper and serious sense of discourse, it is vitally important to study both the text and context.

There is another sense in which context may be seen as relative to the text: that is, context, just as reality as a whole, can be created and changed through the text. Thus, the text and context are in what Duranti and Goodwin (1992: 31) call 'a mutually reflexive relationship to each other, with talk, and the interpretive work it generates, shaping context as much as context shapes talk'. For example, the text can be employed to create context for the appropriate or preferred interpretation of one's text and conduct (see Gumperz 1982 for 'contextualization cues'). This also means that the speaker and hence the text are not passive with respect to context.

Let me illustrate my various points about context by recalling a chain of 'verbal' and 'contextual' events surrounding the war in Iraq. To start with, shortly after the terrorist attacks in the USA on 11 September 2001, the American and British governments warned Afghanistan that they would bomb the country if the latter's government refused to hand over Bin Laden, whom they had accused of planning the September 11 attack. After the verbal warning and thereby also psychological preparation for the international community, the American and British military action began. Trouble came, however, when some media showed pictures and accounts of loss of innocent lives and subsequently humanitarian aid was sent into Afghanistan (for the first time in history). Then the US President, Bush, went on the TV and said, from one side of the Atlantic, 'We Americans are a generous people.' From the other side of the Atlantic, the British Prime Minster, Blair, told his countrymen that British children are dying of the drugs that are grown in Afghanistan. When Afghanistan's government was toppled, Bush and Blair's wives went on the TV and condemned the abuse of women by that regime.

With this example, I want to show, just as I suggested in describing the relation between reality and discourse above, that context and text must be understood together. The threat of war at the start was good for preparing the war, psychologically and politically. Telling the world that America was sending humanitarian aid was good for continuing the war (sending the aid was good for saying that Americans are a generous people). The televised condemnation of the Afghanistan government's abuse of women was good for ending the war. There is an important sense in which without these verbal acts the military action could not have taken place, continued or finished. Text and context together – or discourse – constitutes our experienced world; through text and context together, we make sense and live a meaningful life. Finally, let me try to give an analysis of the various possible dimensions of context. The general characteristics of context I outlined above should then be seen as a caveat for such a description – any context is a function of the particular discourse research process and so the present account can only serve as a rough guide. The different dimensions of context are termed here as intersubjective, interpersonal, situational and symbolic, respectively. They are interrelated in fact but, for the sake of exposition, presented separately.

Intersubjective context refers to the knowledge that participants bring to bear on the discourse in question. It is 'what I know' and 'what I know that you know' and so on inside the discourse situation. Such knowledge includes personal, social and cultural knowledge. One effect of such knowledge is that the text may be indirect, implicit and 'incomplete', for example, hence presuppositions and inferences are part of the discourse in question. Take the following conversation exchange, for example.

A: I have been to Kobe.
B: Before or after?
A: Before, fortunately!

Without access to the information about what the participants in the conversation know mutually – namely the earthquake in Kobe, Japan in 1994 – it would be incomprehensible to the outside researcher.

Interpersonal context includes the characteristics of the participants involved, such as their personal biography and their relations with each other. An insider participant may take as benign in import a remark by a habitually sarcastic person, but someone who does not have the knowledge of the speaker's personal trait may misinterpret the 'same' statement as malign in intention. Similarly, an insider participant may take as commanding a remark by a person in power, but someone who does not have the knowledge of the power imbalance may fail to see its authoritarian nature.

By *situational context* is meant the temporal, spatial and hence interactional circumstances or settings in which the text is embedded. They are basically aspects of the specific time and place of the text in question, the purposes of the text (for example, buying postage stamps, making a political move or delivering a lecture). Aspects of the situational context are also embodied in the specific domains of social and cultural life, for example economics, religion, politics or medicine. Information about relevant specialist fields such as these can help with interpretation as well.

Symbolic context refers to various forms of symbolic activities surrounding the text under question. These can occur previously, simultaneously and subsequently with respect to the text, for instance pictures alongside a news article. They can appear in different modes (written, spoken, singing, signing) and medium (audio and visual, hence journalism, film, digital media). Further, they can be different in kind (music, fine art, dance, or indeed linguistic communication, which can be further divided into genres of ordinary conversation, fiction, legal documents and so on). What is said before, what is said after, how it is said (pitch, tone, laughter and so on), gesture and posture, are all related to the text in question and important for the researcher's sensemaking. A particular kind of symbolic context that may be mentioned here is the background discourses relating to the text in question. People's discourses are not individual or unique; they are often directly or indirectly associated with previous or surrounding discourses. This has been termed as intertextuality (Fairclough 1992: ch. 4; Gee 1999: ch. 3). To understand discourse, then, one may be informed by intertextual sources.

Finally, there is what I call *the researcher's context*. This is frequently removed from or at best kept implicit in researchers' professional discourse (Blommaert 1997). The researcher, research and resultant discourse are embedded in personal, institutional and cultural context. Thus, the discourse of enquiry and the object of enquiry are inextricably bound. The researcher who studies any discourse cannot escape from this all-encompassing context. From another perspective, the discourse being investigated is also reflexive of the scholar and his or her wider context. Consequently, scientific, academic, professional discourse cannot be merely a transparent report (or for that matter description and explanation) of external objects, people or events. It is important then that in any discourse research one must be aware of the effects of the researcher's context on the research process and product.

In sum, let me stress that context is not an objective entity, just as the text is not. Rather, it is the same sort of meaningful, intentional phenomenon as the text, subjective to individual and cultural interpretation (Gadamer 1989). Just as the researcher selects particular texts to study, so he or she chooses particular aspects of context as relevant and significant and interprets them in particular individual and cultural perspectives. The understanding and appropriateness of the context is closely associated with the characteristics of the researcher, for example their knowledge and aims and their worldviews and theoretical perspective. The implications of context as a social cultural construction will be discussed in Chapter 3.

Conclusion

In this chapter I have given a first, preliminary account of discourse with special reference to the relationship between discourse and reality. I started by offering a critique of the traditional though popular conception of linguistic communication, representationalism, and pointed out some of the deleterious consequences for research and human cultural development. My central argument followed two main lines. On the one hand, the presumed distinction and separation of linguistic communication from reality render it impossible to study the complex and dynamic interrelationship between language and reality (for example, how reality is created linguistically and rhetorically, how language is used to change reality). On the other hand, separation of the two domains makes it difficult to research into ways to struggle against the monopoly of truth and repression of alternative views and to create new discourses in order to transform, enrich or harmonize our inner experience, social relationship or other human cultural realities.

In opposition to representationalism, I redefined linguistic communication into a broader notion, termed as discourse, in which both text and context, both language and the world, are included as part of the same meaning-making activity or process. I argued that discourse and the world make each other up, such that the former constitutes the latter; I called this perspective the thoroughly reality-constitutive view. In light of this new perspective, I went on to reconsider a set of key relations in discourse and highlighted the performative, relational and moral-rational character of discourse. In addition, I reopened the questions of meaning and context and stressed their dialogical nature with special reference to the discourse researcher. In a nutshell, discourse is at the heart of personal, social, historical and cultural reality and the construction of and action upon reality are at the heart of discourse.

This thoroughly reality-constitutive view leads us beyond the search for objective descriptions of the world (forget what the 'world' really is!) and causal explanations of discourse behaviour (forget what the 'social (psychological) structure' really is and how it 'determines' text and talk!). Instead, we can take up discourse as a legitimate topic in social, psychological, historical and cultural research. Here we can ask a number of new, practical and useful questions:

1. What kind of reality is constructed and through what textual and contextual means?
2. What action is performed and how is this done?
3. Who is the producer of the discourse in question?
4. What purposes are achieved and what consequences follow?
5. How is power imbalance maintained or reinforced and what power practice (for example, domination, repression and resistance) is exercised and how?
6. How are relationships formed, maintained or improved?
7. How are new, better or more useful realities created?

Now readers must be wondering what status my perspective has. Having deconstructed the representationalist view of language and reality, do I then supply another realist account of my own? Does the kind of discourse I have sketched out here have a universal form? Does it function universally? Can there be a universal theory of discourse? What is the relation between my account here and those of others, real or potential? To answer questions like these, we must now consider the more fundamental issue of culture and its consequences.

2
Discourse and Culture

Introduction

At the end of the last chapter, I raised the reflexive issue of the status of theoretical discourse in relation to alternative versions, real or potential. The question there related to my own account of discourse, of course: I rejected the realist position of representationalism and then suggested a different, reality-constitutive one. Is my own version not realist in nature? If not, what is its specific status, or that of any such anti-representationalist position, in relation to other, different versions? However, when I raised that question, I also had a further, larger question in mind. Namely, what is the relation between such a theoretical discourse to culture? Is a universal theory of discourse possible, or even desirable?

Lying at the heart of these questions, I believe, is a more fundamental, but hitherto much marginalized, issue in discourse studies – and it is a motivating one for the present chapter: the general relation between discourse (ordinary and disciplinary) and culture. Are they discrete entities separable from each other? Or, on the contrary, are they intermeshed so that you cannot say this is where discourse begins and that is where culture ends? The discipline of discourse studies, however, has tended to assume culture as basically an epiphenomenon, external to discourse. Discourse 'itself' is universal: that is, across human cultures, the 'underlying' forms and functions of discourse are more or less the same. This conception explains why discourse analysts usually present themselves as objective and neutral, dispassionate and impersonal – acultural, so to speak.[1] In the same way, it explains why textbooks and handbooks commonly paint a universal image of the models and methods they proffer. This view of discourse and culture further accounts for the fact that discourse studies continues to be preoccupied with making itself a cross-disciplinary, interdisciplinary, multidisciplinary, transdisciplinary enterprise, but not concerned with the cultural diversity of human discourses. As the result of the marginalization of culture and hence owing to the grand master discourse of all discourses, a hegemonic order of the discipline is established and maintained and culturally alternative theories repressed or silenced.

How can we then construct a culturally pluralist theory of discourse? Further, once such a theory is adopted, how can we uphold the multicultural perspective and at the same time keep the dialogue between diverse theoretical discourses critical and productive? In order to find a conceptual tool for the job, I shall draw on a range of critical insights from cultural studies. These currents highlight the diversities and interconnections, power and dynamic that saturate contemporary culture, including discourse, its quintessential medium and embodiment. From these, it becomes clear that it is neither possible, nor desirable, to formulate, 'from above', a universalist theory or, 'from below', a particularist theory. So, instead of continuing to tackle the issue from the binary, universal–particular standpoint, I propose that we theorize discourse *from in between cultures*.

To take an in-between-cultural stance on (discourse) theoretical articulation is not to describe or explain anything from any representationalist and universalist point of view. Rather, as a theory-conceptual strategy, the in-between-cultural stance places culture at the heart of understanding and critique of discourse, ordinary and disciplinary alike. It also creates an opportunity for cultural-political intervention. In this way, the individual theorist will be able to draw attention to the special, complex and all-important question of cultural relationship and common cultural fate, whether it regards East and West, West and Rest, North and South, America and the Third World, or white and non-white. The researcher will also be able to construct, not certain or true knowledge, but a culturally dialogical, creative, double vision. Most important of all perhaps, the theorist will be in a position to find and formulate innovative values and cultural-political objectives in their intellectual work.

Adopting this proposed conceptual strategy, I explore the cultural nature of discourse as I outline, in a preliminary and suggestive way, a *culturally pluralist* theory, on top of the reality-constitutive view I developed in Chapter 1. Thus, I shall suggest that discourse, or discourses rather, be seen as a set of diversified, competing and dynamic ways of speaking of and acting upon the world associated with particular communities of speakers. Like Wittgenstein's (1968) 'games' of various kinds, such cultural discourses share 'family resemblances' but each is incommensurably different from the other in some particular way. Unlike the various games, however, culturally differential discourses are in connection and competition with one another, for the right to speak, over the truth of speaking, about the way to speak it and so on. Unlike the games, too, culturally divergent discourses possess the moral-rational force to reflect upon themselves and others historically and to produce progressive change.

In the following, I shall first examine universalism (as well as aculturalism) in discourse studies in terms of theoretical difficulties and political consequences. Then, I shall go outside of the discipline – to cultural studies – in search of a new position for rearticulating a culturally democratic view of discourses. Next, accordingly, I shall sketch out a culturally pluralist framework of discourse. Finally, I shall make explicit the cultural-political objectives to which CAD is committed. (The corresponding methodological view and research strategies will be laid out in the next chapter.)

The universalist discourse

Universalism

Especially since the 1990s, discourse studies has been one of the fastest growing intellectual movements and has now established itself firmly within the human and social disciplines. More importantly, its ideas and techniques have found their way into most of the other disciplines, ranging from psychology, sociology, anthropology, economics and history to philosophy, and often act as the cutting edge that challenges the basic foundations of these disciplines. The sheer deluge of textbooks and handbooks on discourse studies is testimony to the breathtaking achievements and the signs are that the market will continue to grow. Success stories are many, including discourse analysis, critical linguistics, critical discourse analysis and discursive psychology, whose models are being consumed and applied around the globe.

Underlying various Western lineages, there seems, however, a common thread of universalism. That is, they portray, implicitly or explicitly, discourse, the object of enquiry – 'text', 'talk' and, to an extent, 'context' – as objectively given. Further, they assume that this object functions about the same across human cultures. In the same way, they take conversational maxims, turn-taking, repair systems and politeness as universal. Therefore, they offer concepts and theories as more or less natural, without a trace of historical and cultural specificity. They analyse text and talk into structural and functional levels, dimensions and categories ('words', 'grammar', 'style', 'speech act', 'macro-structure'; 'subject', 'object', 'transitivity', 'identity') as if they were universally true. And they hold out certain types of linguistic, textual and rhetorical questions and even 'social problems' as the standard and proper objects and objectives for discourse analysis.

This universal image of discourse is in keeping with an implicit, rationalist assumption about scientific discourse and ultimately the scientist as well. That is, the scientific discourse user is dispassionate, impersonal and neutral, whose identity as ordinary person and as member of some social, cultural community is irrelevant to scientific discourse. Their scientific discourse, in turn, proceeds from universal reason and evidence and is therefore objective and more or less accurate. To crown it all, the powerful business of international publishing, globalized marketing, transnational and transcontinental conferences and travels, and the World Wide Web reinforce, consolidate and amplify the universalist discourse.

Universalism in discourse scholarship is not isolated thought and action; it is bound up with the broader Western modernist intellectual trend, especially that in the cognitive sciences. For example, in universal grammar, language is understood to be a set of universal cognitive mechanisms for human speech. In cross-cultural semantics, human languages are assumed to be governed by universal concepts. In cross/intercultural communication theory, too, competent speakers share a common language and their misunderstandings are caused merely by culturally variable expressions. It is important to note, too, that theoretical formulations such as these are proffered, not as reflecting the writers' own (anglophone) language and *Weltanchauung*, but as universal representations.

Aculturalism

At the back of universalism, of course, is what might be called aculturalism: they are two sides of the same coin in discourse studies, only the latter is more implicit in the universalist discourse. After all, the fact that universalism is widely accepted in language studies has at least logically to do with an exclusionist notion of culture. To thoroughly understand the universalist discourse, then, it is important to examine the other overshadowed term of the dichotomy.

Although antecedent Western intellectual traditions have placed culture at the heart of language and thought, an idea which can be traced at least to Boas (1966), Sapir (1949), von Humboldt (1988), and Whorf (1956), the modern scientific discourse, especially since the rise of the cognitive sciences in the 1960s, has generally discredited the relevance of culture and managed to push it to the margins of language scholarship. Thus Carey (1992: 19) comments on the place of culture in this way, when he explains the favoured notion of language and communication as transmission in America:

> the concept of culture is such a weak and evanescent notion in American social thought. We understand that other people have culture in the anthropological sense and regularly record it – often mischievously and patronizingly. But when we turn critical attention to American culture the concept dissolves into a residual category useful only when psychological and sociological data are exhausted.

A number of properties of this stereotyped sense of culture may be highlighted here. First, culture is objectively given. As such, it manifests itself in emotions, patterns of behaviour, symbolic expressions and evaluations. According to this essentialist notion, it will be possible to describe and clearly distinguish (so compare and contrast for that matter) 'Irish culture', for example, as opposed to other cultures. Here one may think of those approaches to language and communication where different cultures are identified and used as explanatory resources.

Second, consistent with the essentialist notion, culture is thought to be pure in that it has a primordial and uncontaminated form and content originating in some particular space and time. In this view, 'Irish culture', 'Dutch culture' or 'ancient Chinese culture', for example, can be determined and defined according to the language spoken, hence the group of speakers, and the geographic location and/or the time frame of the people involved. Because of this authentic quality, culture is distinctive and so can be distinguished from other cultures. According to this version, there would be some such well-defined thing as 'Chinese culture', distinct from other cultures.

Third, culture is a collectively shared consciousness of particular groups or regions and therefore homogeneous. As such, it shapes the behaviour of individual members of the group. In this sense, it is supra-psychological: that is, it is outside the individual and so beyond individual control. In this view, all 'Irish' or 'Chinese' people for example would be the same kind of beings and expected to do the same sorts of things, at least in principle.

Cutting across these assumptions is a further notion that different cultures coexist in an equal relationship to one another. This view is attested to by the liberal notion of multiculturalism where worldviews, perceptions, feelings, symbols and ways of saying and doing things of different cultures are regarded as merely relative to each other. For example, the notion seems to underlie cross-cultural communication research and certain forms of educational and cultural reform. Thus, when members from different cultures come to communicate with each other and experience problems, these are attributed to respective cultural differences. For this reason, too, cultural differences are sought after in communication studies (hence cross-cultural communication), linguistics (hence cross-cultural semantics and psycholinguistics) as well as psychology (hence cross-cultural psychology).

Last but not least, in favour of valued individual reason, culture is implicitly assumed as a drawback, prejudice or inaccuracy, a concept which can be traced to nineteenth-century European philosophical and literary thought, as well as colonial history. Because it is supposed to derive from local conditions, historical traditions and, for some at least, specific languages, it prevents individuals and societies from seeing the inevitable, the true and the natural, hindering communication and understanding.[2] But through reason, rigorous methods and evidence, culture can be transcended and overcome. When cultural idiosyncrasies are detected and when the inevitable, ultimate enlightenment of scientific progress is achieved, universal truth, modernity and globalization will arrive.

Precisely because culture is conceived of as lying outside the structure of linguistic communication, it becomes possible to portray a universal picture of discourse. Further, because culture and rationality are presumed to be detachable from each other, it becomes possible to present scholars' own scientific communication as dispassionate and accurate.

Various critical approaches in the human and social sciences have found the sort of view of culture described above flawed. For one thing, the notion of culture as objective, primordial, homogeneous, relative and irrational is not a universal one, but a western, historical construction (as alluded to above); it is one among many other potential and real constructions at that. For another, since the notion of culture, which has been used to distinguish truth, objectivity and science, is itself culturally penetrated, the validity of the latter notions becomes questionable. It creates false foundations for truths, objectivity and science. Moreover, it excludes the possibility that every culture may have the creative power to regenerate itself, including its own values – the 'good', the 'right', the 'true' and such like (Taylor 1999; see also Shweder 1984 for the Romantic view of culture). In addition, the notion of culture as bounded and static fails to recognize processes of hybridization and consequently cultural dynamic and complexity (Ang 2001; Clifford 1992). Our world, especially in the age of globalization, information technology and network society, is experiencing accelerated border-crossing and border-remaking: human migration, hypermedia, Europeanization, tourist travel, international business and global conflicts. Consequently, dynamic and diversity exist not merely between cultures, but also within cultures and subcultures. Last but by no means least, the relationship between different cultures throughout human history has never been symmetrical. The domination, repression, marginalization, exclusion and prejudice of other, different cultures have been practised since antiquity, from slavery and imperialism to contemporary neocolonialism. They are also manifested in today's relationships between the First World and Third World and between the (especially American) west and its non-western others.

Resounding silences: peculiarity, whiteness and exclusion

Concerning the universalist discourse, I want to suggest, however, that crucial, intellectual, theoretical and political aspects of the discipline have been glossed over. The resulting, strategic silences render the universalist discourse natural, its dominance effective, and the marginalization of alternative cultural discourses permanent.

First, there is a set of (inter)textual features of the disciplinary discourse that are seen but unnoticed. One concerns the culture-specific origins of discourse studies. Here the concepts, theories and methods stem from the reactions to formal linguistics which occurred in the 1970s and 1980s in Western Europe and North America (for example, text linguistics, functional grammar, conversation analysis, pragmatics). In its current boom, discourse studies assimilates more, largely Anglo-America-dominated, social sciences (such as philosophy, literary criticism, history, psychology and sociology). It is now a standard expectation that Western, but not non-Western, intellectual traditions are referenced (think of de Saussure, Wittgenstein, Austin, Goffman, Chomsky, Halliday, Foucault, Derrida, Habermas and so on). Another is the particularity of its object of enquiry. In mainstream discourse studies, data predominantly come from Western European and American societies. Of course, they are supposed to be in American or British English. The analytical focus is supposed to be the linguistic form (lexical choice, grammatical structure and textual process, style, conversational turn-taking and so on). The topics of interest are expected to reflect Western academic concerns and debates (for example, style, politeness, conversation, subjectivity, and, of course, identity of a myriad of kinds). Still another unique feature of discourse studies is that it is done in the American/British English language. I will come to my view of what English is and amounts to in a moment.

Outside discourse studies, other forms of language studies are characterized by Western traditions and perspectives in much the same way. Influential theories of communication (for example, the transmission model, encoding–decoding model and negotiation model) can be traced to a set of distinct Western European values and desires, ideas and discourses (Carey 1992; Hall 1981). The notion of communication as 'neutral' representation, dominant in much of inter/cross-cultural communication education and research, is constructed by the powerful elite and serves merely to explain away power practices and to reinforce the institution of linguistic and cultural knowledge transmission (Shi-xu 2001; Shi-xu and Wilson 2001). The notion of 'human language' in modern western linguistics, similarly, is infiltrated by the metaphor of western, valued natural science (Shi-xu 2000a).

Second, there is an important contextual property of the disciplinary discourse that has seemed to be smoothed over. Discourse studies itself acknowledges the importance of context, for example the identity of the speaker, in understanding language use. But at the level of its own disciplinary discourse, paradoxically, it would seem irrelevant to ask or to speak about who, in the international academic arena, can and *do* do discourse analysis, publish in it and control the communication system. Here the context of the author/speaker and the larger institutional and cultural order and so on is usually presumed to have little to do with the 'discourse' itself that is theorized or the 'methods' that are used. But were we to pause and think who the producers are of the theory and methods, hence the master text/handbooks, in discourse analysis, then it would become clear that whiteness is not only a sign of cultural power, but also a condition of our current discipline. In his *There Ain't No Black in the Union Jack* (1987), Gilroy insists that 'race' must be analysed at the heart of contemporary intellectual work (see also Stratton and Ang 1996; Gilroy 1992; Hall 1999). Then, the silence over colour in professional discourse studies should be broken, too.

Third, when white, Anglo-American Western discourse studies universalizes and markets itself globally, discourses in other languages, in other cultures, in other parts of the world, intellectual and everyday alike, are marginalized, repressed or excluded. Here I am thinking especially of those in non-white, non-Western and Third World cultures (for example, Dissanayake 1988; Gumperz and Levinson 1996; Heisey 2000; Kincaid 1987; Shen 1999; Silverstein and Urban 1996). 'Discourse', as envisioned in the 'integrated' and multidisciplinary version, may not be a relevant topic, or even a recognizable notion, in other cultural intellectual traditions and everyday life. The toolkit and template proffered for discourse analysis, consequently, may not generate locally useful or even meaningful results. As has been shown (for example, Ngŭgĭ 1986; Pennycook 1998), the predominance of the British/American English language, which is required of discourse studies and indeed of any scientific discourse the world over, a result of British colonialism, will only overshadow other local cultural experiences and realities. The political consequences of such theoretical imperialism are described clearly when Gergen (1999: 17) reminds us:

> it is clear that the family of suppositions and practices in question [science, objectivity, self, truth, reason, morals, and the present author ventures to add 'discourse'] are all byproducts of Western culture, and chiefly byproducts of recent centuries. If we simply take them for granted, we stop asking questions. In particular, we fail to ask about the downside – what are the negative repercussions for society. Further, we fail to address whether these beliefs and practices can successfully function within the new century. For example, with the development of globe-spanning technologies of communication and transportation – from telephone, radio, television and jet transportation to computers, satellite transmission, the internet, and Word Wide Web – the world's peoples increasingly confront each other. And rather than the *global village* for which many hoped, we confront increasing numbers of contentious factions, expansionist movements, exploitative practices, animosities and resistances. Under these conditions we must ask whether any culture – and particularly a powerful one – can afford commitment without question? ... As elsewhere, we in the West typically presume the university of our truths, reasons, and morals. Our scientific truths are not 'ours' in particular, we hold, but candidates for universal truth.

So he warns us (Gergen 1999: 17):

as we presume the reality and truth of our own beliefs, so do we trample on the realities of others. We unwittingly become cultural imperialists, suppressing and antagonizing.

In highlighting the resounding silences in discourse studies, I do not mean, however, that there has been no reflexive, self-critical effort on the cultural issue of theoretical discourse (see, for example, Bazerman 1998; Cameron 1992; Carey 1992; Milhouse *et al.* 2001; Newmeyer 1986; Sherzer 1987; Urban 1991). Nor am I saying that there has been no theoretical attempt to take note of non-Western, non-white and Third World discourses (see, for example, Gumperz and Levinson 1996; Ngũgĩ 1986; Silverstein and Urban 1996; Young 1994). But endeavours such as these are few and far between and often come from the margins of language studies or have origins from outside the discipline. Indeed, given the current international cultural imbalance and disorder in the social sciences and humanities, the struggle against cultural imperialism in general and universalism in particular will be a gradual, long and arduous process. To resist the rampant and dominant universalist discourse in the field and to combat the continuing marginalization of non-Western, non-white and Third World concerns, materials, methods, theories and worldviews, much more effort is called for.

I should like to caution against the dangers, too, of conflating the West with whiteness. Just as the West is not a homogeneous whole, so not all whites are domineering. Moreover, because the anti-racist movement, like feminism, does not spread evenly across the globe, the cultural struggle within academia in general and in discourse studies in particular varies across space and time. In addition, there is the further complication of the specific post-colonial and neocolonial condition of America as the world's single superpower. My own use of the terms 'white', 'whiteness' and so on, therefore, is subject to specific contexts such as these.

Critical studies of culture

In this section, I shall consider some critical insights from cultural studies which will lead us to a notion of culture as saturating the entire social life, all acts, facts and artefacts, the professional domain of discourse research included, and not just discourse as object. If this is true, then we shall have to create a new way of thinking and speaking about discourse, beyond the universalist discourse. In the following, I shall first describe these ideas on culture developed in cultural studies as well as linguistic anthropology and then spell out accordingly a new way to construe discourse.

Cultural studies: culture as saturation of social life

Indeed, I believe, and shall argue below, that new forms of knowledge and theorization in discourse studies, beyond universalism and aculturalism, are possible and good beginnings can be made, if different speaking positions are taken up. These positions consist in a radical rethinking of culture in general and the intellectual projects of post-colonialism and diasporicism in particular, which are being worked out in cultural studies. In the following, I shall sketch these out and consider how they provide the vantage point from which to generate a culturally oppositional and pluralist form of discourse theory. Debates on culture, post-coloniality and diaspora are broad and complex; here I will offer a particular, selective uptake, with special reference to discourse theory formation.

To start with, cultural studies (CS) as an intellectual project, since its inception with the founding of the Centre for Contemporary Cultural Studies (CCCS) in Birmingham, UK, in 1964, has been growing steadily, spreading first to North America, then Australia and finally much of the rest of the world. It has its origins in a variety of human and social sciences and to some extent overlaps in topic and approach with them. Dissatisfied with the exclusionary notion of 'high culture' and its consequences, CS attempts to involve the whole way of contemporary life as its object of enquiry by adopting a populist and more democratic notion of culture (Hall 1996a, 1999; Hoggart 1958; Williams 1981). Thus, culture, in the words of Williams (1976: 90), is defined as 'a particular way of life, whether of a people, a period or a group', where the way of life is understood as primarily a process of constructing and acting upon reality. Here, culture is not seen as in harmony, but rather from a left-wing, Marxist perspective, as characterized by social division and asymmetry of power. Consequently, CS chooses as its objective to change the existing ways of life (CCCS 1982; Hall 1977; Hoggart 1958). Specifically, it attempts to address the 'central, urgent, and disturbing questions of a society' (Hall 1996a: 337), in the interests of the repressed and underprivileged groups of people. Its alliances with social movements such as feminism and anti-racism are typical manifestations of this political motive. Thus, CS is a new, political project with the 'deadly seriousness of intellectual work' (Hall 1999: 108).

There are a number of interrelated aspects in CS's definition of culture that may be unpacked and highlighted here. It will then be seen that linguistic communication or discourse is not separate from, but inextricably related to, culture. First and foremost is the notion that culture is not an independent element or dimension or aspect of society, but involves the whole way of life of a people. Culture penetrates entire human experience, 'internal' and 'external': artefacts, events, peoples, their patterns of thinking and feeling, speaking and acting, understanding and evaluating, and so on and so forth. Human reality is cultural reality. This notion emphasizes the *permeating* or *saturated* character of culture in people's lives. In particular it may be pointed out that this cultural stance opposes grand, totalizing theory (Foucault 1980; Lyotard 1984).

At this point, I would like to observe in particular that scientific knowledge, including that on discourse, is no exception to our general condition of cultural saturation. It is not free from cultural relations, actions and consequences, but a product of the interaction of the person with the relevant cultures. As such, it also has cultural consequences, often through its impact on the academic readership. My criticism above of the whole discipline of discourse studies as a systematically western, white and non-west-exclusionary discipline is just one example of the cultural saturation of knowledge and science. Other critical approaches to the social sciences have also disclosed the Eurocentric dimension of western scholarship (for example, Bloor 1976; Fenton, *et al.* 2000; Knorr-Cetina 1981; Mulkay 1979; Woolgar 1988).

Second, CS's understanding of culture stresses *social practice* (Williams 1981: 64–50), a notion also endorsed by Geertz (1973).[3] That is, culture does not consist in some fixed and essential structure. Rather, human activity has a pivotal role in producing, maintaining and transforming it. People and things *are* cultural, but they are so only because they are always involved in the carrying out of practical tasks in life. People create, reproduce, change and utilize cultural reality – symbols, beliefs, facts, or whatever – by performing various forms of social action. That also implies that all reality, be it self, identity, race, gender, or whatever, is a *cultural* construction.

Third, the social action that forms, sustains and develops culture is accomplished through use of various symbol systems or *symbolic action* more generally. People use various sorts of tools and methods – such as art, music, science, religion and linguistic communication – to construct and act upon experience or reality; all the devices that people use, all the representations they produce and all the actions they perform become symbolic, that is, expressing meanings and being assigned meanings. This semiotic notion of culture runs parallel to Geertz's (1973: 5) understanding, too, when he tells us:

> The concept of culture I espouse ... is essentially a semiotic one. Believing, with Max Weber, that man is an animal suspended in webs of significance he himself has spun, I take culture to be those webs, and the analysis of it to be therefore not an experimental science in search of law but an interpretive one in search of meaning.

Fourth, CS's definition emphasizes that culture is *patterned* and *diversified* (as is the social practice that makes it up). Culture is patterned in that it can be seen as a collective property of groups of people in particular types of context and that it can guide individual action (see below). It is diversified, however, in that culture, as patterned ways of constructing reality and acting upon it, may not match one another. Cultures may have their own and so different ways of looking at the world or, better, worlds, and different ways of acting upon them. Different cultures may even be irreconcilable, because cultures have the intrinsic spirit or force to reinvent and refashion themselves (Taylor 1999). It may thus be realized that different cultures do not, and cannot, see themselves and others objectively, if there could ever be such a thing (Bhabha 1994).

On top of this cultural diversity, there is a fast-expanding complexity in the contemporary formation of culture: cultures 'travel' (Clifford 1992). Historical, local, national, regional, diasporic and global processes, especially those in mass (hyper)media and migration, crisscross in human culture so that cultures become ruptured and hybridized (Ang 2001; Appadurai 1996; Bauman 1998). Consequently, cultures should be seen as located in the 'Third Space' (Bhabha 1990, 1994), in which they interact with and upon each other and create new meanings and realities.

Immediately, I must add that, in CS, cultures are seen as not merely 'different' from each other, but in *tension, competition* and *contestation*, both within and without, often along the borders of gender, race and class. In everyday life, where cultural differences are perceived, they are usually not seen in the cultural other's perspective (and, strictly speaking, cannot be), but often from one's own and hence as deviations, deficiencies, or sources of trouble. Here we may be reminded of the historically evolved relations of domination, exploitation, exclusion, prejudice and resistance between ethnicities, classes, genders, East and West, the North and the South, the empire and the colony, the super-power and the Third World, and so on. In that connection, it may be pointed out, too, that the world's poverty-stricken populations grow faster than the wealth of the rich few. So, 'cultural' differences are basically differences of power; culture *is* a site of power struggle.

Finally, culture, as collective patterns of thinking, speaking and acting, is not independent of *individual persons* and *subgroups acting to reproduce, sustain and transform it*. Culture on the one hand and the person and subgroups on the other are dialectically linked: the former guides the latter in social practice and at the same time is reproduced, maintained and changed by the latter. Further, there is also a possible multiplicity and dynamics of subject positions and ways of meaning articulation to recreate culture and identity (Butler 1992). Consequently, culture is not stable or homogeneous, but dynamic and creative. A new generation in a culture, for example, does not merely passively acquire cultures through the authority of parents and the educational system, but, as a socio-genetic human developmental process (Valsiner 1989), may refashion cultural landscapes.

Post-colonialism and diasporicism: culture as history and hybridity

Under the general heading of culture, two more recent critical and strategic developments can be particularly useful for a theoretical rethinking about discourse studies. These are post-colonialism (Appiah 1992; During 1987; Fanon 1967; Harrison 2003; Hutcheon 1989; Mishra and Hodge 1991; Ngũgĩ 1986; Said 1993; Young 2001) and diasporicism (Ang 2001; Bhabha 1990, 1994; Gilroy 1987, 1990; Hall 1990, 1992). They are closely related to each other and both involve a complex of new concepts and approaches. For the present purposes, I shall be concerned with them as intellectual strategies and as part of the broad cultural politics within cultural studies.

Post-colonialism, on the one hand, is a broad intellectual current that proceeds from the view that the present world order or condition is part and continuation of the *historical*, Europe-initiated, colonialism and subsequently neocolonialism or, more broadly, imperialism (Harrison 2003; Said 1993; Young 2001). The central feature that runs through this historical imperial process is the domination, repression and discrimination by the American/European West against the Rest. Accordingly, post-colonialism insists on a political intellectual strategy to deconstruct, subvert or neutralize the hierarchical and hegemonic practices and relationships existing between the 'centre' and 'periphery', the 'core' and 'exterior', the colonizer and the (de)colonized, and so on, by relating these repressive practices and relationships to that brutal historical context.[4]

Diasporicism, on the other hand, is an intellectual movement that proceeds from the understanding that, as part of the broad imperial order, different cultures, nation states and communities do not have pure essences or fixed identities but are interconnected and interdependent, hence diaspora. This view recognizes not only cultural diversity across space but also cultural change through time (Ang 2001; Stratton and Ang 1996). As an intellectual project or strategy, it aims to undermine fixed, binary and exclusionary notions of culture, language, 'race', ethnicity, nation and so on and ultimately to promote human cultural unity by stressing diversity, complexity, fluidity, hence *hybridity*.

A set of relations between post-colonialism and diasporicism is in order. First, post-colonialism and diasporicism are intellectual currents or projects born out of and so in keeping with CS's rethinking about culture. Whilst the notion of culture is more general, post-colonialism and diasporicism are more particular. The former provides a pluralist and oppositional way of thinking about human conditions and practices, the latter are concerned with their specific historical and geographical conditions. Second, just as post-coloniality and diaspora as historical conditions are linked by colonialism, so the intellectual projects around them, post-colonialism and diasporicism, share a common political commitment, namely to combat cultural imperialism. However, they are different in that whilst post-colonialism emphasizes power difference and struggle, diasporicism emphasizes cultural interconnection and pluralism (Stratton and Ang 1996: 384–5). Still other positions of enunciation may be found or formulated, for example feminism and post-communism, but to redress universalism and its theoretical deficiencies and political consequences the present proposed ones are particularly relevant.

Culture as discourse

Finally, let me consider how culture is related to discourse. If culture permeates the whole ways of life of groups of people and if it is itself constituted in social semiotic practice (Geertz 1973; Shneider 1976), then discourse, the most pervasive and quintessential part of such practice, is culturally saturated, too. Other semiotic activities, such as art, music and sport, are doubtless an important part of culture, but their meaning, value and emotional charge would be overshadowed if discourse were not mobilized to describe, explain, sustain, promote, sensationalize and coordinate them. Similarly, it would be hard to imagine how science, religion, education or other such symbolic activities can proceed and succeed without discourses to embody, maintain and execute them. Conventional and new media, too, which now literally inundate people's lives, would lose their functionality without discourses to partake of them. Indeed, people spend most of their daily, and hourly, life, reading, writing, speaking or listening to each other. As McQuail (2000: 93) puts it, 'Perhaps the most general and essential attribute of culture is communication, since cultures could not develop, survive, extend and generally succeed without communication'. Similarly, Duranti and Goodwin (1992: 2–3) have expressed the centrality of discourse in the organization of culture vociferously when they say, 'it would be blatantly absurd to propose that one could provide a comprehensive analysis of human social organization without paying close attention to the details of how human beings employ language to build the social and cultural worlds that they inhabit'. So Barker and Galasinski insist (2001: 4), 'To understand culture is to explore how meaning is produced symbolically through the signifying practices of language within material and institutional contexts'. The arguments I offered in Chapter 1 on the discursive constitution of reality apply to *cultural* reality in much the same way.

Despite its 'linguistic turn' or the (re)discovery of textuality, CS has been less than explicit in the analysis of discourse, even less about creating and promoting new forms of discourses. In particular, there has been little systematic and explicit study of how culture may be discursively constituted (Barker and Galasinski 2001: 1, 21, 62). Although many attempts have been made from various intellectual traditions contemplating the discursive constitutive nature of culture (for example, Bakhtin 1981; Blommaert and Verschueren 1998; Cassirer 1944; Duranti 1997; Geertz 1973; Gumperz 1982; Gumperz and Levinson 1996; Kluver 2000; Lutz 1988; Sarangi 1995; Sherzer 1987; Urban 1991; Vološinov 1986; Wittgenstein 1968), a more specific and explicit formulation in terms of discourse remains to be made. Cultural studies cannot be serious about culture without paying attention to discourse. To study culture, one must perforce study discourse.

Theorizing from in-between cultures

What do these insights into culture imply for the practice of discourse theory formation and development? They are not necessarily centrally concerned with the discursive forms of cultural practice. We need to find their links with the theoretical analysis of discourse. Further, how can individual researchers then formulate a non-ethnocentric, non-imperialist theory of discourse? The links between culture and discourse-theorizing could be multifarious. We need to translate them into a new, specific and principled way, or conceptual strategy, for informing the articulation of discourse theory. Let me take up these questions one by one.

The new cultural insights described above imply, first of all, that in the international academic world the construction of any discourse theory, my own as well as those of colleagues, cannot be natural, impartial or free from (imperial) cultural power. Therefore, the theorist must go beyond ambitions of grand narratives and attend to local, particular, especially hitherto marginalized, forms of discourses. These include not only ordinary discourses, but also the discourses of intellectual traditions. Thus, the theorist must depend on not only western intellectual traditions, but non-western ones as well; they must analyse not only western discourses but non-western discourses as well. In the same process, the theorist must place cultural power at the centre of attention.

Second, the discourse theorist must take 'race', ethnicity and culture, hence racism, seriously in theory construction. These properties must not be treated as if they belong only to other ordinary people; they exist at the core of the elite, disciplinary profession itself (for racisms in other social sciences see Gilroy 1992; Hall 1999; Said 1978, 1993; van Dijk 1993b). Such a new form of theory formation should make explicit its ethno-historical specificity, on the one hand, and, on the other hand, attempt to involve multiracial/coloured participation, collaboration and critical reflection as well as analysis of culturally diverse discourses, including local languages and issues.

Third, culturally different theories must genuinely interact with each other, not from the 'centre' to the 'periphery' or the other way around, but on an equal footing, not from fixed positions but with an open and critical mind, not merely to enrich local understanding but to integrate global perspectives as well. Thus, theorists must formulate their theory in such a way as to include local and global perspectives and to be open to intercultural negotiation and dialogue.

Last but not least, any position of theoretical enunciation has to be assumed by individual researchers. This means in particular that the person still has agency in the employment of these positions and consequently a role to play in the theoretical reconstruction. Different researchers have different backgrounds and qualities and so will use them differently.

So, I want to suggest, tentatively, that there is a strategy to take these positions up in a coherent and effective way. Namely, since cultures are diverse, competitive and dynamic, the theorizing individual can best proceed, not from any one particular culture, or from above all cultures, but from *in between cultures*. Theorizing from such in-between-cultural spaces enables the person not only to relativize and to transcend different cultures, thereby avoiding laying any universal and objective claim to truth, but also, more importantly perhaps, to intervene critically in the intra- and intercultural process. In addition, the in-between-cultural position compels the theorist to seek cultural coexistence and cohesion. As Rorty (1991: 14) has suggested, 'our best chance for transcending our acculturation is to be brought up in a culture which prides itself on not being monolithic – on its tolerance for a plurality of subcultures and its willingness to listen to neighbouring cultures'.

A pluralist account of discourse

That brings me, finally, to theory. From the above formulated stance, it will be clear that the version of discourse that I shall be sketching out here will have to do with the specific topics of interest I choose and the cultural political objectives I favour. That also means that it will bear the mark of personal intervention *vis-à-vis* wider culture and that it is not exhaustive or conclusive but open and developing. The properties of discourse I shall specify here are obviously interlocked but for the sake of exposition I will deal with them separately.

Discourse as cultural political construction

From the interstitial space between cultures, it can be seen, first, that what 'discourse' consists in is not something essential, pre-given, screaming for our attention. It does not have a fixed identity or boundary. It does have not such objective structures, processes and strategies as structuralist models tell us. Potentially, there can be any number of descriptions and any (bit of) discourse can be interesting. Any particular choice of discourse is then not a natural object or topic of enquiry. It is a meaningful and motivated semiotic phenomenon par excellence. Consequently, the definition of discourse(s), including the present one, is suggestive and subject to negotiation and contest.

In the present case – the result of personal initiative and cultural double vision – discourse, as object of enquiry and topic of interest, is essentially a (researcher's) construction of (human) construction and a cultural political construction at that. It involves the point of view, interest and circumstances of the researcher. By the same token, it involves the context of individuals or groups being studied: for example, the purpose and consequences, local situations and backgrounds of the language use in question. Further, such a construction will direct attention to, describe and act upon reality in a particular way, as opposed to culturally other, alternative ways. Discourse is thus an 'ideological product' in the sense of Vološinov (1986: 9):

> Any ideological product is not only itself a part of a reality (natural or social), just as is any physical body, any instrument of production, or any product for consumption, it also, in contradistinction to these other phenomena, reflects and refracts another reality outside itself. Everything ideological possesses *meaning*: it represents, depicts, or stands for something lying outside itself. In other words, it is a *sign*.
>
> (Emphasis original)[5]

From this perspective, we discourse researchers can expect and be expected to play a pivotal role in the selection, redescription, evaluation and recreation of discourses. Thus, in the culture-recreative process, we shall be able to keep reflexivity as a constant concern and common cultural benefit a conscious commitment. Out of the mass of discourses surrounding us, we can decide as our object of research on discourses about a particular issue, by a particular group of people, in a particular setting, in a principled and prioritized way. Further, instead of following a set or prescribed model of analysis, we can draw on methods eclectically and cultural contexts sensitively and examine those features or follow those procedures that may best suit practical research objectives. In addition, we shall be able to take an even more proactive approach to discourse studies and construct, like a critic or artist, meta-discourses or new discourses that may lead to adoption of culturally 'better' discourses in wider society. In Chapter 6, I choose to focus on the discourses of 'troubled' cultures, in this case the two opposing communities in Northern Ireland, and study them through a historical-contrastive method in order to seek out signs of hope. I compare and evaluate the discourses from different historical periods on the basis of a chosen parameter, namely, the degree of antagonism *vis-à-vis* the 'other' group. By identifying the abandonment of traditional themes of animosity, the adoption of new identities of equality and the assumption of a cooperative mode of speech, the analysis demonstrates the moral-rational agency of human cultures and beacons a possible, positive and promising future for Northern Ireland which has been dogged by the myth of a sectarian past. In Chapter 7, I experiment with a futuristic, transformative mode of discourse research. Here, other than practising the conventional work of analysing some past or existing discourse (data), I take an interventionalist approach to the wider cultural landscape of discourses and contemplate future, alternative or new discourses that have not become widely accepted. Identifying and highlighting a set of culturally divisive discourses as urgent cultural issues on the one side, I formulate and justify meta-discourses or new discourses that favour the virtues of cultural cohesion and common prosperity on the other side. It is hoped that once academia accepts such discourses, through writing, teaching and research, it could bring about greater cultural transformation.

Discourse as cultural ways of speaking

From the in-between-cultural standpoint, we can see, too, that discourse is not a unified and universal phenomenon, but, as configurations of texts and contexts, consists in a variety of incommensurably different ways of constructing meaning. Discourse, sociolinguistic and linguistic–anthropological work (for example, Hymes 1974) has long shown that 'language usage, norms for what counts as appropriate speech behavior, as well as the very definitions of such events vary from culture to culture and context to context' (Gumperz 1982: 3). In Chapter 1, I have already referred to the contested talk of Bin Laden. When we look at such talk, or any other discursive constructions, whether on democracy, individual freedom, women or the Arab world, across cultures and different groupings, the contradictions between discourses become sharper.

A parallel may be drawn here between this kind of pluralist understanding of discourse and Wittgenstein's (1968) notion of language as games. He shows that games as a whole have nothing in common but merely 'family resemblances' and maintains that it is these family resemblances that define the essence of language. As Wittgenstein explains it (1968: 31–2):

Look for example at board-games, with their multifarious relationships. Now pass to card-games; here you find many correspondences with the first group, but many common features drop out, and others appear. When we pass to ball games, much that is common is retained, but much is lost ... I can think of no better expression to characterize these similarities than 'family resemblances'; for the various resemblances between members of a family: build, features, colour of eyes, gait, temperament, etc. etc. overlap and criss-cross in the same way. – And I shall say: 'games' form a family.

Recent advances in the language-oriented approaches to culture, especially linguistic anthropology (Gumperz and Levinson 1996; Lucy 1992; Lutz 1988; Sherzer 1987; Urban 1991), provide further weight for understanding discourse as diversified. Here, as elsewhere in language studies, the assumption of linguistic universals, with the emergence of cognitive sciences, had until recently been dominant and languages and hence cultures were studied largely as variable systems of something more general. But especially with the new developments in the study of the reformulated linguistic relativity hypothesis, it is argued that meaning is not encapsulated in grammar and lexicon (think of the meaning of 'Will you bring back this book tomorrow?'). There are many (re)sources of meaning-making; contextual features of language use, including the characteristics of the speaker/hearer, their interests and desires, strategies of interpretation, power relationships, can all become part of cultural meaning-making practice. The cultural structuring of contexts, with which text and talk are indissolubly bound up, makes a universal notion of language (or discourse for that matter) untenable.

So, we should say, without denying the commonality that all humans speak and deserve a voice, that it is important to see discourse as *a diversity of discourses*. Different discourses embody different experiences and realities, much the same way that Whorf's (1956) specific languages embody different worldviews. On the one hand, different cultures have different histories, conditions, problems, issues, aspirations and so on. Consequently, the different cultural discourses which constitute them will have not only different objects of construction or topics, but also different categorizations, understandings, perspectives, evaluations and so on. They make up different cultural worlds, so to speak. On the other hand, such cultural discourses have not just different symbols and strategies of constructing meaning, but also different norms for using them (May 2001). As differentiated patterns of speaking and acting with culturally specific norms and values, discourses (re)define objects of knowledge and constrain what is sayable and what is not (Foucault 1972, 1980) and 'compel' relevant communities of speakers to think and act in particular ways (Grace 1987). In western cultures, for instance, people often use language as an expression of valued individual reason and self-identity (Bellah *et al.* 1985; Carbaugh 1993; Carey 1992). But in eastern cultures, people generally hold speech communication as a tool for maintaining relationship and harmony (Chen 1998, 2002; Liu 1996; Young 1994). For similar kinds of reasons, women and men can be said to possess and use different discourses (Tannen 1990).

If discourses are varied and diverse ways of constructing meaning, then we must not be content with reading and listening to our own, familiar arguments and explanations. Apart from that, we should pay attention to the discourses, including their contexts, from other cultures and communities, even if this may mean that we learn other tongues and study unknown history and geography. The multicultural view also means that (on top of reading travel literature and listening to foreign songs) we should also be actively involved in intercultural intellectual dialogue and communication, on philosophy, theory, method, findings and so on. Needless to say, we must try hard to preserve and maintain endangered languages and cultures. Only in this way can we hope to develop a genuine globalism or internationalism without lapsing into imperialism and crude universalism. In Chapter 5, I call on mainstream language scholarship to study marginalized, non-Western discourses and, against the background of dominant Western discourse on Hong Kong's decolonization in 1997, highlight the marginalized, unfamilar and oppositional voices from China and Hong Kong. In Chapter 7, I suggest, among other things, that we language researchers try to create the need for intercultural communication, debate the common rules of intercultural engagement and improve the (social, cultural and technological) conditions for it.

Discourse as cultural power struggle

From the in-between cultural vantage point in general and postcolonialism in particular, we can see that culturally diverse discourses are not a multicultural mosaic, however. The most crucial difference between cultural discourses is difference in power. The world's different discourses are not in harmonious relation with one another, but in tension, competition and opposition to one another. They embody hierarchical and hegemonic relations and practices, both internally and externally (Fairclough 1989; Foucault 1980; Fowler 1985). Discursive relations and practices of power, such as dominance, control and resistance, occur most often along the borders of 'race', gender, class and nation. For example, the gender-dichotomizing tendency in both everyday and professional English discourses (for example, 'chairman', the notion of men as rational) reflects historically rooted sexist hierarchical relationships and thereby represses alternative discourses of women's experience (Cameron 1992). Similarly, dominant western forms of language, through their demeaning metaphors, narratives, stereotypes and so on, discredit, ignore and exclude non-White, non-Western, Third World discourses (and hence experiences and realities) (Spivak 1988b). The English language for one, and one of colonialism at that, has domineered over the discourses of the rest of the world for centuries (Pennycook 1998). At the same time, it may be observed that marginalized, repressed and racialized groups, countries and regions endeavour to find and form alternative discourses to resist or subvert the western discourses of domination, prejudice and exclusion, for example new narratives of hybridity identity and (anti)colonial history (Ang 2001; Ngũgĩ 1986; West 1993). In this sense, discourses can be seen as also different and differentiated in power relationships.

In the postmodern, post-colonial and post-communist discorder at the threshold of the twenty-first century, discursive antagonism and struggle have intensified and saturate every aspect of contemporary human culture. The US and British governments' discourse of justifying their war in Iraq is confronted everywhere in the world by discourses of justice and peace. Against the discourse of global economy, including that of 'business going south/east', there is a discourse of anti-global capitalism. In opposition to the discourse of keeping jobs and man's interest, there is a discourse in many parts of the world in favour of the environment, sustainability and the future of mankind. Apart from such voiced/heard discourses, it should be recognized, too, that there will be many other or alternative discourses to the existing ones out there which have been silenced, ignored or otherwise repressed. For example, Said (1993: xi–xii) summarizes European writings on Africa, India, parts of the Far East, Australia and the Caribbean thus:

> What are striking in these discourses are the rhetorical figures one keeps encountering in their descriptions of 'the mysterious East', as well as the stereotypes about 'the African [or Indian or Irish or Jamaican or Chinese] mind', the notions about bringing civilization to primitive or barbaric peoples, the disturbingly familiar ideas about flogging or death or extended punishment being required when 'they' misbehaved or became rebellious, because 'they' mainly under-

stood force or violence best; 'they' were not like 'us', and for that reason deserved to be ruled.

The culturally oppositional perspective on discourse highlights the difference between the diversity of cultural discourses as essentially the difference in *power*. The power differences may take the form of unequal relations between cultural discourses and discursive practices of domination, discrimination and exclusion on grounds of 'race', colour, ethnicity, language or 'culture'. To study cultural discourses – discourses about 'us' and 'them', intercultural discourses, international communication and so on – is then to study the asymmetry of power and practices of power that are constituted through discourse. To study discourse is also to find new and non-hegemonic ways of speaking of the Other. In Chapter 4, I draw attention to western discourses of its cultural others and show how they typically construct culturally other places as contradictions. It will be seen that such rhetorical constructions of contradiction are premised on a sense of the West as the norm and standard. Further, they function to reaffirm the authority and supremacy of the West on the one hand, and effectively to undermine and discredit cultural others on the other hand. In Chapter 7, drawing on a variety of forms of cultural politics, I suggest a set of themes for speaking of the Other and justifications for those themes. For instance, to create a condition and relation of equality between cultures, it will be useful to speak of plurality and common goals of human cultures. Further, these appear to be better forms of speech than existing ones because they not only reflect the themes that have been obscured or suppressed, but also represent the best chances for mutual, maximum benefit.

Discourse as culturally dynamic

If we conceptualize discourse from the space in between cultures, we shall see that discourse is neither pure nor static. It does not emanate from some singular origin and it does not maintain a self-identical form through time and space. It cannot, therefore, be subjected to a 'uniform', 'systematic', 'comprehensive' analysis. Words and ideas travel all the time (Clifford 1992). The Chinese language, for example, has been characterized by borrowings and combinations of alien elements since its very beginning (Shen 1999). The same can be said of the English language. As we enter the twenty-first century, what we encounter is accelerated globalization, through conventional and digital media, migration, international trade and so on. Consequently, interconnections and interdependencies between cultures and hence between discourses multiply, so that discourses continue to refashion themselves. From another perspective, there is an increased level of external pressure for discourses of different cultures to continue to evolve and change.

At the same time, more importantly perhaps, discourse is itself not passive in the process of intercultural interaction *vis-à-vis* other cultural discourses. In Chapter 1, I already argued that, from a historical point of view, discourse has the inherent moral rationality, or critical consciousness, to reflect upon and reinvent a better self on the basis of its past discourses. Here, with the double-cultural consciousness, I would like to contend, with Taylor (1999), that culturally different discourses have an intrinsic dynamic, not to merge into a 'singularly rational', 'uniform', 'modern' discourse, but to recreate themselves continuously from out of their own historical and cultural traditions as well as interaction with other cultural discourses. Consequently, cultural discourses become not just hybridized or diaglossic (Bakhtin 1981), but, at the same time, progressively transformed as well.

Discourse studies is typically concerned with structures and functions of linguistic activity at a given point or relatively short period in time. Rarely does it consider discourse in relation to cultural transformation through large spaces of time (cf. Fairclough 1992[6]). In particular there has been relatively little attention paid to how change might come from within discourses and hence from the speaking individuals and communities of the discourses. From the in-between cultural standpoint (especially the post-colonialist perspective), we cannot possibly understand the power struggle between culturally diverse discourses in general and in particular the anti-imperialist discourses, for example from within the West and the rest of the world, without taking into account the immanent moral rationality of discourse and its speakers. The same principle applies to the rise of the feminist discourse and the anti-racist discourse amongst certain social and scholarly groups and the resulting transformation of societal discourses. It is the distinctly human ethical reflexivity or critical consciousness that leads to the abandonment of culture-specific less 'good', 'right', 'free' discourses and the adoption of better ones. The prophetic discourses produced by such avant-garde thinkers and authors as Frantz Fanon of Algeria, Lu Xun of China, Maxim Gorky of Russia and Paulo Freire of Brazil who stood up against their time are multicultural cases in point. In Chapter 7, I shall demonstrate how the two traditionally opposing communities in Northern Ireland, through time, transform their discourses from mutual animosity to coexistence and collaboration. There we shall see that traditional themes are relinquished, novel identities adopted and the mode of speaking with the Other changed.

The goals of CAD

If discourse is not free from culture but shot through with it, then scientific and intellectual discourse cannot be 'innocent', either. It is political, inadvertently or consciously: that is, its action will be characterized by particular values with respect to particular groups of people. Other than neutral or merely descriptive discourse will involve not only culturally relevant motivations and consequences, but also the potential to bring about cultural transformation. This means that we discourse researchers should then be mindful of our responsibilities and obligations as producers of academic, professional discourse (for a similar position see Eagleton 1983, 1991; Fairclough 1992; Hoggart 1958; van Dijk 1993a).

From the in-between cultural stance, the cultural political choice in a research project is the product of the interaction between the individual researcher's interventionalist initiative and the relevant, diverse cultural discourses. This means that there is no universal, timeless cultural politics. West (1993: 3–4), for example, has suggested that the most novel kind of cultural politics is the one that is the 'creative responses to the precise circumstances of our present time'. And he has identified what he calls 'the cultural politics of difference' as 'to empower and enable social action and if possible, to enlist collective insurgency for the expansion of freedom, democracy and individuality' (1993: 4).

So, finally, I want to make explicit the cultural political objective, or *cultural politics*, of CAD. My account of discourse above has highlighted diversity, power struggle and critical consciousness as the central characteristics of contemporary discourse. More broadly, our new global culture, as I described in the Introduction, is characterized by a changed (dis)order: increasing interconnections confounded by growing antagonism and resistance, so much so that the basic existence of many of the world's cultures and populations is under threat and erosion (see also Appadurai 1996; Bauman 1998; Huntington 1998). This changed global cultural context requires an urgent, new purpose in discourse and cultural research. Accordingly, I propose that *cultural coexistence and common cultural prosperity* be the ultimate objective of our discourse research, CAD.

Political ideals will remain a phantom unless they are translated into concrete, practical strategies of action, in this case, discourse research strategies. For the present objective, I have two broad strategies in mind; they specify the object and mode of discourse enquiry. On the one hand, CAD strives to undermine culturally repressive discourses, that is, those discourses that dominate, exclude or discriminate against groups and communities on the ground of 'cultural difference', be it historical, geographical, ideological, racial, ethnic or linguistic. I shall call it a deconstructive strategy. On the other hand, CAD endeavours to create and advocate new or alternative discourses that are inclusive, non-hegemonic and collaborative with regard to cultural 'others'. I shall call it a transformational strategy. Collectively, they make for a pragmatically motivated, interventionalist project (Bennett 1998), beyond mere description, explanation, interpretation or 'analysis' of just any text or talk.

The cultural political objectives described here must not be taken dogmatically, however. They are linked with the particular researcher's experience, skills and circumstances and the specifics of the research context. Moreover, the cultural politics proposed here must be negotiated dialogically and continuously with the groups of people or communities involved. In other words, the cultural politics of CAD must attempt to construct what Bhabha (1994: 57) describes as the 'modes of political and cultural agency that are commensurate with historical conjunctures where populations are culturally diverse, racially and ethnically divided – the objects of social, racial, and sexual discrimination'.

Conclusion

I began this chapter with the marginalized issue of cultural diversity and contest between human discourses within the discipline of discourse studies. Here I argued for the need of complementing its celebrated multidisciplinarity with cultural pluralism. To that end, I identified several obscured features of the disciplinary discourse. Thus, I revealed its western-historical particularity, beneath the veil of universality. I pointed to the whiteness of the profession, through the invisibility of colour. Further, I drew attention to the much ignored cultural diversity of communication and context, beyond the totalizing theory of 'integrated', 'unified' and formalized discourse.

In order to produce a culturally pluralist reconceptualization of discourse, I turned to cultural studies for a new position of theoretical articulation, over and above the universalist and aculturalist stance.

Rendering its radical insight into culture in general and its post-colonial and diasporic strategies in particular, I advocated an in-between-cultural strategy for reconceptualizing a culturally inclusive and dynamic theory of discourse. This strategy urges the researcher to go beyond their familiar and comfortable cultural confines, recognize the new global cultural conditions and take a personal initiative on the cultural division.

Speaking/writing from this in-between cultural position, I formulated a notion of discourse as culturally saturated and so pluralist: human discourses are incommensurably diverse, competitive and creative constructions and configurations of meaning through the use of linguistic symbols in particular contexts. Further, since discourse is not an independently given object but involves the researcher's interest, desire and other characteristics on the one side and social, cultural consequences on the other, I made explicit the specific cultural political motivation behind the current account. That is, the current theory is designed to achieve cultural harmony and common progress through deconstructing discourses of cultural repression and promoting discourses of common cultural prosperity.

In conclusion, let me stress that the notion of discourse that I have outlined here is neither purely western nor purely eastern, let alone being universal. It is supposed to be a product of personal intervention from within a particular space between western and eastern cultures. It reflects personal experience and initiative; it is connected with perceived global cultural conditions. As a scholar in discourse and cultural studies, I have travelled through eastern and western educational and intellectual systems (in China, the Netherlands, Singapore and the UK), lived across the encompassing cultures and seen cultural domination, discrimination and resistance. This personal cultural trajectory has doubtless helped shape the vision of discourse being unfolded here.

It may be noted, too, that this is a partial, provisional and 'floating' perspective. It offers one possible kind, and site, of envisaging discourse studies and cultural politics, amongst personally and culturally diverse and dynamic versions. It is tied to the current actuality of the world and particular issues involved therein. This means that other researchers, adopting such an in-between cultural stance, have the freedom of taking up other spaces between other particular cultures and have the choice of setting up other particular cultural political objectives. I am thinking of individuals with their particular personal biographies and cultural positions who find themselves in Asia, Africa, Australia, Europe and North and South America.

And yet, given the broad cultural political objective and its corresponding strategies, there remains a question as to what scholars and
students of language, communication and discourse can do in order to
achieve the desired cultural politics. This question of methodology and
methods I shall try to answer in the next chapter.

3
Political Ethnography

Introduction

Towards the end of the last chapter, I declared that the present reality-constitutive and culturally pluralist perspective on discourse is motivated to achieve an explicit form of cultural politics: to help facilitate cultural cohesion and common prosperity. More particularly and specifically, the current proposed theoretical position of CAD is oriented towards two, interrelated discourse research objectives. On the one hand, it aims to undermine existing discourses of cultural repression, domination and exclusion. On the other hand, it seeks to initiate and advocate subversive, alternative and creative discourses in favour of harmony amongst all cultural, ethnic and 'racial' groups.

Now the time has come for us to consider the corresponding questions of how we, in CAD, can effectively carry out discourse research and achieve those cultural political goals. These are three in kind and they have to do with different aspects of social research. First and foremost, how do we understand the nature of social (discourse) research? Is it truth-seeking, interpretive or political? Second, what would be our best angle of approach to it? That is, what concrete discourse research strategies, or in conventional parlance 'methods', are available or required to achieve the intended cultural politics? Here one might want to be still more concrete and ask what norms or policies, procedures, techniques, questions, concepts and so on we should resort to in pursuit of those cultural political objectives (but see later). In addition, by what criteria can we CAD researchers, our academic colleagues and students (who identify with our research field and so to whom we direct our research) assess the degree of success, or failure for that matter, in the chosen cultural politics? Or from another perspective, to what explicit research standards, accessible to the involved and relevant academia, should the researchers of CAD aspire in the cultural political research process?

These are issues of methodology and method; they will form the focus of the present chapter. Here 'methodology' is understood as the general view of and approach to social science, as well as the corresponding standard for evaluating research results (Crotty 1998; Feyerabend 1993; Giddens 1976; Giorgi 1970; Polkinghorne 1983). 'Method', on the other hand, is seen as the specific norms of research observed, procedures of investigation followed, types of question asked, concepts and categories of analysis employed and so on. Considered as a whole, they are the research principles constructed, selected or utilized for finding the best answers to research questions.

Methodology and method are not however isolated, autonomous tools of research; they are shaped by their specific intellectual context. So, before I describe what sort of methodology and method I shall be aiming to develop, let me briefly introduce this context. First, it may be observed that methodology and method are themselves constituent components of some larger research system and therefore related to the rest of that system (to a greater or lesser degree at least). Specifically, which methodology and method one adopts have to do with not just the theoretical perspective that one subscribes to, but also the epistemological stance that one adopts, as well as the research objectives. The latter co-determine the former (Crotty 1998). Regarding the present case, it may be recalled that representationalism and universalism were rejected and instead a culturally pluralist and anti-imperialist stance is advocated on discourse, including the scientific discourse on it (Chapters 1 and 2). Further, it was indicated that CAD is committed to a particular kind of cultural politics: cultural cohesion and common prosperity. These epistemological, theoretical and political stances will have a distinct impact on the shape of the methodology and method that I am going to develop; I shall spell this out where appropriate later.

Furthermore, from the present culturally pluralist stance (Chapter 2), it may be realized that there are different and competing methodologies and methods in the social sciences across cultures. Any particular choice of methodology or method will not therefore be impersonal, neutral or culturally inconsequential. Currently and generally, the Western human and social sciences operate on two broad, dominant though opposing methodological paradigms, namely, foundationalism and interpretivism. Further, the methods they apply are Western in origin and are used predominantly for Western materials and reality. At

the same time, however, there have been other, non-Western methodological approaches to social science but they have basically been
shunned. For instance, there has been a long and dynamic Chinese
intellectual tradition, beginning at least with Zhuang Zi (*c.369–c.286*,
philosopher: http://www.apophaticmysticism.com/tttpractice.html),
through to Lu Xun (1881–1936, author and social critic: www.rwor.org/
a/v20/970–79/970/luxun.htm), which treats knowledge and research
as overcoming categorization and as political struggle, respectively
(Needham 1954–95). Any attempt to 'integrate' or 'systematize' such
culturally diversified, competing and dynamic methodological discourses, then, would be to totalize knowledge against culturally
different intellectual traditions, impoverishing science and research
consequently.

So, what sort of methodology and method shall I be developing here?
First, as one primary task of this chapter, I shall attempt to argue for a
methodology that generates scientific knowledge and discourse, neither
from a culturally singular tradition nor from a culturally omniscient
standpoint, but *from in-between cultures*. Knowledge produced from this
strategic position will then be a cultural 'double vision', uncertain yet
interventional. The in-between cultural stance implies, among other
things, that social research should not rely on rigid, fixed, singular,
'impersonal', 'universal' and 'timeless' methods. Rather, it ought to seek
and draw upon flexible, personal–cultural, local–global, strategies and
to do so in dialogue with the relevant academic community as well as
the one under investigation.

As the other central task of the chapter, I shall sketch out two sets of
concrete principles or strategies of discourse research corresponding to
the intended cultural political objectives.[1] The first, termed 'deconstructive', directs researchers' attention to past and present discourses
of cultural difference and discrimination and helps the researchers to
undermine them through various discourse analytic techniques. The
second, named 'transformative', orients to potential, future discourses
and suggests ways of initiating and advocating discourses of cultural
harmony and prosperity. Different from the universal and impersonal
methods which purportedly identify, describe, explain or criticize
'given' discourses, the concepts and procedures that I offer are suggestions, illustrations or pointers to other, possible alternatives. They are
eclectic in origin, flexible in application, syncretistic in interrelation and
mindful of local and global contexts. Therefore, they are essentially
open, provisional and experimental. Later in the chapter I shall call
these strategies 'political ethnography' and explain why. The entire

system of the general view of and approach to social science ('methodological stance') and the concrete discourse research strategies ('method'), as well as the criteria for assessing research, constitute the methodological component of CAD.

In what follows, I shall first critically review the main Western methodological approaches to human and social science. Then, drawing upon the critique developed thereof, I shall go on to outlining the in-between-cultural stance on social research. Finally, I shall spell out the deconstructive and transformative strategies of cultural studies of discourse. In conclusion, I shall reflect on the evaluative criteria guiding the quality of practical research.

Foundationalism versus interpretivism

The foundationalist impasse

In modern western social science, the dominant methodology seems to hold a twofold view that serves as its foundation. On the one side, the object of social enquiry is a neutral fact. In other words, the meaning of social facts inheres in an independent, discrete, object world. On the other side, there are possibly neutral, transparent and impersonal methods that scientists can use in order to obtain true knowledge. The methodological view of this kind is usually called 'foundationalism'.

Proceeding from this position, researchers often use the principles of 'validity' and 'reliability' – the foundational two notions borrowed from natural science – in their research practice as the yardsticks for selecting, designing and implementing methods and evaluating research results (Silverman 1993). 'Reliability' refers to the degree to which research findings are replicable by different people studying the same phenomenon or by the same person on different occasions (Silverman 1993: 145). Under this rule, it is expected that different people looking at the same phenomenon, when using the same method, will arrive at the same conclusion. 'Validity' refers to the extent to which a description is accurate about the phenomenon it characterizes (Silverman 1993: 149). According to this standard, it is supposed that impersonal methods are possible.

What is glossed over, however, is that social research, from research questions, recognition and selection of suitable data, through analysis to the presentation of research findings, also has to do with the characteristics of researchers, formulation of questions, the nature of data source and selection, context-dependent interpretation of data and the manner of presentation. For one thing, data material is indeterminate: due to particular interests and assumptions, it is subject to different interpretations. For another, scientific writing is not merely descriptive; it may be argumentative with respect to professional rivals. Consequently, it becomes impossible to disentangle the researcher from the researched, the researcher's discourse from that of the researched. In other words, the foundationalist approach fails to recognize not only the problem of the constitution of reality, on the one hand, but also, on the other hand, the problem of the construction of knowledge. For these and other reasons, reliability and validity of scholarly description and argumentation are unprocurable. As Habermas (1972: 68–9) states:

> The positivistic attitude conceals the problems of world constitution. *The meaning of knowledge itself becomes irrational* – in the name of rigorous knowledge. In this way the naïve idea that knowledge describes reality becomes prevalent. This is accompanied by the copy theory of truth, according to which the reversibly univocal correlation of statements and matters of fact must be understood as isomorphism.
>
> (Emphasis original)

The foundationalist position is challenged with post-positivist arguments, too, as in Popper (1959), Kuhn (1970) and Feyerabend (1993) (see also Hammersley and Atkinson 1995; Marshall and Rossman 1995). These thinkers insist on the historicity of the natural and human domains. They expose the inconsistencies between scientific claims and actual practices. They point to the theoretical assumptions on which scientific research findings are based but not all of which are verified or verifiable. Thus for them, science is a continuous process of improving on our understanding. But because post-positivism, especially *à la* Popper and Kuhn, has its foundations in a posited world, I shall not take it further here.

And yet foundationalist assumptions and practices seem to run deep in the mainstream of discourse studies, which itself has been inalienably bound up with modern western linguistics in general and linguistic structuralism in particular. The most typical and obstinate manifestation of such foundationalism is that 'language', and for that matter linguistic 'structures', 'strategies', 'processes', 'levels', and a host of other 'properties' or 'features' are held to be pre-given, objective facts. For this reason, practitioners take such to be the basis of discourse studies as an empirical science. As a partial consequence, they proffer their methods as 'universal', present linguistic features identified as 'neutrally given', and provide explanations as 'indubitable'. Take conversation analysis (CA) as a specific example. Here conversations are posited as having objective rules and structures. The task of the analyst is to discover them, by going through observable conversational material. Only observable data (often in the form of transcripts) count as reliable evidence (the analyst must not bring in their own pre-understandings and assumptions). Other types of discourse analysis, similarly, take structures and processes of discourse as independent of the individual analyst and the wider cultural framework. They present and prescribe methods in such a way as if they were the standard, correct, universal. They put a premium on grammatical/textual structures or strategies and cognitive structures (for example, 'attitudes', 'ideologies') at the expense of contextual connections.

In sum, the foundationalist methodology is ill-suited for social research in general and the meaning-making activity of language in particular. It ignores the intentionality and the cultural diversity of discourse as object of enquiry. It conceals the creativity and authority of professional individuals. In addition, it represses the need for intercultural dialogue and thereby monopolizes truth.

Interpretivist alternatives

Now let me turn to the other, oppositional but increasingly accepted, or rather revived, methodological view in modern western social science, interpretivism. Interpretivism is not an internally homogeneous and externally discrete tradition in methodology, however. The term is used rather loosely to refer to a range of methodological positions that are attributable to various, more research process-conscious, Western systems of social science, beginning at least with Dilthey. These include such diverse lineages as post-structuralism and postmodernism (Derrida 1976; Foucault 1980; Lyotard 1984), social constructionism (Berger and Luckmann 1967; Gergen 1999), feminism (Butler 1992; Spender 1980; Stanley and Wise 1983), phenomenology (Husserl 1931; Heidegger 1962), hermeneutics (Gadamer 1989) and critical theory (Adorno 1974; Horkheimer 1982; Habermas 1984, 1987). In the following, I shall consider them briefly and mainly in terms of their methodological orientations. Where appropriate, I shall consider their relevance, as well as hindrance, to the goals of CAD and to the particular methodological stance that I shall develop.

Phenomenology: intentional and cultural worlds

Phenomenology is an intellectual current that drew attention to the intentionality and cultural framing of reality (Heidegger 1962; Husserl

1931; Merleau-Ponty 1974; Sartre 1969). Let me explain. On the one hand, the notion of intentionality refers to the necessary interaction between the subject and object, hence the interpenetration between the two. This being the case, the distinction between the subject and the object is then dismantled. The blurring of the distinction, or the merging of the subject and object, can be clearly seen by analysing the different 'places' of the 'insider' participants who produce 'raw' material and the 'outsider' researchers who study it within the research context. Thus, first of all, the objectives of the researched and researchers are different. For instance, whereas the 'insiders' orient their activities to practical, complex and often multiple purposes, the scholars may not be interested in everything that is going on there. For instance, they may focus on their opinions only. In fact it is not possible for them to take everything into consideration. Second, the range of contextual information that is available to the insider participants and the outsider researchers is at variance between the two parties. The researchers cannot have all the personal, ethnographic and organizational information to the same extent as the participating interactants themselves do. Moreover, because of the trade-off between analytical details and extent of observation, the discourse data for scrutiny are usually (de)limited. For example, video recordings 'omit' broader cultural and historical context. Audiotapes 'omit' facial expressions, gesture and posture. Transcriptions may generalize umming and ahing. Extracts for analysis exclude surrounding texts. Consequently, the researchers' readings are only relative to the available, chosen data. Third, the temporal–sequential process of discourse data is different between the participating interactants and the research analysts: interactants' discourse and understanding evolve temporally whereas the analysts do not have this constraint. Think of the fact that the viewers of a film develop and change their perceptions and understandings as the vista unfolds. Conversation moves in the same way. But the discourse analysts are not restricted in this way. Instead and in fact, they can read pertinent, sometimes discontinuous, fragments of discourse recursively and control their own speed of reading.

On the other hand, it is argued that reality, experience or phenomena are culturally framed – defined, categorized, evaluated and classified. Consequently, human social worlds are diversified and shifting, such that it is futile to seek universal, enduring entities: think of 'justice', 'food' or 'loneliness'. They are socially constructed and saturated with human emotions and desires, cultural values, historical ideas, theoretical preferences, and so on. Consequently, it will be illusory to sort out the socio-cultural and discursive dross from 'scientific facts'.

More specifically, the discourse of social human science imposes meanings on the phenomena under study and thereby has social consequences for them.

Hermeneutics: historical interpretation

Hermeneutics was originally concerned with the exegesis of scripture, but was later extended to become a theory of human understanding in general (Gadamer 1989). Central to hermeneutics is the notion of interpretation as historically situated. The historicity of scientific interpretation can be seen from several perspectives.

First of all, researchers and the research activities they carry out – from selection of topics, formulation of questions and data collection to research presentation or publication – are embedded in historical context. This means that the social and human scientists function within particular personal, institutional and cultural settings and arrangements. The traditions, habits and customs that are embodied in such contexts constrain individual researchers and thereby their research activities. In particular, it may be noted that such conventional organizations, whether in terms of assumptions or overt practices, constitute power relations and individual or institutional interests. The same, by the way, may be said of the individuals, groups or institutions that are being investigated: they, too, are susceptible to contextual historicity.

Second, it will be realized that the researchers cannot detach themselves from the object of research or the researched. For one thing, researchers are also human beings and cannot free themselves from their own individual and social desires and agendas when they look for research topics, choose theories and methodologies, or present research conclusions. For another, the amount of knowledge available to the researcher/analyst about the phenomenon under study is to a greater or lesser degree limited and that will consequently shape the quality of their interpretation. More importantly, meanings themselves are not fixed or given but 'represent a fluid multiplicity of possibilities' (Gadamer 1989: 268). Consequently, Gadamer suggests (1989: 268–9):

> All that is asked is that we remain open to the meaning of the other person or text. But this openness always includes our situating the other meaning in relation to the whole of our own meanings or ourselves in relation to it . . . *The hermeneutical task becomes of itself a questioning of things* . . . That is why a hermeneutically trained con-

sciousness must be, from the start, sensitive to the text's alterity . . .
The important thing is to be aware of one's own bias, so that the text
can present itself in all its otherness, and thus assert its own truth
against one's own fore-meanings.   (Emphasis original)

From the above it will be clear that interpretation has multifarious
dimensions. It is inextricably bound up with the researcher/interpreter,
the researched/producer, the social milieu including interests and
power, and traditions, such that discourse studies cannot be mere
description but is an interpretative business (or, to use Weber's term,
Verstehen). Furthermore, it can be deduced from the contextual and historical nature of research that different practitioners may produce variable interpretations. Related to this, too, is the irreducible ambiguity of
meaning. Such is the human and social world that behaviour and events
are, to use Gilbert and Mulkay's (1984: 9) phrase, 'the repositories of
multiple meanings'.

Post-structuralism and postmodernism: genealogy and deconstruction

Post-structuralism and postmodernism are two Western intellectual
movements whose influence spreads across philosophy and social
science as well as a range of other social activities. Whilst post-
structuralism is a reaction to structuralism which originated in
Durkheim's sociology and de Saussure's linguistics, and postmodernism
a reaction to modernism which emanated from West European science
and technology, these two also overlap and inform each other.

Both post-structuralism, as in the later works of Foucault (1980, 1986),
and postmodernism, as in Derrida's oeuvres (1976, 1981), reject the
notion of language as a reference to reality and the notion of reality as
having essential qualities independent of textual mediation. Instead and
to a large extent, both share the view of meaning as consisting in relationships between an unending play of differences in texts and traces
of texts and therefore as being indeterminate, unsteady and deferred,
hence *différance* (Derrida 1976).

Here two major, interrelated methodological corollaries from this
position may be sketched out. On the one side, Foucault (1980, 1986)
points out that knowledge and power are two sides of the same coin,
hence the coinage *knowledge/power*, and that power, which is embodied
in the experience and practice of all human groups, can be not only
repressive but also productive. Therefore, to do critical social science
is to highlight and reverse the power hierarchy in knowledge

construction and wage war against power effects. Further, critical social science can empower people through, for example, re-articulation of subject positions. For these tasks Foucault (1980: 85) constructs a genealogy:

> in contrast to the various projects which aim to inscribe knowledges in the hierarchical order of power associated with science, a genealogy should be seen as a kind of attempt to emancipate historical knowledges from that subjection, to render them, that is, capable of opposition and of struggle against the coercion of a theoretical, unitary, formal and scientific discourse. It is based on a reactivation of local knowledges – of minor knowledges, as Deleuze might call them – in opposition to the scientific hierarchisation of knowledges and the effects intrinsic to their power.

On the other side, Derrida (1976, 1981) advocates the strategy of deconstruction. For him this is a philosophical position, a political strategy as well as a critical form of reading. For our purpose here, let us consider it as a mode of reading and interpretation. Given that meaning is in flux, it is possible to destabilize, take apart, subvert meaning, thereby fixation and certitude, by uncovering hidden assumptions. Deconstruction is especially directed at such hierarchical binaries as reality/appearance, object/subject, self/other, centre/margin, reason/madness, good/evil, where the 'superior' term is used to exclude the 'inferior' term in order to monopolize truth. Culler (1983: 86) summarizes the strategy succinctly:

> to deconstruct a discourse is to show how it undermines the philosophy it asserts, or the hierarchical oppositions on which it relies, by identifying in the text the rhetorical operations that produce the supposed ground of argument, the key concept or premise.

However, since post-structuralism and postmodernism conceptualize meaning only as confined in texts, they generally avoid research into context, personal, historical and institutional, with which texts interact. For the same reason, they also overlook audience and readership, hence interpretation, including that of the researcher. At the heart of these problems are their roots in the structuralist notion of meaning as residing in the linguistic signs, on the one hand, and the associated relativism whereby they refuse to make explicit valued judgements, on the other hand.

Feminism: political values and debate

Feminism is similar to postmodernism in that it opposes foundational-ism and positivism, but it does so through attacking patriarchal reason and rationality (Spender 1980; Stanley and Wise 1983). But it is also different from postmodernism in that it rejects relativism by emphasizing feminist consciousness and feminist politics (Butler 1992; Gill 1995).

Feminism is a diversified intellectual (and social) movement. However, two general methodological trends may be distinguished and they converge on the same feminist cause. On the one side, a strand of work argues for a distinct form of knowing which is different from that of men. Consequently, there will be a *feminine* form of research and a special place in knowledge-making. On the other side, a body of work maintains that research is necessarily political (Butler and Scott 1992) and therefore opts for explicit and specific agenda, values, concerns or commitments. Consequently, there will be a *feminist* form of research. All the same, both these methodological starting points are oriented to the same political ethics and action. Namely, feminist research seeks to reduce or eliminate social inequality and injustice inflicted on women and to achieve emancipation and freedom for women.

Since feminist methodology is defined by the specific values it chooses, as just mentioned, there is the question of warranting and accountability. Instead of 'reason' and 'truth', and in the absence of ontological guarantees, feminist researchers rely on open and explicit debate, or what Butler calls 'contingent foundations', to sustain and advance the women's cause for freedom and justice. Gill (1995: 178–8) expresses its strategies well:

> Political action . . . may not be best served by asserting truth . . . in fact, the impetus for social transformation may call equally upon empathy, anger or disgust . . . Claims about domination are claims about injustice, and as such they belong on the terrain of politics and in the realm of persuasive speech and action . . . We make social transformation an *explicit* concern of our work, acknowledge the values which inform it, and situate all interpretations and readings in a realm in which they can be *interrogated* and *argued* about.
>
> (Emphasis original)

Critical theory: interests and norms of discourse

From critical theory, especially the one developed by Habermas (for example, 1972, 1984 and 1987), two methodologically significant themes may be highlighted. First, it is the human interests that guide all activity, including the social sciences, so that it is not possible to separate value from fact (Habermas 1972). From a slightly different perspective, researchers are part of the same historical, moral, political order that they study. As Habermas puts it (1972: 181):

> Whether dealing with contemporary objectivations or historical traditions, the interpreter cannot abstractly free himself from his hermeneutic point of departure. He cannot simply jump over the open horizon of his own life activity and just suspend the context of tradition in which his own subjectivity has been formed in order to submerge himself in a subhistorical stream of life that allows the pleasurable identification of everyone with everyone else ... An interpretation can only grasp its object and penetrate it in a relation in which the interpreter reflects on the object and himself *at the same time* as moments of an objective structure that likewise encompasses both and makes them possible.   (Emphasis original)

Consequently, for Habermas, the goal of social research should be self-reflective, practical and above all socially critical (see also Giddens 1984: ch. 6).

Second, in order (for critical theory) to exercise social critique, that is, negative evaluations of social practices, one needs to reconstruct the norm for undistorted human communication (Habermas 1984, 1987). So based on ideal speech situations Habermas sets normative standards, which are thought to be immanent in all language use, communication free from constraint and representative of the common good. These are then to be used as the criterion for social and cultural criticism. This requirement means that social researchers are faced with, and ought to make, moral and normative choices.

Social constructionism

Social constructionism is a relatively recent intellectual development; it is becoming increasingly influential within the social sciences on the understanding of knowledge and enquiry (Burr 1995; Gergen 1999). It argues that all knowledge, whether as internal consciousness or the external world or both, is constructed in and through situated, human cultural and historical interaction. Knowledge is not a mere copy of reality, nor is it free from interest; rather it is constructed through social interaction between the subject and the object. In particular, such construction reflects power. These properties of knowledge consequently make it imperative that discourse researchers refrain from making truth claims and that they be mindful of the ethical consequences of their scientific practice. That is, they need to be clear whose interests their methodology serves. By implication it cannot be separated from specific time and space or social context more generally. Thus, it is irrelevant, or rather a mistake, to make a distinction between the 'objective' and the 'subjective'.[2] Similarly, Crotty has formulated social constructionism as follows (1998: 42):

> It is the view that all knowledge, and therefore all meaningful reality as such, is contingent upon human practices, being constructed in and out of interaction between human beings and their world, and developed and transmitted within an essentially social context.

Furthermore, social constructionism maintains that knowledge is linked with power relations and practices (Foucault 1980). In the above, I indicated that phenomenology and critical theory both view knowledge as a historically and culturally contested field of the human realm. Here in social constructionism, similarly, the production, circulation and consumption of knowledge are understood as linked with powerful institutions: science, the government, education, religion, language and so on.[3]

At this point, I could move on to doing the same exercise on the Chinese methodological approaches (see Hart: www.stanford.edu/dept/ HPS/RethinkingSciCiv/etexts/Hart/BeyondSciCiv.html) but my purpose here is not to offer a cultural comparative analysis. Rather, I want to suggest that Western approaches in social science methodology have not shown sufficient cultural awareness, let alone a willingness to engage in interculturally egalitarian and democratic communication and reconstruction. So to this problem I turn.

Western bias in social research methodology

The Western interpretivist currents of methodology all seem to converge on the view that social science is a historically and culturally situated, knowledge-creative, social activity, rather than a neutral, objective facsimile of reality. Accordingly, they generally adopt an approach to social science that is dialogical in nature and orientation. And yet, this interpretivist reaction, ironically, has not led to a dialogical interaction with culturally different, especially non-Western, methodological traditions, let alone the adoption of non-Western methods at an international academic level. (Critical) discourse analysis, for example, has not yet seen the beginning of cultural pluralism in its methodological approach. Instead the issue of 'uniformity' and universalism remains a barrier to a culturally more inclusive form of methodology and consequently to the cultural political objectives as set out in Chapter 2.

Part of the reason, at least, has to do with the fact that the various methodological paradigms fail to situate themselves in a broader, global framework of historical–cultural power relations and practices. This in turn has to do of course with political expediency. Often implicitly and indirectly, they denigrate non-western views of knowledge, science and methods to an 'inferior' and 'substandard' class. On the other side, through the troupes of ever more 'integrated', 'systematic' and 'universal' grand narratives, they effectively maintain, consolidate and perpetuate the Anglo/European/American Western dominant position in the international system of communication in the social sciences. In so doing, they also stamp out non-western differences. A moment of reflection here will reveal the underlying, historically derived, culturally asymmetrical relations of power between the West's and the Rest's intellectual, academic, professional discourses. I have already discussed this issue in the last chapter. So there is no need here to hark back to that problem.

To formulate a culturally less biased form of methodology and ultimately to achieve the intended cultural politics, then, we need a more radical perspective and approach. Such a reorientation must try to resist cultural prejudice, domination and exclusion as its starting point. Rorty (1991: 34) has offered advice on this when he says that the best way to avoid methodological ethnocentrism is to create 'a culture which prides itself on not being monolithic – on its tolerance for a plurality of subcultures and its willingness to listen to neighbouring cultures'. From another perspective, Feyerabend (1993: viii) suggests:

> science should be taught as one view among many and not as the one and only road to truth and reality. There is nothing in the nature of science that excludes such institutional arrangements or shows that they are liable to lead to disaster.

Further, he admonishes us (1993: 12):

> the world which we want to explore is a largely unknown entity. We must, therefore, keep our options open and we must not restrict ourselves in advance.

At this point, I might as well refer as an example to a different, ancient Chinese version of ascertaining knowledge, or indeed, according to Zhuang Zi, *having no-knowledge* (as different from not having knowledge, hence ignorance). To have knowledge of the world, for Zhuang Zi, is to be able to make distinctions between things in it. However, this kind of knowledge is merely commonsensical, external and superficial knowledge, because, in ordinary life, people's points of view are finite and therefore their opinions partial and one-sided. At the same time, Zhuang Zi believes in the relativity and interdependency of all things in the universe. Where there is life there is death. There is something good because there is something bad. The construction of a table is the destruction of the tree. A thief can steal a piece of gold but the gold can merely be moved somewhere in the same universe. To reach a higher level of knowledge, that is, the Tao, therefore, is to discard ordinary differentiations and identifications, hence having no-knowledge. When all distinctions, including the one between self and others, disappear, 'I' reach the centre of the circle of movement, no longer affected by external changes. (No-)knowledge obtained at this level is unthinkable and inexpressible (since there is always something beyond whatever is thinkable and expressible). Thus an imaginary conversation in *Zhuang Zi* that takes place between Confucius and his favourite disciple Yen Hui illustrates well the method of obtaining a higher level of knowledge (Fung 1948: 116):

Yen Hui said: 'I have made some progress.' What do you mean?' asked Confucius. 'I have forgotten human-heartedness and righteousness,' replied Yen Hui. 'Very well, but that is not enough,' said Confucius. Another day, Yen Hui again saw Confucius and said: 'I have made some progress.' 'What do you mean?' asked Confucius. 'I have forgotten rituals and music,' replied Yen Hui. 'Very well, but that is not enough,' said Confucius. Another day, Yen Hui again saw Confucius and said: 'I have made some progress.' 'What do you mean?' asked Confucius. 'I sit in forgetfulness,' replied Yen Hui.

At this Confucius changed [his] countenance and asked: 'What do you mean by sitting in forgetfulness?' To which Yen Hui replied: 'My limbs are nerveless and my intelligence is dimmed. I have abandoned my body and discarded my knowledge. Thus I become one with the Infinite. This is what I mean by sitting in forgetfulness.' Then Confucius said: 'If you have become one with the Infinite, you have no personal likes and dislikes. If you have become one with the Great Evolution (of the universe), you are one who merely follow its changes. If you really have achieved this, I should like to follow your steps.'

The point of this philosophical excursion is that different cultures have different ways of searching for knowledge and the culturally different ways, each being finite but in a different way, make different sets of distinctions. These different sets of distinctions are partial, biased and power-ridden and consequently constrain the searching of 'no-knowledge'. It will be methodologically productive then to break down cultural borders and boundaries of methodologies and transcend culturally singular discourses in general and distinctions in particular.

An in-between cultural stance

What specific form then should a culturally diversified social (discourse) research methodology take? What I want to propose here is a conceptual strategy, or principle, for social (discourse) science methodology. Namely, we attempt to seek and to produce scientific knowledge, not from a culturally singular and stationary position, but *from in-between cultures*, especially western *and* non-western. Let us call it the *in-between cultural* approach.

This approach has a few specific implications for the methods and process of discourse research to which I would like to draw attention here. First, the in-between cultural approach implies that one must not rely on just one cultural tradition of methods. Confinement to just the western, or just the non-western, methodology will only result in totalizing research, thereby impoverishing rather than enriching it. Moreover, since existing models of discourse analysis are concerned to describe, explain or interpret and to study mainly American/ European/Western/English phenomena (even if sometimes these include social problems), their methods are not sufficient or even relevant for the cultural political problems in the realm of East/West, white/ non-white, (neo)colonizer/(de)colonized, superpower/developed/Third World countries. Thus, from an in-between cultural stance, researchers should always try not only to draw upon existing, familiar traditions but also to resort to other methodological paradigms. In this way, researchers can benefit from concepts and techniques from diverse cultures and thereby be equipped to reach a culturally open, dialogical and enlightened form of understanding.

That does not mean, however, that researchers merely mechanically combine methodologies from different cultural traditions. Rather it means they must make choices that are best suited for reaching the intended cultural political goals. Thus, the in-between cultural position aspires to what Polkinghorne (1983: xi) has called 'a syncretic approach which integrates the results obtained through multischematic and multiparadigmatic systems of enquiry'.

Second, the in-between cultural position rejects any 'universal' form of methods. According to this approach, researchers must not stick to the same, fixed or preferred set of methods, independently of the local, cultural and linguistic contexts. Rather, they need to shift methods as they research into different cultural discourses.

Third, observations, findings or conclusions enunciated from the in-between cultural position are not absolute truths or norms. Rather, as products of cultural 'double vision', they are rearticulations, creations, interventions. For this reason, the in-between cultural approach is designed for innovative research. This leads to my further point about innovation.

Fourth, given that appropriating culturally different but particular frames requires individuals' choices, this principle renders it possible for individual researchers to create and intervene in the scientific activity as a cultural process, thereby facilitating cultural transformation. By taking such an in-between cultural stance, researchers can avoid proceeding from predetermined categories and levels of analysis of any one particular cultural tradition. That is, individual researchers need not be bound by any one methodological tradition but are encouraged to change the research culture by introducing methodological diversity.

Finally, this approach also emphasizes that discourse researchers should pay attention to not only the local context, including the concerns of the researched (Blommaert 1997), but also the global perspectives, not only personal experiences but also (multi)cultural insights (Bloor 1978; Cappella 1991).

It may be conceded though that this approach would expect researchers to go out of their way to learn about other cultures' intellectual traditions and to do so continuously. But, at another level, it is precisely the point of this approach. That is, methodological approaches of different cultural lineages, just as theoretical perspectives, ought to interact with, complement and inspire each other, in order to achieve academic democracy, produce scientific innovation and enrich the international research culture as a whole.

In another sense, the in-between cultural stance is a pragmatic one in that it encourages the use of research strategies that best accomplish the goals of cultural politics. Not merely western concepts and procedures are used, but non-western issues and accordingly appropriate non-western methods are drawn upon as well, all for the sake of intercultural and international cohesion, communication and cooperation. As Barker and Galasinski (2001: 46) have suggested, cultural discourse researchers should produce knowledge, not as 'a matter of getting a true or objective picture of reality', but as one of 'creating tools with which to cope with the world'. They illustrate this pragmatic approach thus (2001: 47):

> since discourses of freedom and discourses of determination are socially produced for different purposes in different realms it makes sense to talk about freedom from political persecution or economic scarcity without the need to say that agents are free in some metaphysical and 'underdetermined' way. Rather, such discourses are comparing different social formations and determinations and judging one to be better than another on the basis of our socially determined values.

To schematize, the in-between cultural principle favours those strategies that

- help identify and challenge discourses of cultural imperialism in ordinary and professional life
- focus research on the discourses of the subaltern or the disadvantaged in order to help them
- help formulate and advocate discourses of cultural cohesion and prosperity.

The in-between cultural position of enunciation has a number of advantages. First, it allows academic individuals to play a more creative and culturally interventionalist role in changing the scientific research culture. For example, individuals adopting such a research position can bring in or draw on different cultural methodological principles eclectically, thereby creating broader perspectives and innovative modes of research. Second, it may open new research ground. For instance, in-between culture-minded researchers may be able to introduce fresh topics of enquiry, draw attention to new phenomena of cultural concern and ask unconventional questions which would be out of the question from a monocultural position. Third, it may help advance the cultural politics of CAD at the level of scholarship. As I argued in Chapter 2, international social science in general and discourse studies in particular are not culturally neutral but themselves saturated with power im-balance. Thus, individuals in favour of researching from in between cultures may become critical of 'universal' knowledge fabricated out of particular cultures and initiate debates on those intellectual traditions that dominant cultures have suppressed. In so doing, they facilitate and constitute cultural dialogue and diversity within social science as well as discourse studies.

Political ethnography

What would the concrete research strategies under the auspices of the in-between cultural stance be like then? In this section I will describe the general nature of the research strategies proposed and in the next their individual forms, contents and conditions. Taken as a whole, these strategies can be described as at once ethnographic and political in character. Let me explain.

On the one hand, these strategies are ethnographic in a number of senses. First and foremost, they go beyond the (post-)structuralist prac-tice to confine meaning to (inter)text and talk irrespective of their context and study not only verbal forms but also characteristics of their speakers, listeners, historical circumstances and global connections and so on (Atkinson 1990, 1992; Widdicombe and Wooffitt 1995; Willis 1978). Second, they not only encourage the researcher's role and per-spective as an individual and cultural member, but also give credit to the concerns and perspectives of the researched (During 1999: 17–18; Hammersley and Atkinson 1995; Jessor *et al.* 1996; Widdicombe and Wooffitt 1995; Willis 1978, 1980). Moreover, these strategies are eclec-tic and open to a *combination* of *any* theories, approaches, concepts and data, across disciplines and across cultures, as long as they contribute to the cultural politics of CAD.

It needs to be stressed that 'ethnographic' is not used here in the classic – realist and naturalist – sense (for a critique see Clifford and Marcus 1986; Hammersley 1992). On the contrary, the intended ethnography is explicitly politically motivated. Thus, other than being 'descriptive', 'explanatory', 'interpretive' or otherwise 'objective', the strategies guided by the in-between cultural stance are responsive and conducive to the cultural political goals of CAD. Thus for example, one central strategy here is to focus on the researcher's own choice of the discourses reproducing cultural tension, repression or cohesion.

In this respect, these are also different from the interpretivist approach, which lets research questions determine methods (though unlike foundationalism) but has no constraint on the sort of questions to be asked (see, for example, Polkinghorne 1983: 3):

> Science is not seen as an activity of following methodological recipes that yield acceptable results. Science becomes the creative search to understand better, and it uses whatever approaches are responsive to the particular questions and subject matters addressed. Those methods are acceptable which produce results that convince the community that the new understanding is deeper, fuller, and more useful than the previous understanding.

That leads me precisely to the point about the politics of the ethnography. The discourse researcher here takes reflexivity seriously and puts cultural politics before any ethnographic interest and innovation in theory, method, data and so on. More specifically, the researcher invents, borrows, concocts and applies research methods with a view to subverting discourses of cultural prejudice, domination and marginalization and advocating new discourses of cultural coexistence, cohesion and cooperation. This parallels the social politics of critical discourse analysis, as expounded by, for example, van Dijk (1997: 23):

> Beyond observation, systematic description and explanation, they [discourse scholars taking a political stance] decide to make one crucial further step, and see the discourse analytical enterprise also as a political and moral task of responsible scholars. They emphasize that it is not always possible, or desirable, to neatly distinguish between doing 'value-free' and technical political critique on the other. They will claim that one can no less study racist discourse without a moral position about racism than a medical researcher can study cancer or AIDS without taking a position about the devastating nature of such diseases, or a sociologist can study the uprising of exploited peasants without being aware of the nature of their oppression and the legitimacy of their resistance . . . Critical scholars of discourse do not merely observe such linkages between discourse and societal structures, but aim to be *agents of change*, and do so in solidarity with those who need such change most.   (Emphasis original)

Discourse research strategies

Finally, the discussion turns to the discourse research methods or strategies. But a few caveats about them may be stressed at the outset. First, the categories of the methodological strategies below are not to be seen as fixed rules or procedures. They are suggestive: depending on the nature of research (data, context, objective and so on), researchers can modify, supplement or replace them. The strategies are also evolving: with the advancement of research researchers can enrich, strengthen or change them. The thing is that the strategies they use should be suitable for and responsive to the particular research objects and objectives at hand. In that connection, second, the strategies provided here are far from being exhaustive. There will certainly be other kinds of strategies in the intellectual traditions across cultures which may be equally well equipped to confront the sorts of cultural political problems highlighted here. Third, the strategies described below may in some cases be interconnected and complementary to one another. For example, what is instrumental to being 'deconstructive' in the following, first category may also serve the purpose of being 'transformative' in the subsequent, secondary category. Thus, whilst 'to take the perspective of the disadvantaged' may contribute to the *deconstruction* of the discourses of the dominant, it can help to create alternative discourses at the same time, thereby inducing *transformation*. For the sake of space and exposition here, however, the strategies will be placed under separate headings.

It may be mentioned, in addition, that, although the strategies outlined below are suggested mainly for discourse and cultural studies, what transpires may also be relevant to the other *critical* social sciences as well, be it anthropological, historical, psychological, political, economical or legal.

Deconstructive strategies

The general 'deconstructive' type of strategies is defined in terms of the object of enquiry it takes up, the tasks it performs in relation to that object and the objectives it achieves through those tasks. In the following, I shall describe these with special reference to concepts, categories, approaches and techniques found in current language, communication and discourse studies. But here, very generally, we may say that deconstructive strategies are designed to identify, highlight, confront and alleviate the problems of cultural prejudice, discrimination or domination which are produced through discourse. I use the general phrase 'cultural imperialism' to refer to that class of culturally repressive discourses upsetting our twenty-first-century world order. Acts of identifying, highlighting, confronting and alleviating, performed by discourse researchers, are oriented toward the same, broader goal, that is, subverting or undermining discourses of cultural imperialism. We hope that, ultimately, academic cultural members, groups and institutions, who engage with our intellectual project, become critical of and distance themselves from such discourses. How these strategies are practised in empirical research is illustrated in Chapters 4 and 5.

Identify and characterize discourses of cultural imperialism

A first discourse research strategy I would like to recommend is that we try to identify and characterize discourses of cultural imperialism. Thus, this mainly resolves the issue of topic or object of enquiry in CAD. Many discourses and aspects of them can be 'interesting' and worth studying. Following from the cultural politics of CAD, however, one specific and central interest is the problem of cultural imperialism, constituted in and through discourse, hence the discourse of cultural imperialism.[4] Although cultural imperialism can be realized through various forms of social symbolic practice (economics, diplomacy, visual art or architecture), the central object of enquiry advocated here is the discursive production of cultural imperialism. (One can argue, as is done in Chapter 1, that discourse is central, and not peripheral, to social cultural life, including practices of cultural imperialism.) Cultural imperialism can be created, reproduced, facilitated, maintained, concealed, legitimated, perpetuated, mitigated, or more generally constituted, through text and talk. Such roles of discourse in the realization and reproduction of cultural imperialism are considered to be an essential part of this first research strategy. Such discourses as may be added can be found in various discursive forms, as in the media, fiction, politics and everyday conversations, and therefore we should explore all types, genres and contexts through which cultural imperialism operates.

Because not all discourses are imperialist and especially because the discourse of cultural imperialism is often implicit, indirect, covert, hidden or legitimated, there is obviously a problem of how we can detect the discourse of cultural imperialism. Here a moment of reflection will reveal that imperialist discourses are more often than not associated with tensions over the signs of 'race', colour, gender, nation, ethnicity and colonial history, the West/Rest and so on (Hall 1996a, 1999; Harrison 2003; Pratt 1992; Said 1993; Young 2001) and frequently derived from (ab)uses of these signs. Therefore, as part of the strategy, special attention should be directed at discourses where these signs are constructed, utilized and acted upon.

The discourse of cultural imperialism, put simply, is characterized by oppression of other cultures and the resultant asymmetry in power between cultures. However, it can take a myriad of forms and performs a variety of specific functions. As the apparatus of cultural power, it can dominate, demean, repress, stereotype, discriminate, marginalize and/or exclude cultural 'others', though the object of imperial power is nearly always non-Western, non-White and Third World cultures. Therefore, detailed analysis needs to be done on the specific nature of concrete discourses of cultural imperialism.

The discourse of cultural imperialism often gets the upper hand under the current, international communication order. This means, for example, that about a particular, 'same' issue, other relevant discourses are marginalized in one way or another. Sometimes, certain forms of discourse are detrimental to certain other groups and communities and thereby imperialist, not necessarily because they are ostensibly so, but because they are effectively so in relation to alternative discourses, real or potential. Therefore, it would be useful and productive to identify what discourses are available and dominant *in relation to* the other discourses that have been repressed, silenced and discredited. We may try to illuminate how cultural authority, objectivity and truth are established; who is monopolizing the truth, for what purposes and with what consequences. In close connection with that, it would be equally important to identify *which group's* discourse is more widely spread, influential and powerful than that of other (thereby subordinated) groups. Here we may examine, further, how the dominant group negates, discredits, marginalizes, excludes or simply silences the powerless.

Investigate and confront cultural imperialism in diverse modes and settings

Cultural imperialism is not a form of thought and action that is found merely in editorials, political speech, diplomacy, colonial administration or some other such political arena. It is a much wider, more fundamental and prevailing phenomenon: it permeates all facets of our contemporary global life (Chapter 1). Thus it infiltrates and saturates the multitude of semiotic modes, media and genres surrounding us every day: conversation, speech, newspaper, radio, television, digital (multi)media, film, music, literature, textbook, magazine, and so on and so forth. Moreover, cultural imperialist practices in and through such modes, media and genres are not confined to merely such societal domains as politics, economics and the military. They also penetrate everyday and professional life, be it schooling, academic and scientific institutions, publishing, interpersonal and intergroup communication, public entertainment or the World Wide Web. It is thus the whole network of communicative channels and settings across the globe that continues to maintain, reproduce and consolidate the historically evolved domination, discrimination and marginalization of non-Western, non-white and Third World cultures and communities, thereby constituting the international web of cultural imperialism.

In this case, my central recommendation is that there is a variety of semiotic modes, media and genres and a diversity of sites that we can and should study. Thus, this strategy is meant to indicate the scope of deconstructive research. It will be realized that language use plays a part in virtually all the forms of semiotic activities mentioned above; further different modes and genres of language have a role to play as well. Therefore, the use of language constitutes an important part of the current discourse research strategy. But it can also be easily seen that research can become better informed when surrounding or simultaneous semiotic practices are studied at the same time. Sometimes we can look at one kind of practice or one setting in detail, but often it may prove productive to take the semiotic diversity and complexity of cultural imperialism into account.

Uncover and undermine 'common sense'

A second research strategy I would like to suggest here is one that renders transparent, interrogates and subverts or undermines those taken-for-granted, matter-of-fact, commonsensical assumptions, notions, categories, definitions and evaluations or other forms of thinking and understanding that effectively help to maintain or reproduce cultural hierarchy and oppression. Common sense is often presupposed and therefore unexpressed or left implicit in text and talk. Where such hidden common sense is used, whether consciously or inadvertently, which contributes to the domination, stereotyping and exclusion of other groups and communities on cultural grounds, we need to pay special attention. This kind of 'common sense' may often be found in (post/neo)colonial, imperialist discourses of otherness or the Other, as stereotypes, 'universals', 'truisms'. Therefore, we should examine how such 'common sense' renders possible and supports cultural equality and injustice (see below).

Stereotypical and repressive 'common sense' is, however, frequently rendered through linguistic, rhetorical devices as if it were natural, universal, justified. It may be recalled that, in Chapter 1, I refer, as ideological discourse, to those ways of thinking and speaking whereby one group dominates, coerces, excludes or discriminates against another but whereby such power practices are smoothed over or rendered 'natural' through *common sense* (Billig 1991; Fairclough 1989; Shi-xu 1994a, 1995). When such discourse negatively affects the well-being of particular cultures, it becomes imperialist ideological discourse. That is, imperialist ideological discourse can be defined as the ways of speaking and thinking that demean, dominate and discriminate against other groups and communities on the basis of 'race', colour, ethnicity, nation and tradition, and yet render those repressive practices imperceptible through common sense.

The strategy to confront and combat imperialist ideological discourse may contain two steps. One is to identify, make transparent and highlight them by reconstructing the underlying commonsensical view or standpoint. This can be an important and effective tack for power struggle because such discourse is implicit, indirect, covert, elusive, mystifying or ambiguous and therefore might otherwise be unheeded and so go unchallenged (Billig 1991; Fairclough 1989; Kress 1991; Blommaert and Verschueren 1991; Mey 1985; van Dijk 1993b; Wodak 1996; cf. Eagleton 1983: Conclusion). A further step is to challenge ideological discourses by locating the fallacies in argumentation and explanation (van Eemeren and Grootendorst 1992, 2004), tracing the cultural origins of 'universal' common sense (Shi-xu 2000a) and revealing the rhetorical processes of 'truth'-making (Derrida 1976; Simons 1989; see also Shi-xu 2000b). Similarly, West (1993) has suggested strategies of *deconstruction, demythologization* and *demystification*.

Expose and contradict hidden meanings, silences and inequalities

Ideological 'common sense' is but one, though a major, form of discourse that contributes to the continued subordination and marginalization of non-Western, non-white and Third World cultures and therefore must remain a persistent focus of attention and analysis. And yet there is also a host of other discursive forms and devices which may be no less productive of imperialist power. Such forms and devices of cultural difference and discrimination are in fact complex and therefore require a multifarious approach. Cultural imperialist discourse may conceal its hegemonic intent through indirect speech acts, for example. It may manipulate perception by keeping silence about certain topics or silencing alternative versions. It may perpetuate the same negative story about other cultures through repetition, fantasy, cliché or 'They are all always like that'. It may hierarchize and totalize knowledge by rhetorical ploys of 'integration', 'systematization' and universalization of cultural knowledge on the one hand and of exclusion of alternative forms of knowledge on the other hand, creating consequently an asymmetrical relation between this dominant discourse and other marginalized or silenced discourses.

In the face of this diversity of elusive or concealed forms of cultural dominance and coercion, my central suggestion is that we try to make them transparent and, further, contradict in order to reduce or undermine their effects. This means that we may try, on the one hand, to tease out the inferences, implicatures, implications, purposes, effects and consequences of imperialist discourse by reference to verbal and non-verbal evidence. On the other hand, we may try to identify inconsistencies, discrepancies or oppositions through intertextual and sequential analysis of discourses and contexts (Billig *et al.* 1988; Fairclough 1992). Such relevant discourses and contexts as may be noted can occur either between one's own versions, or between socially and culturally differential versions, for example those between the underprivileged and the powerful. They can also occur between different levels of discourse, for example between explicit statements and underlying assumptions. This strategy can be effective and fruitful because the order in which groups and institutions operate is a moral one and held accountable in terms of 'logic', 'consistency' and 'truth' (Shotter 1993).

Transformative strategies

Inspired by the activist forms of research in feminist and anti-racist studies, CAD goes beyond the conventional norms of social science methodology and strives to put forward concrete proposals for discursive change in favour of cultural harmony. Thus, in addition to the deconstructive strategies described above, the political ethnography of CAD also proffers more proactive research strategies, called 'transformative strategies'. These strategies are intended and committed to help generate and establish across the international, multicultural community alternative or new discourses which are conducive to cultural coexistence, solidarity and common prosperity.

As may be recalled, discourse analysis is usually concerned with analysing or, for that matter, describing, explaining, interpreting, criticizing or even interrogating discourses. Its object of research is either past or present text or talk. The political ethnography of CAD, in contrast and addition, is also concerned with future, new discourses, and it is committed to creating and advocating them. From another perspective, CAD has an added expectation of its scholars and students: they try to play a prophetic, activist and generative role in the academic, professional and educational community (see also Rorty 1991; West 1993). For, as Barker and Galasinski (2001: 47) have argued:

Change is possible because we are unique inter-discursive individuals about whom it is possible to say that we can 're-articulate' ourselves, recreate ourselves anew in unique ways by making new languages . . . In so far as this applies to individuals, so it applies also to social formations. Social change becomes possible through rethinking the articulation of the elements of 'societies', of re-describing the social order and possibilities for the future.

The application of transformative strategies has a caveat, however. Future, new discourses, while requiring critical consciousness and imagination, cannot be completely cut off from past and present discourses. They can be responsive, reflexive, critical or creative, but always in one way or another related to what has been said before or is being said now. Therefore, transformative strategies and hence transformative research need to be informed by deconstructive research, directly or indirectly. After all, deconstructing discourses of cultural repression and discrimination is ultimately for contributing to their reconstruction or transformation in future human cultures.

Furthermore, but not less importantly, because transformative research is designed to promote discursive and cultural change on the part of particular groups and communities, we also endeavour to include their own concerns and voices as part of the ethnographic–political process. In addition, transformative research may be informed by the researcher's own deductive and retrospective experience, personal and cultural. Both these principles are in keeping with the general in-between cultural stance in that, respectively, the perspective of the researched is taken into account and individual initiative mobilized.

Rethinking, proposing and (re)formulating discourses is one thing; but having them accepted and adopted in the wider society is quite another. Traditions, ideologies, common sense, power and interest may well be in the way. Therefore, while they need to do much deconstructive work in that regard, researchers committed to the cultural politics of CAD have also the necessity – and professional expertise – to find the grounds or arguments to warrant and advocate the discourses they proffer. That means that they need to seek, create and formulate the rationale, benefit, advantage, interest, wisdom, morals and so on to justify the new ways of speaking and acting which were previously not known or sufficiently grounded. New ways of speaking may, however, encounter oppositions. It will be necessary therefore to prepare counter arguments as well. This means, for example, that we may think about and point out consequences and disadvantages if our proposed discourse were not adopted or if the counter discourse were to be adopted. In the following, I will briefly describe these strategies; I will detail the practice of these strategies in Chapters 6 and 7 of the book.

Investigate and reclaim the voices and identities of the subaltern

Social research, as discussed earlier, has hitherto often been guided by its own theoretical, methodological and broader institutional concerns, to the neglect of the interest, concern and conceptions of the people it is supposed to examine. In the transformative part of political ethnography, a first strategy is to turn attention to the group and community under study and put a premium on their own views and experiences. In this case, researchers can use various ethnographic methods to gain insights into their lifeworld. For example, they can try to solicit information from different contexts across a length of time. To that end, too, it will be useful to broaden one's knowledge and perspectives as much as possible.

Here it may be pointed out in particular that across the international and multicultural community certain discourses are dominant; many others are repressed, excluded or discriminated against on the grounds of some cultural signs. At the same time, diverse human cultures are being increasingly interconnected at other levels. There is a sense indeed in which intercultural conflicts and disasters result from the refusal of the dominant cultures to listen to and conduct dialogue with the powerless groups. Therefore, researchers of CAD are committed especially to identifying, making known and reclaiming the voices and identities of those subordinated and silenced groups and communities. Thus, for instance, we try to find ways to understand the opinions and wishes of the non-Western, non-White and Third World cultures. Even from a practical point of view, the latter's discourses may contain not merely dissenting or different opinions, but also fresh perspectives that can enrich one's own vision and understanding.

Create conditions and need for intercultural communication

International and intercultural division, antagonism and exclusion are maintained through not only voiced discourses of cultural imperialism but also, as part of the underlying, implicit, imperial order of communication, lack of mutual, egalitarian reading, writing and dialogue. A most important research strategy, then, is to try and devise ways to enhance communication between groups of different backgrounds and traditions in favour of what Geertz (1973: 14) has called 'the enlargement of the universe of human discourse'. More specifically, we may try to create possibilities and improve conditions for such intercultural communication (Shi-xu 2001; Shi-xu and Wilson 2001). For example, we can help produce contexts and tools for such contact and communication. Further, because mutual and genuinely equal communication between groups, communities and cultures is a 'good' and necessary, though impossible, thing, we can do equally well by highlighting, researching, even creating the needs for such communication. For instance, we may demonstrate and highlight the necessity and benefit for such intercultural contact and communication in not only everyday life but also scientific research. Equally important, we may help formulate commonly acceptable rules for intercultural communication and interaction. For instance, we may work with different cultural groups to elicit and negotiate common rules of communicative engagement.

Create and advocate discourses of cultural cohesion and prosperity

Still another important strategy of research is to proffer and justify new kinds of discourse that are subversive to existing ones and may therefore change the status quo and bring forth new action and relationships amongst different cultural communities. Such proposed new discourses may include new concepts, new perspectives and new bases or arguments for creating new or alternative versions or concepts or ways of speaking. Thus, for example, we may try to open up new possibilities of reality description or illuminate hopeful signs of human cultural development, especially where gloomy views reign, thereby creating 'good' or 'more human' experience for the oppressed and underprivileged. To undermine or subvert the dominant formation, we can inject 'impure' elements into hegemonic definitions. To destabilize the established order of power relations we can try to 'blur' boundaries and promote transculturalism and transnationalism (Ang 2001; Bhabha 1994; Gilroy 1992; Hall 1999; Trinh 1991). Further, we can show the fluidity, diversity and variation of 'cultural', 'national' and 'ethnic' boundaries and categories.

Cultivate the willpower to speak for cultural cohesion and progress

As stated in Chapter 2, our late-modern world is saturated with capitalist, colonial, racist, sexist, sectarian and other oppressive and conflicting kinds of discourses. And yet this does not mean that they will not change. On the contrary, the current perspective takes it that discourses, hence their communities of speakers, have the 'critical consciousness' or 'moral rationality' to transform themselves towards cultural harmony (see especially Chapter 6). And they do change through time and space, constantly under the moral pressure to subvert or deconstruct the discourses of cultural repression.

However, changing the status quo of discourses, especially those of cultural power and repression, can be difficult, because, for instance, they may be against one's immediate interests. Discourse researchers can play a vital role in stimulating or arousing moral motivation or willpower by formulating and warranting non-repressive or common cultural discourses (Chapter 7). This can be carried out, for example, in the context of education and training.

Conclusion

Methodology and methods are created to achieve certain research purposes. There must then be criteria for judging the outcome of research; from a different perspective, there must be standards of research practitioners can aspire to. So finally, I shall consider what criteria, or principles, should be employed to guide and evaluate research.

To begin, let me mention some elementary requirements that social scientific discourse ought to meet. First, it must uphold the standard of 'accountability'. By that is meant the degree to which research procedures and claims are made explicit or transparent to the intended scholarly (sub)communities. This means that the researcher should be explicit about the context of the research(er), ways of argumentation or reasoning, circumstances of data collection, research goals and possible negative as well as positive consequences (Gill 1995; Tracy 1995). Second, it is necessary to accurately define one's perspectives (Surra and Ridley 1991). For instance, the researcher should, where appropriate (for example, in a journal publication, research report or course assignment), indicate their theoretical orientations and presuppositions and relevant personal academic background. In addition, the researcher should actively utilize their personal experience to make their account credible (Stanley and Wise 1983: 150). Finally, presentation of the research should be generally accessible to the intended scholarly communities and coherent (Tracy 1995). For this will make further scholarly argumentation possible.

Beyond those minimum expectations, there is a more specific and difficult question regarding CAD: how can we measure the degree of success of discourse research in the attainment of the cultural politics of CAD? From the theoretical and methodological viewpoints outlined so far, it should be clear now that the 'last word' does not lie with the discourse researcher alone. The researcher offers discourse research findings and suggestions as discursive constructions, which are open to argumentation. The assessment, rather, ought to come out of the researcher's consultation with at least two communities. On the one hand, because CAD is an intellectual project meant for convincing and mobilizing scholars, researchers and students in language studies and cultural studies, this group should form one of the parties for making the evaluative judgement. As Polkinghome (1983: xi) has suggested:

> What is needed most is for practitioners to experiment with the new designs and to submit their attempts and results to examination by other participants in the debate. The new historians of science have made it clear that methodological questions are decided in the practice of research by those committed to developing the best possible answers to their questions, not by the armchair philosophers of research.

On the other hand, because the CAD work is intended ultimately to undermine cultural domination and to promote common cultural freedom in wider human cultures, this latter community should take part in the negotiation process. This procedure can be carried out through many channels: for instance, interviews, field observations and subsequent investigations into the resulting discursive changes in the relevant contexts. Moreover, such a feedback process should be conducted continuously.

Part II
Practical Studies

4
Deconstructing the Other Place

Introduction

In Chapter 3, I suggested that one of the useful ways to confront cultural power and prejudice is to reflect on a culture's discourse about other cultures, or the discourse of cultural 'otherness' or Other. More particularly, I proposed that efforts should be made to identify or rearticulate culturally domineering and demeaning discourses and, furthermore, to try to undermine them from various local and global positions. Highlighting a culture's oppressive language about other cultures, peoples and places can be a first and important step towards critical cultural awareness. Moreover, such critical reflexivity may help create new conditions for discursive and cultural transformation and for new and genuinely intercultural and international communication and relations.

Many a critical approach in the social sciences and humanities – for example, cultural studies, literary criticism, media studies, history, politics, anthropology and pedagogy – has pointed out the dominance of the modern Western discourse of cultural 'others'. This discourse, it has been claimed, has stereotyped the colonized, decolonized, nonwestern, Third World 'others' as inferior, deviant and perverse and has done so through the signs of origin, race and colour (Bhabha 1994; Clifford 1988; Said 1978, 1993; Spivak 1988b). At the same time, it reaffirms the Western assumption of itself as the 'superior', 'standard' and 'centre' with regard to the 'Other'. Thus the Western discourse of the Other provides for a vitally important topic of cultural political and discursive research and constitutes a field of sustained and continuous engagement.

In this chapter, I shall accordingly take up some empirical cases of Western discourse of cultural difference and discrimination. These are specifically an American socio-political and cultural analysis of Singapore, Dutch travel literature on China and Western journalism on Hong Kong, respectively. By analysing these data from different genres and different sites, I want to demonstrate, first of all, that there is an alternative but recurring pattern of modern Western discourse that constructs the cultural *Other Place* as *contradictions*. Specifically, I shall be examining how the other place is routinely and typically presented as a site of tension or conflict that breaches some underlying 'rational', 'natural' or 'universal' standard. It will be seen that this discourse of contradiction takes a variety of semantic forms: as self-contradictory, temporally contradictory, locally contradictory, globally contradictory and so on, hence the plural form of the noun; and contradictions appear in variations: contrasts, oppositions, incongruities, inconsistencies and so on. Thus the Western discourse of the Other consists of not only the strategy of stereotyping, but also the strategy of constructing cultural other places as contradictions.

Beyond highlighting this contradicting strategy, I want, second, to make explicit how the 'contradictory' states of affairs involved are bundled together and judged to be contradictory. Contradiction does not come alone, as alluded to above; normally it presupposes or relies on some implicit system of norms or expectations to which something is deemed contradictory. It is thus a three-part structure: two contradictory states of affairs plus the underlying principle breached. So, as will be observed, in the construction of contradictions, certain 'normal' or 'universal' models, morals or mores are invoked, indirectly or explicitly. I shall therefore scrutinize such rhetorical and psychic bases for 'discovering' and 'judging' pairs of phenomena as 'contradictions'. In the process, I shall pay particular attention to the reasoning process, and the cultural assumption, whereby the normalizing judgement is made and, in turn, the contradiction made present and real. Thus, it will be observed that the contradictions in the non-Western Other Place are not so much given facts as artefacts fabricated through employing preferred standards, concepts, definitions of the West's own. There is a sense then in which the western universalizing discourse of colonialism and imperialism turns culturally 'other' places into chaos and contradictions.

Sighting and representing 'contradictions' in the non-Western Other Place is not just a visual and linguistic exercise, but can serve ideological functions of desire and derision. I have no better proof than the intimation by the American journalist Sesser (1994, whose accounts I shall study in detail below) when he says:

The constant tension between the charm and the cruelty of life in Southeast Asia *lured* me as a journalist, and *left me with memories* of both fond encounters and endless tragedies. I became *fascinated* with Southeast Asia during two trips to Burma as a tourist in 1985 and 1986. Burma reflects the dichotomy between charm and cruelty in a way that *mesmerizes many Western visitors . . .* But the *curse* of Southeast Asia – the oppression inevitably intertwined with a country's allure – appeared as poignantly in Singapore as anywhere.

(Sesser 1994: xi–xv; italics mine)

So, in examining the structures and processes of the discourse of contradiction, third, I shall be particularly concerned with its forceful functions of power and pleasure. Thus, it will be seen that the contradiction of the cultural Other is also strategically oriented to anxiety, discovery, surprise, puzzlement and such like. That is, the contradiction renders the unknown Other absurd, primitive or untrustworthy in times of ambiguity and uncertainty. Effectively it achieves effects of contempt and derision towards the Other. It becomes only a short step then to the conclusion that the Other needs to be taught, corrected, governed, disciplined and, if it refuses, to be destroyed.

The cultural politics of CAD does not stop here. It is also committed to creating new, possible discourses of cultural cohesion, or what Fanon (1986: 218) calls 'reciprocal recognitions'. So, after a deconstructive analysis, I shall finally be concerned to seek alternative lines of cultural realignment. A first, obvious form of discourse I shall thus advocate is one which states that the 'contradiction' of the Other is not natural or self-evident but that there is an intrinsic interrelationship between the west as the beholder and a place (or people) as the cultural 'Other'. Another line of discursive alignment I shall suggest is to speak of the cultural Other (Place), not merely from one's own cultural perspective but also in the other's own, local, historical terms. Still another relevant, culturally cohesive form of discourse I shall try to formulate is one that speaks of the cultural Other Place, beyond contradictions, as precisely the embodiment of cultural diversity and course for truly intercultural dialogue.

The construction of the Other Place and contradiction

Before I go on to the empirical study, I need to discuss some of the relevant theoretical and analytical notions. These revolve round the construction of the cultural Other Place and the discursive strategy of contradiction, respectively. The central themes I shall be developing here are twofold. First, the construction of the sign of the Other Place is an important form of cultural Other differentiation and discrimination in modern western discourse, along with the other notorious – originary, gendered and racialized – modes of representation and repression. Second, central to the construction of the Other Place is the strategic device of contradictions which, just like the strategy of stereotyping, is a powerful apparatus of power and pleasure.

The Other Place

The construction of culturally other places is a growing area in discourse and cultural studies (see, for example, Clifford 1997; Duncan and Ley 1993; Greenblatt 1991; Pratt 1992). There is a sense in which it is a subject that is being revived (see Bakhtin 1981; Briggs 1985; Clark and Holquist 1984: ch. 13; Foucault 1999). Yet in comparison with 'race', ethnicity, culture and gender, the cultural Other Place is still a marginalized topic of research. More often than not it is largely confined to discussions to do with travel literature and ethnography.

Here I can only be brief, general and speculative about the form, meaning and minimal conditions of the discourse of culturally other places or the Other Place. Thus, as a provisional definition, the *Other Place* refers to a textually and contextually constructed spatial locus that is different from that of one's own culture. Such a spatial domain is, of course, not merely physical, spatial or 'geographical' but associated with particular times (past, present and future), events, people, political institutions and so on. For this reason, it is always attached to particular values and emotions. Such apparently geopolitical entities are often constructed in the form of region, nation, country or community, circumscribed with borders and boundaries and measured in terms of the distance from the 'centre' and 'margin'. As such, it typically has certain social, political, moral and religious systems. For these reasons, the construction of the Other Place is frequently interwoven with 'race', ethnicity, origin and gender. The sign of the Other Place, in the discourse of (post)colonialism and cultural imperialism, has usually signified the non-western, non-white or Third World place. It is not just an inferior, degenerate and chaotic place, but also a distant domain of desire. Consequently, this has also meant that it is the place to rule and to control, as well as to fantasize. Thus, along with 'race', colour, gender, origin, and so on, place and space have functioned similarly to dominate, demean and discriminate against the world's non-western, non-white and Third World cultures (Shi-xu 1997).

Contradiction and uncertainty

It may be observed that theoretical and analytic work on the western discourse of cultural imperialism in general and (post)colonialism in particular has commonly identified stereotype, or more specifically fixity, as its central strategy and constitutive feature (Bhabha 1994; Hall 1997; Said 1978, 1993; Tomlinson 1991; van Dijk 1987; Wetherell and Potter 1992). Marked by what Said (1978: 72) called 'radical realism', it continuously fabricates the same sort of stories about the Other and confidently monopolizes truth. Furthermore, its stereotypical knowledge is always negative in content and demeaning in effect. Bhabha (1994: 70–1) characterizes the discourse of the Other thus:

> It is an apparatus that turns on the recognition and disavowal of racial/cultural/historical differences. Its predominant strategic function is the creation of a space for a 'subject people' through the production of knowledges in terms of which surveillance is exercised and a complex form of pleasure/unpleasure is incited. It seeks authorization for its strategies by the production of knowledges of colonizer and colonized which are stereotypical but antitheoretically evaluated. The objective of colonial discourse is to construe the colonized as a population of degenerate types on the basis of racial origin, in order to justify conquest and to establish systems of administration and instruction . . . [co]lonial discourse produces the colonized as a social reality at once an 'other' and yet entirely knowable and visible.

However, I think that, seen in a broader framework of the Western discourse of the Other, the stereotypical mode of thinking and talking may have a significant antithesis to it. That is, the Western discourse of the Other, in addition to its fixed knowledge and representation of the cultural Other, may also contain uncertainty, suspicion or puzzlement with regard to the Other. Further, this epistemological disavowal may often be connected with *anxiety, surprise* or *fear*. As my examples below will show, the non-Western Other Place can be a site not of certain knowledge but, on the contrary, the unfathomable, the unknown or the puzzling (Shi-xu, 1995, 1997). In this sense, I concur with Bhabha (1994: ch. 3) when he claims that the stereotyping discourse itself can be ambivalent.

However, I do not think that stereotype is the only, or even an important, strategy of discourse within the Western discourse of the Other which is routinely deployed to deal with ambiguity and ambivalence.

Rather – and this is the other theoretical claim of the present chapter – I want to contend that it is the *contradiction* that plays a significant, functional role in times of want of knowledge or certainty. Contradiction, as any dictionary will tell you, is a condition of incongruities, inconsistencies, contrasts or oppositions; it is a state where things do not hang together. Because it signifies misfit, chaos and instability, contradiction, as a rhetorical and psychical strategy, can help discredit, repress and exclude the Other, especially when the latter is perceived to be incomprehensible, unreliable or surprising. Contradiction can take a variety of forms and be accomplished through multifarious discursive means, textual and contextual (as will be detailed when we come to the empirical analysis). This leads to my next point.

At the heart of contradiction is the underlying principle that has been infringed. So contradiction is a three-part, argumentative structure: the two opposing components (X and/but Y) plus the underlying rule being broken. The rule or principle in question may take the form of a theory, law, norm, assumption and hence expectation about how things ought to 'hang together'. It is either implicitly or explicitly formulated in the discourse of contradiction. It can be about virtually anything in individual, social and cultural life. It is most important to point out here that such a model or moral order of things is culturally and historically embedded. That is, it has its own historical and cultural origins. Moreover, as part of discursive practice, it reflects the interests of the speakers of contradiction and has practical social consequences.

The data selection

The Western discourse of colonized, decolonized, non-western, non-white, Third World 'others' or Other is a vast and fuzzy field. For this study, I have chosen (1) an essay on Singapore from a socio-political and cultural analysis of Southeast Asia written by an American journalist,[1] (2) two travel books on China by a Dutch travel writer[2] and (3) journalistic writings on Hong Kong by western reporters, as alluded to earlier. These choices are limited and to some extent at random. They only represent a fraction of western discourse, its discourse on other places and the discourse of other places as contradictions.

However, the purpose of this chapter is to draw theoretical and empirical attention to the discourse of cultural other places in general and the discourse of cultural other places as contradictions in particular. More specifically, I want to *illustrate*, theoretically and empirically, the study of the discourse of cultural other places as contradictions as part of a broader cultural political and discursive project. Given this consideration, the range of genres (socio-political analysis, travel literature and journalism), the spread of western positions of enunciation (America, Holland, Britain, Austria and so on) and the amount of data (three books in the first two cases and hundreds of articles in the third case) are sufficient. Moreover, it might as well be mentioned that these choices reflect my personal–cultural trajectory as a discourse and culture researcher: I have lived in China, the Netherlands, Singapore and the United Kingdom. I was exposed to the discourses under study as I was daily involved with the respective countries and cultures.

Imperialist pleasure and prejudice

Below I will show that in the Western (post)colonial discourse the construction of the non-western Other as contradictions is not merely a description; it is a figure that is based on western perspective, concept and desire and further it effectively turns the non-Western Other into an irrational, immoral and outdated subject.

Singapore: on whose model?

The first case I want to present is material from the book by the American journalist Stan Sesser, entitled *Lands of Charm and Cruelty* (1994). The book as a whole is a sort of socio-political analysis and the object is Southeast Asia. The author has been a journalist with the *New Yorker* and the *Wall Street Journal*. His writings, whether for magazines, newspapers or as in the present book, display a strong interest in political and social affairs in Southeast Asia, especially in the field of human rights. To write this book, Sesser travelled through five countries in Southeast Asia: Singapore, Laos, Cambodia, Burma and Borneo, interviewing key political figures and other personalities. The book contains a chapter on each of these countries.

The individual chapters, and the book as a whole, are filled with accounts that portray at once admirable and deplorable aspects of the region; the positive and negative sides are organized almost symmetrically. The apparent semantic ambiguity or ambivalence is so dominant and prevailing that an isolated, superficial reading may often lead the reader to wonder whether the writer likes the place or not and whether he is merely trying to be neutral and objective. Actually, parts of this account are quoted with approval by both the Singaporean government and its opposition (Sesser 1994: xxvi). But, from the new perspective I outlined above, what the author is presenting, throughout the book, is not a neutral, 'two-sided story', but rather an image of this part of the world as a *place of contradictions*.

The discourse in question consists in a set of interrelated verbal forms. A first striking feature is that the image of contradiction appears repeatedly and in variation (that is, in terms of topic); sometimes these images are functionally related as statement and supporting argument. Another is the juxtaposition of apparently contrastive terms: 'charm' and 'cruelty', 'enchantment' and 'tyranny', 'suffering' and 'allure', 'pleasure' and 'pathos', 'fond encounters and endless tragedies' and so on and so forth. This is also found in larger textual structures: the yoking together of apparently contrastive narratives of one cause and one unexpected effect (as either lack or other effect). A third supporting feature is the definitional term of such apparent juxtapositions: 'dichotomy', 'contrast', 'tension', and so on. A fourth related device is the disjunctive conjunction, such as 'but' and 'yet', and the connective conjunction 'and' which functions pragmatically in the same way as 'but' (as in 'charm and cruelty'). The most crucial feature in the network is the invocation, implicit or explicit, of the law of how things belong together or the expectation of what the normal case is. The title of the book sets the tone (*The Lands of Charm and Cruelty*) and then follows a long string of instances of contradiction, such as the one below:

Example 4.1

> Much about Long Leng [a settlement in Borneo] represents in a microcosm my experiences elsewhere in Southeast Asia. The rain forests of Borneo are but one of the many features that make Southeast Asia perhaps the most intriguing part of the world: nations of beautiful people who warmly welcome a visitor, of ancient cultural traditions that still thrive, of great religious monuments and works of art. But Southeast Asia is also a place of tyranny and repression, where governments dismiss democracy and human rights as indulgences of the West, and view the most severe environmental degradation as a small price to pay for economic growth.
>
> (p. xi, Introduction)

Let me now turn to a random section of the book: the chapter on Singapore. It is based upon the author's one-month stay in Singapore, under the commission of the former prime minister, Lee Kuan Yew. The material initially appeared in the *New Yorker* in 1989. A first noteworthy feature of the chapter is its title: 'Singapore: the prisoner in the theme park' is metaphorical in the sense that, by equating 'the prisoner in the theme park' with 'Singapore', the author stereotypically portrays Singaporeans as prisoners. It is metonymic at the same time in the sense that the 'prisoner', while referring to Chia Thye Poh, the most well-known political prisoner in Singapore, is a reference to the people of Singapore as a whole. And yet this 'ugly' side is juxtaposed with a 'beautiful' side of the country: the particular prisoner, Chia Thye Poh, is locked in the 'theme park', Sentosa, an offshore island that serves both as an international tourist attraction and a recreational park for the locals. As a consequence, a semantically contrastive and so psychically incongruous or contradictory image of Singapore emerges.

This semantic contrastive structure is sustained in the rest of the chapter (and the book as a whole). On the one hand, there is a recurring theme of Singapore as an economic wonder in contrast to other 'comparable' countries and cities, especially in the same region. Singapore emerges positively thereby as an exemplary city and country in the world; admiration for Singapore by the West/USA/author is also displayed. On the other hand, a parallel theme of a completely different side of Singapore is introduced: it has a repressive and cruel sociopolitical system. Further, it should be noted that particular Western theories of social and economic development are also invoked at the same time and hence particular expectations of Singapore (for example, it should have a 'democratic' political system as well) and then that there is a lack of what is expected. As a result of this invocation of 'our' norms and 'their' lack of compliance, Singapore as a country, city and people becomes a contradiction. This 'global' structure is reinforced by countless details in the chapter. Let me illustrate this discourse of contradiction by a detailed analysis of a couple of examples (the bold type in all the samples below embodies features that make up contradiction).

Example 4.2

> Singapore is a prosperous nation with little racial animosity, no external threat, and a government that is genuinely popular, because of the economic growth it has brought. **In the eyes of many Westerners**, Singapore **should have achieved** political, cultural, and social freedom as **an inevitable companion** to the high level of economic development. **But** Singapore's record **lags not only in contrast to the records of Western democracies but also when it is compared with the records of its neighbours**, who have their own problems with human rights. (pp. 35–6)

Here the American journalist places two sorts of states of affairs next to each other. On the one hand, there is a particular, 'desirable', side of Singapore; on the other hand, there is a 'lack', a lack on the part of Singapore at that. The lack is constructed, as may be noted, through implicit as well as explicit means, namely the subjunctive mood (as in 'should have achieved'), the verb ('lags') and the contrastive and comparative phrases ('in contrast', 'compared with'). Through the lack, the American writer articulates otherness or difference (see below). Further it may be noted that what Singapore 'lacks' is not just anything, but precisely something which is *expected* (note the subjunctive mood 'should have achieved'). Thus, there is also an 'undesirable' side to Singapore.

However, the juxtaposition of the 'desirable' and the 'undesirable' is neither a natural yoke of 'facts', nor a show of a random contrast. And it is important to point out, too, that there is more to the juxtaposition than a demonstration of journalistic objectivity and neutrality. Here there is a particular, underlying logic applied to the dichotomy and in this instance the American writer makes it explicit. Namely, on the one hand, the author shows the dichotomy to be unexpected, surprising, disappointing. The disavowal is rendered through a variety of expressions: 'In the eyes of many Westerners . . . should have achieved. . . . But . . . but also.' On the other hand, he invokes some *rational* and *appropriate* principle with regard to it. He uses not only the Western yardstick ('In the eyes of many Westerners', 'Western democracies' – he assumes Western democracy to be superior anyway as indicated above), but also the 'more appropriate' standard ('the records of its neighbours'). Notice here that Singapore's level of democracy cannot even match a 'low' standard ('lags . . . when it is compared with the records of its neighbours, who have their own problems with human rights'). Note also 'not only . . . but also' and the lexical construction of the universal law ('an inevitable companion'). As a consequence, the 'two sides' of Singapore become a *contradiction*, two states of affairs that do not belong together.

The construction of contradiction is not the sole point of the game, however. It is not merely a description of some sorry state even. It will be realized that the contradiction involves the *intentional* nature and moral standing of Singapore in general and its government in particular. For, what it 'lacks' is 'freedom' and that is a *valued, ethical* quality of 'any' government (note the subjunctive mood in 'should have achieved'); moreover, freedom should be there *naturally* because it would be an 'inevitable' outcome of Singapore's high level of economic development. In addition, 'Singapore' is (part of) the subject of verbs

('Singapore should . . .' and 'Singapore's record lags . . .'). Effectively, Singapore's 'contradiction' is not some incomprehensible, natural condition, but rather the result of the Singaporean government's *subjective, willing* action. By qualifying the contradiction in this way, the American writer's account presents a perverse, degenerate and cruel Singaporean government.

But how are the 'rational' and 'appropriate' bases for discovering the Singapore contradiction constituted? What is the 'rationality' or 'appropriateness' employed anyway? What is the underlying regime of truth regarding the contradiction? I shall come to this more fundamental question when we have studied the next, similar example. This is one amongst a long list of what the author explicitly names as 'contradictions':

Example 4.3

> Except for Japan, it [Singapore] has the best-educated, most knowledgeable, and most world-wise society in Asia, **but** the government **still** tries in many ways to regulate its citizens' lives . . .   (p. 7)

This example is similar to the one just examined in that here, too, is a 'pleasurable' part in the Singapore 'contradiction'. That is, the first half of the sentence conveys a positive face of Singapore, just like the first sentences of the foregoing example. However, the other half does not construct a lack, but some *other* state of affairs or, more specifically, some *other* pattern of behaviour than what is expected. To schematize and so to compare the formal semantic strategies of constructing contradictory components in examples 4.2 and 4.3, respectively:

X but not Y (or lack of Y)

as opposed to

X but Z

Similar to the underlying structure of the contradiction constructed in example 4.2, here too the writer invokes some principle governing the relation between the two conflicting states of affairs. This is done through the grammatical and lexical constructions of the (un)expected ('but . . . still . . .', respectively). But different from the foregoing example, in this one the writer does not (bother to) state what governs the contradiction or what makes the two otherwise separate states of affairs constitute a contradiction. He takes it for granted, to be self-evident and universal. Namely, any government in the same situation will not regulate its citizens' lives. By rendering 'the order' of things opposed to the 'standard' model of things, the American author effectively makes that order a *contradiction*. The two states of affairs in Singapore no longer belong together.

It may be added that, since the Singaporean government's behaviour is 'contradictory' to the 'normal', 'universal' expectation and, more importantly, *volitionally* so (note the 'government' as the *subject* of action and the verb 'tries'), the Singaporean government is rendered an irrational demon.

It may be noted here that the journalist's account of the contradiction is not an expression of prior, *stereotypical* knowledge but intrinsically produces a consequential effect of surprise in the observing writer and the audience. Note the disjunctive conjunction 'but' and the adverb 'still'. But what I want to point out here is that the construction of the unexpected, surprise or puzzlement about the Other via the apparatus of contradiction is not merely a psychical reaction, but strategically oriented to perform a particular ideological function (Shi-xu 1997: ch. 6). Namely, because the Other breaches the 'basic', 'rational' and morally consequential norm of behaviour, the new discovery also brings about a debased Other. The bizarre becomes the corrupted and contemptuous.

Now, let me return to the analytically more fundamental question: how exactly does Singapore come to be a disordered contradiction and its government an irrational demon? Where, more specifically, does the normalizing principle of subjectification come from?

In example 4.2, it may be recalled, Singapore is portrayed as failing to do what it is expected to, against a 'natural' law of societal development. That law is specifically though implicitly that the prosperity of a country will lead inevitably to the freedom of its people. It is this assumed order of things that enables and sustains the expectation that 'Singapore should have achieved political, cultural, and social freedom as an inevitable companion to the high level of economic development'. What is rendered into oblivion here, however, is the fact that this theory of societal development is not so much a universally proven, recognized or even relevant model as conjured from a particular cultural, and specifically, *American/Western*, standpoint. One may immediately think of the common application of this Western concept and discourse to economic development in the Third World.

In example 4.3, similarly, when the author yokes together the 'facts' of the great intellect of Singaporean society and the government's heavy regulation of its citizens' lives, they are already contradiction-prone. For he has resorted, albeit imperceptibly, to a 'universally indisputable' rule of governance: if a population is well-educated then its government must not regulate its citizens' lives. Whether this is indeed the 'universal' law is not questioned.

What is genuinely worrying, I should like to stress, is the effect or the powerful productivity of such a totalizing, other-contradicting, reasoning discourse. Above we have already seen that, in consequence, a Singapore as a nation full of contradiction and disorder and oddity becomes real. More seriously, because these contradictions, disorders and oddities do not happen to be there, but are rather the result of the intentional and motivated action of Singapore in general and of its government in particular, their agents are rendered deviant, demonic and degenerate.

From another perspective, it may be argued that the sort of contrasts, juxtapositions, incongruities and unexpected lack we saw above makes sense and becomes real only within a particular, wittingly or unconsciously adopted frame of rational or moralistic thinking and speaking. Contradiction is inextricably associated with the beholder/speaker. The reality of a city, a country, a nation, or a place and its people more generally, in turn, does not have an independent, externally knowable, existence, but is tied in with particular cultural and rhetorical configurations.

Here I am of course not saying that we must not criticize social and political repression in other cultures; it should be open to intercultural critique and intervention. Nor am I even saying that one must not use the rhetoric of contrast and contradiction. These can be useful tools to undermine domination and discrimination. My point here is to analyse the discursive, rhetorical and psychic process of identification and subjectification in order to reveal the universalizing and totalizing way of thinking and judging and consequently demonizing the conduct and identity of the cultural Other.

China: in whose past?

In modern Western discourse of difference and discrimination, contradiction may also be created out of metaphorical displacement of the Other Place in time, or more particularly into the (distant) past. 'They still live in the past', we often hear. The metaphor of antiquity can be built in a number of ways (for example, constructions of memories, traces, curiosities, old ways of life or absence of modernity).[3] Its meanings are varied and multiple (for example, cherished, backward or of another world). But in the Western context of constructing the Other Place as contradictions, the archaic metaphor is more often than not deployed as an epochal frame to mark the Other as immobile, outdated, removed from civilization and so on. Effectively, it serves to fabricate cultural distance and maintain power hierarchy.

This way of constructing contradiction is markedly different from the discourse of contradiction in the previous story. There we saw that the underlying principle for identifying a contradiction usually takes the form of a universal norm, law, expectation or such like. Here in the Dutch travel accounts of China, it is the 'common' Time or 'universal' history that is assumed as the standard of societal development but is not followed by the Other.

And yet, on closer inspection, it frequently turns out that the metaphorical discourse of the 'universally recognized' past is premised on a European/Western standard of modernity (Shi-xu 1997: ch. 6). Such modernity and contemporaneity of course represent the progressive, the enlightened, the superior. In this case, a culturally specific measure is used as the universal point of reference just as we saw in the constructions of contradiction in the previous section. Fabian (1983: 35) has called this kind of rhetorical strategy, of depriving other cultures of shared contemporaneity, the 'denial of coevalness'.

Caroline Visser (born in 1956) is a well-known Dutch freelance journalist and has published many world travel accounts in the major Dutch broadsheet newspaper *NRC Handelsblad* and in book form. She has travelled through China regularly, by train, bus, ship, bicycle, often alone, and the two books under discussion, *Grijs China* (Grey China, 1982/1991) and *Buigend Bamboe* (Carrying Pole, 1990), are the results of her several trips made during the 1980s.

In these books, Visser paints a highly critical and negative picture of contemporary China as well as its recent history. Frequently she draws upon colonial, European and Western perspectives in identifying, differentiating and critiquing China, as if they are the 'rational', 'standard', 'superior' models of seeing and speaking. Indeed she has been accused by readers of *NRC Handelsblad*, where *Grijs China* initially appeared, of being 'arrogant' and 'chauvinistic' in attitude towards China.

One predominant rhetorical and psychical strategy which contributes to that overall pejorative picture of China and which I shall attempt to grapple with here is the creation of a temporal gap between China and 'modernity', hence epochal contradiction, through the violence of metaphorical archaism. That is, the Dutch writer upholds the notion that China stands, or stood, still, and remains what it used to be, at least partially. At the same time, she assumes that the West has gone a long way towards the modern, the rational, the progressive.

This historical misfit of China is not incidental in occurrence, but recurrent and repetitious. It is systematic and strategic in the Dutch writer's discourse, as may be clearly seen from the opening chapter of her book on China (Visser 1990). It is about a Dutchman, Johan Nieuhof, who travelled through China in 1655 (translation mine, as in all following instances):

> I went back to the Zeeuw Museum several times because I found Nieuhof's drawings are so simple yet touching; I saw before my eyes what China was really like three hundred years ago, at the beginning of the Qing Dynasty . . . Gazing at the old map, I thought up a plan: I wanted to follow the trail of [nareizen] Johan Nieuhof. I wanted to know what remained of the world that he had covered.
>
> (pp. 7–8)

This position of enunciation determines the sort of regime of knowledge, pleasure and prejudice in the identification and differentiation of China as the Other. Effectively, the discourse of epochal contradiction fulfils, for the Dutch westerner, the desire for superiority, the need for affirmation of modernity and progress and the predilection for original, vestigial discovery, or recovery. At the same time, it banishes China into the other, different and distant world.

Moreover, it may be noted that the contradiction-prone metaphor comes in a variety of forms. It can be a straightforward statement ('They live in the past'), or more indirect forms such as an old story or account of memories, or description of absence of (signs of) modernity. Let me illustrate and specify this metaphorical contradiction of time by examining a few extracts from the books in detail.

Soon after arriving in Chongqing, a city in Southeast China, Visser goes to visit it, accompanied by an incidental, temporary English fellow traveller. She describes the city thus (*Grijs China*, p. 23):

Example 4.4

> Het uitzicht is **schokkend**. Een grijze huizenzee golft tot aan de horizon. Tientallen, honderden schoorstenen steken daarbovenuit. Zwarte rook drijft in slierten traag over de heuvels. De lucht boven de hele stad is nevelig, stinkt, en bijt in de longen . . . De stad **doet**

me denken aan foto's van Manchester tijdens de industriële revolutie. 'Dit **is het land van Dickens,**' zegt Engelse Linda somber. '**Alleen** is er hier **geen** schrijver zoals hij.'
(The view is **shocking**. A grey sea of houses stretches to the horizon. Tens, hundreds of chimneys rise up on high. Black smoke drifts slowly in strings over the hills. The air above the whole city is misty, stinks, and bites in the lungs . . . The city **reminds me of photos of Manchester during the industrial revolution.** 'This **is the country of Dickens,**' says English Linda gloomily. '**Only** there is **no** writer like him here.')

To this description of a place in China, it may be pointed out, the writer attaches a significant dimension of Time. The specific time used here is the *past*. There are several explicit and implicit temporal devices that construct this past time element. One of them is the invocation of photos. A photo is of course a snapshot of history (in this case, of the distant history of the industrial revolution). A related temporal feature is the metonymic specification of a previous time, namely 'the industrial revolution', which, as is well-known, took place in the early nineteenth century. Still another device is a similar, metonymic reference to the renowned nineteenth-century English novelist Dickens. All these old-time signifying devices function metaphorically to characterize the Chinese locale that the writer is visiting. Through these devices, the Chinese Place is pushed back in time.

The use of metaphor here is varied and noteworthy. For one thing, the author does not use the 'photos', 'Manchester' and the 'industrial revolution' as a direct description of the Chinese locale but makes her metaphor explicitly *psychical* and thereby realistic ('makes me think of . . .'). I call such a metaphor 'psychical' (cf. Soyland 1994). For another, the metonyms of 'photos', 'Manchester' and the 'industrial revolution' all signify particular past times. I call this type an *epochal* metaphor. Moreover, an extended metaphor is borrowed from a third person('s speech), the 'English Linda'; such use, as a view shared by another, assumes more authenticity. In addition, it may be noted that the temporal metaphor is subsequently modified in order to construct a more 'precise' image ('Only there is no writer like him here.'). This leads me to my next point.

It is not exactly, or only, the point that 'China exists in the past'. The past can mean different things or have different values (Dickens is Linda's 'valued' part of the past). These metaphors of olden times carry with them a particular evaluative quality. Namely, the photo,

Manchester during the industrial revolution and the country of Dickens without Dickens all stir up memories of bleak and filthy times of the past, materials substantiating her titular 'Grey China'. Therefore the 'temporal' metaphors produce a pejorative image of China.

The writer's narrative of the Chinese locale 'colludes' with the metaphors of the 'past' and the 'backward'. That is, the very construction of the narrative also contributes to the same image that the metaphors conjure up. All the details and instances of the narrative fit in well with the European memory of the hard times of the Industrial Revolution and Dickens's literary creations. In this sense, narrative, too, can act as a metaphor to construct the past and the pejorative.

When the writer pushes contemporary China forcibly though metaphorically into the past, she creates a tension between 'now' and 'then' and hence a contradiction emerges. And yet the contradiction is not there merely for descriptive purposes. It creates delight and derision. 'The view is shocking . . . The city reminds me of photos of Manchester during the industrial revolution', as Visser utters; and as her European companion Linda declares, 'This is the country of Dickens. Only there is no writer like him here.' So the contradiction, contrived through collusion between metaphor and narrative, incites imagination, recalls elapsed time and retrieves exotic space. In the same breath, it gives vent to contempt and abhorrence.

Whilst Visser's metaphor succeeds in producing effects of pleasure and horror, it should be clear that the metaphor on which her denial of coevality and consequently the emergence of Chongqin as an epochal contradiction are premised is not one of universal time past. Rather, it is a narcissistic choice of a culture-specific, European, past. Therefore, that 'Chongqin, China, exists in the past' is not a universally relevant temporal construction, as appears poignantly defended. It is the result of a particular cultural past then. More seriously, the discourse of contradiction differentiates, displaces and distances the cultural 'Other' from the rest of the contemporary Holland, Europe and the world as a consequence. In this sense, temporal contradiction leads to a social consequence of cultural conflict and tension.

Example 4.5

Op de andere oever van de rivier leefden de mensen in een andere eeuw; er was bijna **geen** verkeer . . . In het water stond een brakke steiger, gebouwd van aangespoeld hout. Toen we erop liepen, kraakte het onder ons gewicht. Aan weerszijden lagen kleine visserssampans afgemeerd, fragiel als libellen. Het regende. Onder een klein afdakje zaten een paar mensen te schuilen en kaart te spelen. Ze lachten en lieten hun schitterende gouden tanden zien. 'Naar Qingyuan?' kakelden ze, 'dat is minstens een week roeien en een motor hebben we niet. Ayaahhh, de stroom is veel te sterk door de regen.' **(On the other bank of the river** [the Pearl River in the Southeast of China] **the people lived in another century;** there was almost **no** traffic . . . In the water stood a shaky landing made of washed-ashore wood. When we walked over it, it cracked under our weight. On both sides, small fishing sampans lay moored, fragile like dragonflies. It rained. A few people were taking shelter under a small shed, playing cards. They laughed and showed their shining golden teeth. 'To Qingyuan?' they chattered, 'it is at least a week's rowing, and we don't have a motorcycle here. Ayaahhh, due to the rain the floods have grown too strong.)   (*Buigend Bamboe*, p. 20)

Visser reprises the epochal metaphor here. Different from the example above, however, where the metaphor of the past is accomplished indirectly, that is, through the metonyms of 'photos', 'Manchester' and the 'industrial revolution', is the fact that here the writer makes an explicit metaphorical proposition on the past. 'On the other bank of the river the people lived in another century,' Visser declares.

The subsequent narrative, of traffic, the surroundings, the people, their conversation and manner of speech, provides an illustrative and so ancillary picture of life of 'a different century', as the European/Dutch readers would readily recognize. Thus, the two rhetorical tropes, metaphor and narrative argument, collectively proffer an image of life on the other bank of the Pearl River as a contradiction in time.

Displacing the Other in another, past, time zone fulfils Visser's desire of 'rediscovering' the traces that Johan Nieuhof left of China centuries ago. But the discourse of epochal contradiction effectively ostracizes them socio-culturally from the common, contemporary world.

Indeed it has become a style of writing and a mode of thinking for the Dutch travel writer when it comes to contemporary China. As if there were no better way of characterizing the Other, or sometimes as if there were no proof for a certain characterization, the author resorts to old images. Visser (1990: 163–85) is recounting her train journey with her guide to Kaifen (a city in the middle of China). She tells of surprising stories she hears and surprising scenes she sees on the journey. At one point she makes a generalization and then switches to an ancient, British story:

Example 4.6

> Reizen is voor de gewone Chinees altijd een verschrikking geweest,
> als er geen oorlog uitgevochten werd, waren er hongersnoden, rovers
> en overstromingen. **Ik herinner me een verhaal van een Britse mis-**
> **sionaris die aan het eind van de vorige eeuw op het platteland**
> **woonde . . .**
> (Travel for ordinary Chinese has always been a horror. If there was
> no war, there would be famine, robbery and flooding. **I remember**
> **a story told by a British missionary who lived in the countryside**
> **at the end of the last century . . .**) (*Buigend Bamboe*, p. 163)

Different from example 4.5, this text of China-in-the-past does not
provide a narrative as such; it merely presents a generalizing statement.
In contrast to example 4.6, this example does not give supporting 'evidence' for the notion that contemporary China is still 'in the past'. The
writer constructs the overall situation of China as living in the past in
a way as if she needed no proof. Different from 4.6, too, this example
does not contain a (psychical) metaphor that would do the trick of
linking up the 'seen' to the beholder's memory of the past. The denial
of the Other's contemporaneity or coevality here is more subtle and
ambiguous. Almost habitually and as a matter of course, the travel writer
switches to an apparently separate story of the past ('I remember a story
told by a British missionary who lived in the countryside at the end of
the last century'). What this tale eventually turns out to tell is, almost
expectedly, a man's futile hardships endured in a journey of two years.
Therefore, the story here (or more precisely, the writer's memory thereof) functions as a warrant for her foregoing generalization. Note that it
is not the narrative itself that throws the current China into past. It is
the date when the story was told and a century ago at that.

It may also be reflected that here, again, the 'past' is reproduced
through neither China's own action nor its own self-identification as
such. Rather, the Dutch travel writer avails herself rhetorically, though
almost imperceptibly, of her memory of a British missionary's tale, and
of a tale told a century ago. It is a borrowed, foreign and old story then
that pushes contemporary China back into dire history.

Hong Kong: in whose definition?

The discourse of cultural imperialism has yet another variant form of
contradicting the Other Place. Namely, it a priori defines and fixes the
Other Place in a particular way and then brings up a certain aspect or

property of it as being in conflict with it. Underlying this apparent opposition, a relevant rule or norm of 'rationality' or 'common sense' is invoked, implicitly or explicitly, as being broken. Hence a contradiction emerges.

This form of contradiction may appear to be similar to the first type we found in the American data. But the structure is different in that, there, the two contradictory components are in the form of a cause and (unexpected) effect (or lack of it) relationship or causal relationship. Here, the dichotomy is based on an evaluation of the perceived impropriety or incompatibility between something whose nature is 'known' and defined (see below) and something else which is new. Further, the difference also lies in the fact that the latter contradiction has less to do with expectation than with desirability.

This form of contradiction typically occurs in the context of the speaker's uncertainty, anxiety or fear of what the Other (Place) is up to. The effective, pragmatic consequence of this ambivalent and apprehensive knowledge is then clear. Because the 'potential' or 'practical' act is inappropriate, the contradiction makes available the inference that what the Other (Place) does or will do must be discouraged, avoided or stopped. Thus, in this case the Other Place is also the object of western injunctions, warnings or threats.

Central to this third type of contradiction is the use of definition. By *definition* I mean a way and unit of speaking that constructs at once a category representation and explicit knowledge of the essential characteristics of that category. Definitional discourse is not merely a matter of using fixed lexemes (or larger units) and cannot be identified simply in terms of linguistic patterns. Rather it may have various and variable forms of construction. Categorizations ('A "chair" is a piece of "furniture"') and characterizations ('A handkerchief is a piece of cloth for blowing your nose into') are the most straightforward kinds of definitional or conceptual discourse; but many other discursive processes can do the job as well (say, the presupposition in the rhetorical question, 'How can you use a handkerchief to polish your shoes?!'). In terms of the content structure, it may be said, definitional discourse consists of a topical domain and a predicate domain: for example, 'English (topical) is a foreign language for the Chinese/is an analytical language like Chinese (predicate)'. Since what is contradictory depends crucially on such prior definitions, to make sense of contradictions is (also) to examine how definitions are made in the first place.

In that regard, it should be pointed out that the speaker of the contradiction-oriented definitions in the Western discourse of the Other is usually not the Other itself, but rather the West. The Other is normally denied the opportunity to describe itself or speak for itself. As a result of this, the discourse of the contradictory Other, including its consequences, turns out to be inextricably linked with the western beholder and speaker, just as the previous two types.

Turning to the specific case of western journalism on Hong Kong's historic transition, I would like to observe that, on the one hand, it offers various definitions of Hong Kong and China's past, present – except the future (see below). These characterizations fix the origin, tradition, nature, interrelations and so on of Hong Kong and China, through descriptive statements, presuppositions or appositions. Thus, western media discourse often defines Hong Kong as the success of colonial administration, a free, modern and democratic society and a 'handover' or even 'bequest' to the Chinese government. Further, it defines for, or instead of, China what its 'own' interests are (for example, leave Hong Kong alone and it will get political and economical reward). These definitions are not only repeated, but also taken for granted, in that they are frequently spoken of as dispassionate descriptions and hardly explained, defended or elaborated.

Then, on the other hand, and almost in tandem, this discourse places those fixations and determinations of Hong Kong against narratives of what China is doing, or predictions of what it is inclined, or destined, to do. Thus, for example, through nominalizations ('suppression of democracy'), stories ('China is stamping out dissent from Hong Kong'), questions ('What will China do to Hong Kong?') and so on, the discourse not infrequently portrays China as acting, or may act, in an authoritarian, imperialist or simply unpredictable way.

By juxtaposing the definition of the situation of Hong Kong or the 'interest' of China on the one hand and the description of a 'counter' action that China is engaged in or prone to against Hong Kong, the western media produce a contradiction. That is, it shows that there is a conflict between what Hong Kong or China 'is' and the latter's present or future 'harmful' action. In this way, it makes available the inference that China is prone to flouting the rule of *appropriateness of conduct*.

To understand this contradiction pragmatically, especially in terms of its purposes and effects, it will be necessary to relate to the wider veil of a discourse that enshrouds this strategy. This discourse is filled with loss, uncertainty, anxiety and above all doubt over China (Lee *et al.* 2002; Shi-xu *et al.* 2005). Routinely and continuously it asks questions about Hong Kong's future after its return to China and formulates various conditionals to map out different kinds of possible future scenarios of Hong Kong and China. In addition, it frequently resorts to speech acts of threat, warning, or command, sometimes coupled with promise of reward. Seen from this larger discursive context, it becomes evident that the discourse of strategic contradiction is motivated by a continued colonial anxiety, an imperialist desire, to conserve colonial privileges, to regiment and control the Other and to prevent changes unfavourable to the West. 'Let Hong Kong remain Hong Kong or else we will . . .', as it is sometimes bluntly put (see Shi-xu and Kienpointner 2001).

Now let us examine a few examples in order to illustrate and detail how this contradicting discourse on Hong Kong and China is manifested in the Western media. The one that follows is taken from an interview with the last British colonial governor of Hong Kong, carried in the major US magazine *Newsweek*.

Example 4.7

> Christopher Patten: . . . It [Hong Kong] **is a very international city.** And I think that **anything which detracts from that in the future would** be very damaging. 'We did a pretty good job'.
>
> > (*Newsweek* Special Issue, 5 July 1997)

In this instance, Patten defines Hong Kong through the copular, 'is', and the attributive phrase, which functions as the predicate of the sentence, 'very international'. Thus, the sentence fixes the nature of Hong Kong against other possible ways of thinking and speaking of Hong Kong. From the following sentence, it becomes clear that the quality of Hong Kong that is being defined is also considered as a valuable one.

Having made that fixation, Patten then introduces imagined possible actions against the valued 'international' character of Hong Kong and makes it clear that such actions are 'very damaging'. From the wider Western media context of the time where China is portrayed as about to suppress democracy, Patten is attributing those actions to China.

Then a potential, future conflict between the 'good' and the 'bad' is made present. Through the construction of the potential moral tension, the dichotomy signals then that China may possibly breach the principle of 'good conduct' in the future. In this way, the contradiction puts up a moral barrier, as it were, to whatever China intends to do, when Hong Kong is reunited with China, outside of what Patten, the former colonial master, through the American Western media, has already defined, delimited and described morally. In other words, the contradictory discourse here is restrictive, preemptive and prohibitive in nature and orientation and its power most effective and productive in times of post-colonial uncertainty and change.

In the next, Austrian example, the injunction, prescription and prohibition are enacted, through the device of contradiction, upon the Chinese government, not less, but more forcefully:

Example 4.8

Ein Satz **sollte** unauslöschlich in das Gedächtnis der Beijinger Führung sowie in das von Tung Chee-hwa, des Regierungschefs der chinesischen Sonderverwaltungszone Hong Kong, eingeschrieben sein: Die Augen der Welt sind auf Hong Kong gerichtet . . . Beijing **sollte** schon **im eigenen Interesse** Hong Kong Hong Kong sein lassen. **Nicht nur, weil es** die vielzitierte Gans **ist**, die goldene Eier legt. China **wird doch**, sollte man hoffen dürfen, auf die Tilgung der einen Schmach **nicht** eine neue folgen lassen: die Zerstörung des wiedererlangten Territoriums.

(One sentence **should** be irreversibly engraved in the minds of both Beijing's leaders and Tung Chee-hwa, the chief executive of the Chinese Special Administrative Region Hong Kong: The eyes of the world are watching Hong Kong . . . **In its own interest**, Beijing **should** let Hong Kong remain Hong Kong. **Not just because it is** the much-quoted goose which lays golden eggs, **but also because**, after the elimination of one humiliation, China **should not** let a new one follow; at least, we may hope so: the destruction of the regained territory.)

(Ein Land, zwei Systeme (One country, two systems), *Der Standard* (The Standard [Austrian newspaper]), 1 July 1997)

Similar to the previous example, the present one also has a semantic contrast between 'what the Other Place's situation is like' on the one hand and on the other hand 'what detriment it is likely to bring about' to that situation. But, different from the foregoing contradiction, here, what an inappropriate action may do to the situation is not constructed through the formulation of possible actions but modal verbs expressing moral obligations ('should'). That is, these expressions, along with the background Western discourse of 'fearing' what China is up to, indirectly construct what 'undesirable' actions China may carry out. Also different from the previous example is the fact that the definitions of the situation are not enacted through descriptive statements here. Rather, they are accomplished through implicit, undefended, assumptions of the Other's 'interests' ('In its own interest') and 'correct rationale for action' ('not only because . . . but also because . . .').

When the 'rationale' for action is defined ('In its own interest . . .') and the 'right' course of action is determined ('should (not)'), any alternative form of action would become, or be seen as, a contradiction to the rule of propriety of conduct. Thus, by projecting a potential form of contradiction through a prior definition of the situation, a restriction or control is exercised upon the Other.

In the western discourse of Hong Kong's transition, the future, potential contradiction on the part of China may also be constructed through signs that *symbolize* possible future actions. That is, such signs indirectly signify possible actions by Mainland China that are in tension of a defined situation. This is reflected in the following extract:

Example 4.9

> At dawn today, China stamped its authority on **its new possession, when 4,000 troops backed by armoured cars and helicopters** crossed into the territory.
> . . .
> At the formal **handover** ceremony, Prince Charles **bequeathed** Britain's last big overseas domain to Jiang Zemin, a former trainee at the Stalin Auto Works in Moscow and now head of the world's last major, albeit zealously capitalist, Communist Party.
> . . .
> The substitute legislature immediately began its first formal session, ready to pass an omnibus law activating a string of legislation, including **curbs ‘on protests and the funding of political parties**, which had been approved before the handover.
> ('Last hurrah and empire that covered a quarter of the
> globe closes down', *Guardian*, 1 July 1997)

The text creates potential as well as present incongruities and incompatibilities in the Other Chinese Place. On the one side, naming through names ('its new possession', 'handover') and the choice of a particular verb ('bequeathed') define and determine, albeit implicitly here rather than explicitly as in the foregoing two instances, the nature of Hong Kong against other, possible characterizations. Namely and specifically, these lexical choices inscribe and fix Hong Kong as a newly gained 'property', a 'gift', something that ought to be cherished and well cared for.

On the other side, there is a narrative of activities that are exactly the opposite of the cherishing and care ('4,000 troops backed by armoured cars and helicopters', 'curbs on protests and the funding of political parties'). Contradiction of propriety is produced on the part of China because the definitions and hence the associated evaluation of Hong Kong would require a completely different type of moral behaviour. In this way, an ethical shadow is cast upon China.

And yet there is no surprise expressed in this case, as we saw in the first type of contradictory discourse. For here no general law of causality is invoked or drawn upon. Instead, the broader Western uncertainty, anxiety and doubtfulness about China's future action with regard to Hong Kong form the rhetorical and psychical basis for the construction of China's conduct as symbolic of a 'feared' future course of action. It is this implicitly suspected or presumed 'harmful' course of action that renders the construction of China's current conduct natural and stereotypical.

Conclusion

In this chapter on modern Western discourse of discrimination, repression and exclusion, I have pointed to a hitherto largely neglected rhetorical and psychical strategy, namely the construction of contradictions, with special reference to the Other Place. I argued that an important sign in the discourse of the Other is cultural others' Place and, further, that at the heart of the construction of the Other Place is the strategy of contradiction, generative of cultural pleasure and prejudice. Empirically, I have critiqued a set of forms of contradiction in a variety of genres of Western discourse of the Other. Here I identified and teased out various features that make up contradictions of different types. Furthermore, I highlighted ideological purposes and consequences of desire and derision in the fabrication of contradictions and uncovered the underlying taken-for-granted but fallacious assumptions sustaining the strategic discourse of contradictions.

Where do we go from here? And how can we go on? At the beginning of the chapter, I already stated that CAD would, on the basis of prior deconstructive work such as we have done here, attempt to seek and advocate subversive, alternative or creative ways of speaking that might be conducive to cultural coexistence and common progress. So finally, let me try and make some preliminary and tentative suggestions as challenges to and replacements of the sorts of contradicting strategies identified so far.

To avoid misunderstanding, I must make it clear that criticizing the strategy of contradiction as I do here does not mean, however, that all forms of contradiction must be avoided or resisted. Contradiction, as a form of rhetorical thought and action, may be one of the most effective and productive ways through which to undermine inconsistency and thereby inequality and injustice and to find and expand common grounds for intercultural communication and critique. But my point here is that the modern Western discourse of the Other contains strategies of contradiction that are contrived and fallacious and, more seriously, that they are motivated to denigrate, alienate and suppress non-Western 'others'.

Thus, a first, new form of discourse of cultural others I would like to propose is to recognize the difference and diversity of cultural formation by having continual dialogue on the 'unexpected' with other cultures in their own terms, including taking note of their own historical and cultural circumstances. This new pluralist form of discourse implies also that, before we contradict other cultures in any way, we should first reflect on whether both relevant cultures share the same underlying model of cultural development. If not, then, we should try to construct shared visions in order to achieve mutually recognizable well-being. For, as we have seen, the cultural Other (Place) can be turned into a disordered contradiction, not as an objective fact, but as a result of deploying particular culture-specific theorems as universals.

A second alternative form of discourse that I would like to suggest here is to stress the temporal coexistence as well as historical connections between the world's different cultures in order to achieve cultural cohesion and promote cultural solidarity. At the same time, this culturally co-temporal discourse should recognize the fact that the past and the present of the non-Western, non-White and Third World cultures are inextricably bound up with the brutal colonial history and the continued neocolonialism or imperialism. For, as we have witnessed, when Western discourse deprives its Other of contemporaneity and denies it Western modernity, it not only degrades the Other, but also banishes it from the rest of the human family.

Third, I want to suggest that a culturally constructive form of discourse be initiated and promoted in which we refrain from authoritative definitions and stereotypical fixations of the Other and instead put a premium on themes of dynamic human cultural development and transformation. This implies that we should go beyond historical determinism in the understanding of human cultures, others' and our own, and advocate cultural agency and action for cultural innovation. In addition, it requires us to use identifications of our own culture and others as truths not in order to suppress or control, but as experimental devices for cultural regeneration. For we have seen how Western media discourse forestalls or threatens 'undesirable' change in the Other in times of uncertainty by imposing Western preferred determinations of the Other.

5
Reading Non-Western Discourses

Introduction

In the contemporary West, the non-Western world is still rarely read about, spoken of, or listened to. If at all, then it more often than not figures as the 'Other', removed from Western self-experience and deviant from 'the norms' and 'the standards'. If and when, for some dramatic reason, the Other is invoked in Western discourse, then it is usually 'we' that speak for 'them' (Said 1978, 1993). Indeed, reading the non-Western Other and letting the non-Western Other speak have yet to become a normal part of Western discourse (Spivak 1988a, 1988b). But as we enter into the new millennium, it has become abundantly clear that whilst the contradictions between the West and the Rest are being deepened, the interconnections between the two worlds also proliferate, in finance and trade, migration, the World Wide Web, environmental disaster and international terrorism. Nowadays problems 'there' easily become problems 'here'; what 'we' say or do 'here' quickly changes or even eliminates lives 'there'. The changed conditions of growing cultural interdependence and hostility call for new modes of communication reaching beyond local, national, linguistic and cultural boundaries.

With regard to this general problem of marginalization, subalternization and exclusion of non-Western discourse in the western world, I have but two modest aims in this study. On the one hand, I want to contemplate, in an explorative and suggestive manner, what constitutes non-Western discourse, why the Western community should read non-Western discourse and how 'western' reading of non-Western discourse can be conducted. On the other hand, I shall take those propositions seriously by performing a practical reading of China's and Hong Kong's discourses on Hong Kong's historic transition. Here I shall employ a particular sort of cultural-contrastive approach, namely, reading against the backdrop of what has been marginalized or excluded in the relevant western discourse. Through this culturally reflective form of reading, it will be seen that unfamiliar, subversive and constructive discourses are revealed. For example, Hong Kong, especially Chinese, discourses stress that the return of the whole of Hong Kong in 1997 would not have been possible without China's increased power – a discourse absent from the Western media and contradictory to its notion that Britain handed Hong Kong over to China, honouring a historical agreement. Furthermore, a new discourse of cultural relation-building emerges, beyond the perennial western concerns with self and identity.

By drawing attention to and redescribing unfamiliar, marginalized or subordinated non-Western discourse, I hope to help the non-western Other to reclaim identity and agency. At the same time, I hope to increase western awareness of the existence of non-Western discourse and so of the plurality of human discourse more generally. By studying the specific case of China, Hong Kong and diasporic discourses, I wish to show the richness and diversity within non-western discourse, and hence the benefits of reading and, broadly speaking, interacting with the non-western discourse community. To some, the present analysis may seem merely a description or a redescription of some of the non-western discourses. And yet (re)description can be a powerful political tool, because it necessarily claims an existence (in this case a different discourse) and because it can become subversive through undermining dominant versions and revealing excluded ones. As Rushdie (1992: 13–14) states, 'description is itself a political act . . . redescribing the world is the necessary first step towards changing it'. It should be clear, too, that such a project as the present one is not to oppose the west or its discourse as such, but to resist its divisive, hegemonic and imperialist tendencies and effects of Western discourse, thereby transforming it into a more inclusive discourse.

Discourse and reading cultural others

Reading the non-Western Other and researching its discourse are not routine activities in the scholarly tradition of language and (media) communication. Consequently, there is very little by way of theory or methodology. Here I shall only outline in broad lines what constitutes non-Western discourse, why we should read it and how we ought to read it. The term 'Other', and for that matter, East and West, or Hong

Kong and China, does not of course presuppose a unified, essentialistic Subject. My intention here is to argue that there is a need and benefit for the West to read what it would regard as its non-Western 'others'; the 'Other' is a metaphor used to encourage intercultural communication beyond participation in dominant western discourse.

What constitutes non-western discourse?

What is non-western discourse exactly? To begin with, it should be cautioned that the concept 'non-western discourse' cannot, in fact, be easily and clearly defined. For one thing, non-western discourse, or in that connection 'China's discourse' or 'Hong Kong's discourse', is not a homogeneous and monolithic entity. It is diversified and dynamic. For another, the definition also depends on, to say the least, the goals, interests and perspectives of the reader and researcher and therefore cannot be a neutral one. For example, such a concept may have presupposed a western perspective and valuation on the cultural Other and its discourse, or, similarly, a third person's (for example, a researcher's) perspective on western and non-western discourses.

The notion of 'non-western discourse' must perforce then be a motivated and contested one. So far as the present project is concerned, the guiding objective or principle is a cultural politics that aspires to transform dominant western discourse by confronting it with discourses from non-western 'others'. Granted, non-western discourse may best be conceived of, first, as discourse produced by a cultural community different from that of the west. That is, it involves a different community of speakers (Wuthnow 1989) and so a different historical and cultural context from that of the west. Second, such discourse may be thought of as on some topic, shared or otherwise, that is of some critical interest to the west(ern readership), say the environment, relation-building, poverty or, in the present case, Hong Kong's historic transition. That means that non-western discourse would be a selected entity, rather than a totality. It is neither possible nor necessary or even desirable to learn everything of non-western discourse. Third, such discourse speaks of 'the same' subject matter in different ways from western discourse (Césaire 1972; Said 1978, 1993). Different cultural symbolic forms may convey different and interesting meanings. Last by no means least, especially such non-western discourse as is marginalized, excluded or otherwise dominated by the west should be the focus of attention.

The last point deserves elaboration, as it is central in the present theoretical claim and consequently will have important methodological implications. In the field of language and (media) communication, national cultures, national ideologies and domestic media 'logic' are frequently assumed to have the dominant influence. So, for example, the reporting on the Hong Kong transition by the British, American, Chinese and Hong Kong media is explained as merely relative to the respective national political economy, national perspectives and domestic media interests. However, as vast amounts of work in cultural and post-colonial studies (for example, Ashcroft *et al.* 1995; Williams and Chrisman 1993) and the more general tradition of cultural studies (for example, Bhabha 1994; Hall 1996a, 1999; Said 1978, 1993; Spivak 1988a) have shown, linguistic communication, including print and broadcasting media, cannot be understood adequately without taking into account the broader human cultural history, especially the history of imperialism (Shi-xu 1994a, 1995, 1997). In communication and cultural studies, one may very well attend to the concrete or the culturally specific discourses, but one may easily run the risk of nationalism if one loses sight of the broader cultural history of dominance and subordination. For the present project, this means that western discourses and those of China, Hong Kong as well as their diaspora cannot merely be seen from national(istic) perspectives. Rather, non-western discourse, such as instances from China and Hong Kong, must be seen as more fundamentally steeped in the broader cultural-historical context of continued and continuing imperialism – or the international power order – through colonialism, post-colonialism and more recently neocolonialism.

It should be stressed that western and non-western worlds, hence their discourses, are not understood here as essentialistically given, homogeneous and monolithic objects and entities. As may be reflected, cultural discourses, because of the complexities of cultural traditions, cultural agency and power struggle from within and in between, are diversified and dynamic. Consequently, categories of discourse (and indeed of any reality) are always contentious and often motivated by interests of power (for example, interests to dominate or to resist) and further there emerge complexity and diversity in the Others' discourses. These would by the way suggest that we should speak of non-western discourses in the plural. But because of the present cultural politics vis-à-vis western hegemonic discourse, 'non-western discourse', I believe, can be a liberating term and concept. For example, new subject positions can then be reclaimed and cultural forms of discourses which have been denied, repressed or otherwise marginalized can be redescribed (see Barker and Galasinski 2001). The same complexity may be said of

'Chinese discourse' and 'Hong Kong's discourse' (see for example, Tu 1994).

Why read non-Western discourse?

A next question that naturally arises is why reading non-Western discourse is necessary and desirable. I have already alluded at the outset of the chapter to the general problem of deficiency in reading, writing and talking with the non-Western Other in the west. Now I want to focus on the relevance of such cross-cultural reading for beginning to tackle that problem and for intellectual and cultural growth more generally. By 'reading', I mean of course communicatively attending to and engaging with non-western discourse just described, by implication the non-western community, rather than merely imagining it and speaking *for* it all the time.

For one thing, it may be suggested that modern European and American western history is by and large a history of colonization and neo-colonization in which the rest of the world has continued to be involved (Young 2001). West and East, including their fortunes and misfortunes, are thus historically and culturally inextricably interlinked (Bauman 1998). For another, under the present globalized, mediated conditions, discourse is interculturally oriented. What 'they' say or do 'there' may be directed at and have consequences for 'us' 'here' (Bauman 1998; Huntington 1998). The problem is not that non-Western discourse has not been written or spoken but it is hardly read or listened to as relevant or worthwhile in the west (Ashcroft *et al.* 1989). In addition, the ways that the non-Western Others relate themselves to 'us' can possibly provide 'us' with different, fresh and inspiring perspectives. Traditionally and habitually, the west has tended to disregard and dismiss its Other's discourses. Identifying non-Western discourses alternative to familiar Western discourses, then, can broaden cultural horizons. For instance, because Western discourse has valued self and identity to the neglect of relationship (Gergen 1994, 1999), it can learn from non-Western, for example Asian, discourses, where discourses of broader, multiple senses of self or indeed relation-building abound. Furthermore, such a discursive and dialogical turn (Bakhtin 1981) to the Other itself can constitute an important new dimension of the Western and Eastern intercultural relationship. The existing, problematic Western and Eastern relationship can also be transformed thereby, through reflections and critique of 'their' discourses and 'ours'. In the present case, it is hoped that studying the discourses by Hong Kong and China may yield insights into how the two non-western geopolitical communities construct their relationship with each other and with the west and the rest of the world. For in the everyday, familiar western discourse on Hong Kong, the latter has been often represented as a unique, British colony, fearful of being handed over to China.

My central, general recommendation in this chapter is for western discourse scholars and students to study non-Western texts and contexts as well as their intellectual traditions. Having said that, I have a modification to make. Trying to speak as neither easterner nor westerner, but as someone in between, I hope that not only western (discourse) intellectuals will be persuaded, but non-western scholars will also actively involve themselves in helping with this intellectual reorientation by, for example, striving to make non-Western discourses heard on the international stage. There is a sense that such work is urgently called for on the part of non-western intellectuals (Munck and O'Hearn 1999; Robbins 1999).

How do we read non-Western discourse?

Closely related to the motivations of reading non-Western discourse and the definition of the latter is the methodological question of *how* we ought to deal with and make sense of it. This of course is yet another complex problem that calls for examination. Traditionally, the scholars who dealt with this issue, as in literary criticism, intercultural communication theory and anthropology, for example, tended to avoid the broader historical, cultural and political circumstances of discourse. They often treated meaning as fixed and so something to be described accurately (hence 'correct understanding' and 'misunderstandings').

It seems to me that the reading of unfamiliar, non-Western discourses can be helped by the notion of discourse just defined: discourse is a way of speaking that constructs and acts upon reality in a particular way. From here it follows that non-Western discourses can provide ways of thinking and speaking that are unknown to the west. Further, the intercultural communication (hence reading and writing) between the East and the West is not merely a communication of linguistic or cultural 'differences'; it is a power-saturated process (Shi-xu 2001; Shi-xu and Wilson 2001). Based on this understanding of discourse and intercultural communication, I would like to suggest, tentatively, that we try first of all to suspend as far as possible traditional universalizing categories, concepts, values and assumptions about discourse and communication. Instead, we must allow for the diversity and complexity of human cultural discourses and of ways of studying and critiquing them. For instance, we need to realize that the non-western Other and their discourse may have their own concepts, experiences, worldviews and traditions and aspirations whose integrity it may not always be possible to translate into western languages and evaluate in western terms. Following from this, our task will then be not so much to provide an accurate, objective reading of the non-western Other's discourse as to help initiate and continue, through research and pedagogy, a dialogical process of communicating with the Other, articulating new discourses and transforming existing cultural identities and relationships into shared communities, for example.

In the analysis and interpretation of non-western discourse, tension will certainly arise between 'elite' methodologies and local cultural material, as existing dominant methods of analysis remain largely western in origin and orientation. In the present culturalist perspective, inter/multidisciplinarity is clearly not enough; it must be combined with *cultural* diversity with respect to worldview, theory, methodology, topics, data, concerns and so on. In the current West-dominated circumstances, it seems that we need to employ analytic notions and tools eclectically and try to adapt them to the cultural data and issues on hand as closely as possible. In this regard, it may be mentioned that direct experience with cultural and ethnocentric tension, diasporic knowledge and expertise from in-between-cultural spaces will come in handy as part of the interpretative resources.

All this means, more specifically, among other things, that, given any topic, issue or aspect of reality we should gather as much potentially relevant discourse material as possible, from the cultural Other's perspective as well as our own. This effectively resolves the problem of constituting non-Western discourse discussed above, at least partially. In this process, a comparative approach would be required that is always conscious of our familiar or taken-for-granted discourses and perspectives (see also Clifford 1992). In this sense, we should be intercultural as well as interdisciplinary researchers. In research practice, this means that we should be looking for the discourses from the 'Other' that are not familiar to us, that are suppressed or marginalized in 'our' own discourse community and that are different from or even contrary to 'our' discourses. (Needless to say, prior knowledge of the target language and culture will be a valuable asset here.) The new attitude also means that we begin to ask new questions. For example, western cultural studies, just like western language and communication research, has for decades been concerned with the issue of identity as one of its most central problems. Such a focus and preoccupation may be appropriate to western culture, but not necessarily useful or even relevant to the non-western

Other and their discourse. Non-Western discourse, in the case of the discourses from Hong Kong and China, may not simply or always be 'inward-looking' and looking for identities, nationalistic or otherwise; but rather it may perhaps be more oriented to (re)establishing relationships, with each other, the West, the rest of the world, and so on. Furthermore, it will be useful to investigate the linguistic, textual, rhetorical and other semiotic means through which the cultural Other constructs its reality and forges relationships, on the one hand, and, on the other, the actions, purposes, consequences and power relations that are involved. With the development of the new media, where sometimes translation is made available, reaching out to other cultural discourses has become greatly facilitated, though such development is far from equally distributed.

In the case of China and Hong Kong, one important implication would be to read discourse data historically, especially in terms of the largely suppressed colonial history and process of decolonization. Thus, when Hong Kong and China refer to their mutual colonial history and to the historic return of Hong Kong and when they express their cultural, ethnic and national pride, such moves need to be understood against the background of colonization and decolonization. Ignoring that context may easily mislead one to read such references and expressions as 'chauvinism', 'extremist nationalism' and so on, as frequently happens in western scholarly accounts of China's discourse.

By the above theoretical and methodological statements, I do not mean to say that good wheels have not been invented or that I am inventing better ones. Rather, they should be put into operation now in the field of language and (media) communication. Literally and specifically, I am trying to say that academic discourse (in this case discourse concerned with culture and communication) must take up its obligation to intervene and to change the existing order of society. The particular order that I have in mind here is, as discussed at the outset, the discursive and thereby social exclusion of the non-western Other from western discourse. The current exercise then is an attempt to play an active part in the discursive development and transformation of culture by turning to engage with and make sense of marginalized non-western discourse.

Contextualizing research on non-Western discourse

As will be clear from the (inter)cultural perspective outlined above, the study of non-Western discourse will perforce be qualitative in orientation. Its aim is not to achieve an accurate or representative description of a community's discourse, if such a discourse exists at all. Rather, such a project is primarily concerned to draw attention to, highlight and so (tendentiously) redescribe and rearticulate the properties of non-Western cultures' discourses, especially those which are unfamiliar yet significant to the west but have been repressed or marginalized in the west. Accordingly, the criteria to select data in the present case will have less to do with what is representative of the Chinese or Hong Kong (HK hereafter) media than with what would be needed in the west in terms of the interest of intercultural communication. Thus, specifically, the data must reflect: (1) what has generally been ignored, marginalized or dismissed in the western discourse community on the historic transition of HK on the one hand and at the same time (2) what has been recurrent in mainstream, non-extreme HK and Chinese print media. Accordingly, I shall give a brief account below of how these criteria are met. I shall do this by describing (a) my relevant intercultural experience as the researcher, (b) the 'same' historical context of the Western and non-Western discourses, (c) the dominant western discourse and (d) the universe out of which the material presented here is selected.

The diasporic and intercultural intellectual

Intercultural reading in general and reading cultural others in particular are intellectual activities that build on experience and critical consciousness in *intercultural* contact and communication. That is, knowledge about the cultures and histories involved, ethnographic experience in them and above all the will-power to achieve common cultural existence and progress (Shi-xu 2001) are important resources for enhancing the advocated forms of intercultural reading. In this regard it may be mentioned that I myself come from China and have since lived in between western and eastern cultures. This diasporic and intercultural experience has taught me that the difference is not just one in the minds, languages or cultures, but essentially one of power relationships, and that future human culture depends on continued intercultural dialogue. In the present case, furthermore, I have kept a close eye on the unfolding of events of the HK transition over a number of years.

The historical context of Hong Kong

The discourses on HK's return, eastern and western, are embedded in the context of the modern history of HK, China, Britain and the world at large. So that history ought to be recounted. Thus, I shall give a brief account of the history, which is virtually excluded in the western discourse but widely available in HK's and China's discourses.

HK is geographically composed of HK Island, Kowloon and the New Territories and historically part of China's Guandong province. In the middle of the nineteenth century, Britain waged two opium wars against China and forced the then Qing government to sign the Treaty of Nanking and the Treaty of Peking, authorizing the island's cession to Britain. Then, in 1898, Britain obtained from the Qing government the lease of the New Territories (91 per cent of today's HK area) for a term of 99 years to expire on 30 June 1997. It is important to note here that these treaties had not been recognized by any of the subsequent Chinese governments. After numerous failed attempts by its past governments and people, finally in 1984 China succeeded in negotiations and signed the Sino-British Joint Declaration, providing for the British withdrawal from the whole of HK on 30 June 1997 and the restoration of Chinese sovereignty on 1 July 1997. According to the Declaration, HK became a Special Administrative Region of China, to be administered by the people of HK, with its existing system to remain unchanged for 50 years. Different from other decolonized nations, though, HK did not transfer through a consultative process with local people. Rather, the colonizer and the mother country from which it was forcibly separated had negotiated the decolonization, whereby HK's sovereignty was to be returned to the mother country. By the time HK was returned to China in 1997, the 156 years of British colonial history in China came to an end (and, with the return of Macao to China in 1999, so did the four centuries of European colonization in Asia) (see also www.info.gov.hk/hk2000/b5/23/c23-03.html).

Western discourse: lost memories and continued desires

In order to define, select, characterize and understand the target discourses – Chinese, HK and diasporic – unfamiliar, repressed but significant for the west, it will be necessary to make explicit the contrasting background of the western discourse on HK. Drawing on existing literature (for example, Flowerdew and Scollon 1997; Knight and Nakano 1999; Lee 2000; Lee *et al.* 2002; Shi-xu and Kienpointer 2001), let me refer to some broad patterns of western discourse on the 'same' topic below.

First, there is an overwhelming discourse of HK's 'uniqueness', hence valued 'Hong Kong identity'. This uniqueness consists usually in a British and international influence in a Chinese cultural context. The point of this discourse is often to refute its Chinese connections and to warn against future Chinese intervention. Another prominent discourse is that of HK's success as a result of the British administration and by extension of the Western social, political and economic system. In this discourse, the role of HK people and that of China are almost entirely excluded. In relation to that, there is also a resounding discourse of doubting China and hence HK's future. Coupled with that, a stern discourse of warning and threat is directed at China, or against any change in HK. Last but by no means least, significant topics and themes are largely absent from the media as compared with the media discourses in Asia: the modern colonial history and why the return of HK to China is possible at the time it occurs. The common use of the term 'handover' throughout the English-speaking western media reflects and reinforces this kind of discourse.

Such discourses effectively erase the inglorious, unjust and brutal colonial history. As a result, it becomes facile to manipulate what the decolonized does or says to satisfy imperial desires. Thus, for instance, not infrequently China is referred to and described as 'imperialist' and 'aggressor' in the western media and even in western academia. Further, such discourses serve to smooth over the broader post-colonial implications and the anti-imperialist significance in HK, Chinese, Asian and world history. It will be realized, moreover, that such discourses are intended to neutralize possible, undesirable influence from China. Thus, the western media discourse on the HK transition manifests the inherent, continued (neo)colonial desires and ethnocentric sentiments of western discourse (Edelman 1988).

As a typical example of erasing the inglorious colonial history and attributing HK's success exclusively to British colonial rule, HK's last governor, Christopher Patten, says the following in his interview in a special issue of *Newsweek*:

> I get thrown back again and again to a wonderful quotation of de Tocqueville, in which he said if you want to know why a country or a city is rich and prosperous don't look at its forests, don't look at its harbours, don't look at other national resources, look at its laws. Does it have laws which encourage people and help people to thrive and excel? And that's precisely what Hong Kong has had.
>
> ('We did a pretty good job', *Newsweek*, Special Issue, 5 July 1997)

Here injunctions are made as to the rule for explaining HK's success (note the authority of de Tocqueville, the imperatives and the question), the causes to be excluded and the causes to be included. The explicit glorification in the title of the article as quoted statement is another case in point.

The discourse of threatening may be exemplified by the next quote:

> Human rights in Hong Kong are already emerging as another focal point for China–American relations, and any kind of crackdown in the territory could trigger a serious downward spiral in relations between Washington and Beijing.
>
> ('Big change is coming – to whom and how?',
> *International Herald Tribune*, 1 July 1997)

Here, because it is understood that China needs a good relationship with Washington, not least because of the issue of Taiwan, the consequence of 'a serious downward spiral in relations' is made explicit as a deterrent. In this way, a threat is accomplished. Because my aim in this study is not to look into western discourse, I shall not dwell further.

Data source and selection

The original data material that informs the present study is enormous. I have tried to keep myself abreast of the media discourse on HK's return in various modes – printed, radio, TV and digital, from various parts of the world, in several languages and over a span of a number of years since early 1997. In presenting this analysis, however, I have focused on texts mainly from mainstream media sources in China and HK between May and July 1997.[1] It should be mentioned, however, that HK's media discourse is much more diversified, often with texts in contentious or negative terms and perspectives (as for example in *Apple Daily* and the *Hong Kong Economic Journal*), than the Chinese media, which is largely state-controlled (Lee 1994). There is no intention here to deny or suppress such 'within' or 'in-between' differences or dissenting voices. Discursive diversity and complexity ought to be a project in itself (see, for example, Chow 1992). But, because my current purpose is merely to introduce to the western academic readership a reading of some discourses of HK and China unfamiliar to and suppressed in the west, and because the HK discourses critical and sceptical of China and of the reunification have already been rehearsed prominently in the western media, I shall refrain from repeating the negative discourses from HK. Thus, emphatically, the present study is not designed to represent accurately 'China's media discourse' or 'the HK media discourse' as 'they really are', but rather to rearticulate for the west some non-western discourses from an in-between cultural perspective. For an overview of the media sources in China and HK and their sociological context, see, for example, Knight and Nakano 1999; Lee 2000; Zhong 2002: 164–6; http://sun.sino.uni-heidelberg.de/igcs/media/intro.htm#; and www.kidon.com/media-link/hongkong.shtml.

The present approach is interested in not so much individual discourses as recurring patterns of discourse and so the present work will be concerned to characterize patterns of them based on multiple instances in the media. It should be pointed out, too, that, although I lay out China's and HK's perspectives below separately, there is in fact a considerable blending of the two because of the spread of the local and global media. A first dimension of such blending to be kept in mind is the mass and digital media available in both China and HK. Another is the fact that the media of China and HK intermingle by carrying articles and speeches from each other's side. This is especially the case with those articles and speeches by public influential figures.

Making sense out of the Other's accounts

To reduce the obvious tension of analysing large bodies of cultural discourses, I have organized my analysis at two levels, one 'general' and one 'specific'. That is, I shall first provide an overview of a discourse in question in terms of the topic and the proposition(s) about it. Then I shall examine a couple of illustrative sample texts with special reference to the textual and contextual devices that contribute to the construction of the discourse being highlighted.

The two sets of discourses from China and HK, respectively, can be analysed and presented in a variety of ways. For example, each set can be analysed further into particular forms, meanings or contexts; or the two sets can be analysed as a whole in order to identify the contrast and forms of otherness as opposed to the relevant Western discourse. Here I have decided to set them apart and in tandem; however, within each set, I have made distinctions between different 'sub-discourses', that is, ways of speaking on specific issues – for the ease of reading (rather than logic) I have referred to these usually as discourses. The sub-discourses from within the Chinese and HK's discourses, respectively, as will be seen below, match each other. This arrangement is intended to make two broad points. First, collectively, they constitute a form of anti-colonialism and anti-imperialism, similar to and in alliance with anti-colonialist and anti-imperialist discourses from other parts of the world. This also means that there are interconnections and interrelations between the two sets. Second, between these two sets of discourses from

China and HK respectively, there are also differences: differences in historical and cultural circumstances, formulations, concerns, objectives and so on. The original Chinese sample texts analysed here are for typesetting and commercial reasons not presented here. The English translations provided below are mine. I have tried to render the translation as literal as possible – to reflect the difference in the ways of thinking and talking across different languages and cultures. It should be cautioned, though, that some English translations here carry very different meanings from those expressed in the Chinese language: in particular, 'the Chinese nation', 'patriotism', 'the motherland' express positive cultural values. The general advice here is to view such in the world historical context of colonialism and anti-imperialist resistance. To highlight the features I want to draw attention to, whether formal or thematic, I have used italics in the English version.

The Chinese media

The discourse of the significance of Hong Kong's return

If we take an in-between-cultural perspective on discourses, beyond pre-scribed formal, linguistic analysis, in this case in terms of what a cultural discourse does and does not do, then we shall discover that one important and conspicuous sort of discourse that is absent from the western counterpart is a symbolic discourse on the return of HK. That is, the Chinese media do not take the return of HK merely as it would other-wise be: for instance, geopolitical change, administrative transition, return of sovereignty or even national reunification. It is not merely a current event, it is not merely an event in HK, it is not merely an event involving two geopolitical entities. Rather, it means more than these. It is a *symbol* that stands for something else as well.[2] More fundamentally different from the Western discourse than the symbolic meanings of the return of HK is the very notion of the return of HK: it does not exist and is not recognized in the Western discourse. Instead, the Western media take the event of 1997 in HK as something different: it is a handing over or transferring of a piece of land and its population and their adminis-tration to another government, as almost exclusively signified by the uniform term 'handover' which I alluded to earlier.

What are the symbolic meanings of the return of HK to China? The Chinese media have a prominent, elaborate and multifarious discourse on these. First, it may be noted that it is a discourse addressed to not only the people of HK and China, but also the people of the rest of the world. Second, several different themes may be identified within this discourse. One is that HK's return to China is a long-awaited reunification of a separated family, or the mother and the child, as it were. Another is that the return of HK is a reassumption of national sovereignty and hence a great historic achievement of the Chinese as a nation. In relation to that, further, it marks the beginning of the marching of Greater China into the world. Last but not least, it means a victory for the people of the world in its cause for national freedom, peace and development. (These meanings are related to the perceived reasons why the return has been possible, which I shall dwell upon in the next subsection.)

To understand how such a discourse is constructed, let us take a look at a concrete example:

Example 5.1

> *The return of Hong Kong signifies* that we Chinese people *have snow-washed* the hundred-year-old *national humiliation* from Hong Kong's occupation and that we *have ushered in a new era* for the joint development of Hong Kong and the mother country. It also *signifies* that we *have made an important stride* in the course of national reunification. And it *signifies* that the Chinese people *have made new contributions to* the cause for peace, development and progress of the world. (Jiang Zemin, Speech to all walks of life in the capital's commemoration of Hong Kong's return, *Wen Hui Bao*, 2 July 1997)

In this instance, at least three sorts of textual properties may be worthy of note as the instantiation or embodiment of that discourse described above. To start with, the topic of this part of the speech is the 'return of HK'; this notion is manifested in and solidified by the very term used (also in the title of the speech) and hence attention is drawn to it. Second, there is also an explicit term, '標誌著' (to signify, mark or symbolize), that highlights the symbolic nature of the return of HK. Observe that the term '標誌著' is repeated three times as part of a syntactic construction, which, as a commoner rhetorical device in Chinese than in English, further accentuates the significance of the symbolic meanings of the return. Third, four specific, different kinds of symbolic meanings are formulated as may be seen from the extract (so I will not repeat them here). They relate to or involve Mainland China, HK, other Chinese communities (for example, those in Macao and Taiwan) and the world as a whole. These symbolic meanings reflect the great scope and depth of the significance of the return of HK. In that connection, it may be worthy of special note, too, that most of these new meanings are constructed through *metaphors* (雪洗了⋯國恥, have snow-washed ... the national humiliation; 開創⋯新紀元, have ushered in a new era; 邁出了重要一步, have made an important stride). These metaphors add a further dimension of symbolism to the discourse and thereby highlight the special significance of what might otherwise be an incidental geopolitical event. There are contextual aspects of the discourse that should be highlighted here, too. One of these is the brutal, shameful past, when the British defeated the Chinese in two opium wars, that the text makes reference to (through, for example, 雪洗了⋯國恥, have snow-washed ... the national humiliation). The other particularly important piece of context is the decolonization of HK from the British colonizer, hence part of the historical process and moral progress of the international community (世界和平、發展與進步事業, the cause for peace, development and progress of the world). I mention these because the Western media, while predominantly preoccupied with expressing scepticism and issuing warnings to China (Shi-xu and Kienpointner 2001), are nearly completely reticent about them. In this case, the indirectly invoked context serves to accentuate the historic and internationally relevant significance of the return of HK.

The discourse of anti-colonial struggle

Another prominent discourse within the Chinese media, which is nearly completely absent in the western counterpart, is the account of why the return of HK becomes possible at the time it occurs. Specifically, the Chinese media routinely and elaborately recounted the prior circumstances and the previous Chinese governments' efforts leading to the return of HK on 1 July 1997. Thus, all the previous Chinese governments rejected the unfair treaties signed between Britain and the Qing government. Moreover, the previous Chinese governments attempted persistently but failed to reclaim HK from the imperial power. More significantly – this is given more emphasis – at the start of the long-drawn-out negotiations in the early 1980s, the British government continued to refuse to relinquish the territories obtained on the basis of those unfair treaties. Eventually, however, because of its increased economic and political power and because of its newly regained international position, China succeeded in negotiating and reclaiming all the lost territories of HK from the British colonizer. If one were to see the Chinese discourse from the *nationalist* perspective, one would fail to recognize the on-going post-colonial and anti-imperialist struggle; it is only through the in-between-cultural spectacle that such a broader cultural contest can be seen. The total silence on the part of the British western media on this issue, on the other hand, is further testimony to the western preferred dismissal of its colonial history and injustices and smoothes over the continued colonial desires and imperial consciousness. Let us read a concrete piece of such discourse:

Example 5.2

> For this day, after the founding of New China, our country's government repeatedly solemnly declared that Hong Kong has been an inextricable part of the Chinese territory since ancient times, that it does not recognize the three unequal treaties that the British imperialists imposed on China . . . After the 3rd plenary session of the Party's Eleventh Committee, the country entered a new era of reform, opening up and building socialist modernization: it had achieved greater productivity, strengthened the overall national capability and raised its international status. As the most dynamic developing country in the world, China rose up in the East. *These created the necessary conditions for the smooth return of Hong Kong.* For this day, *the Chinese government*, in the paramount interest of the motherland's reunification and in the paramount interest of maintaining Hong Kong's stability and prosperity, following the principle of 'one country, two systems', *provided a practical and feasible solution to the problems of Hong Kong, Macao and Taiwan and, ultimately, to the problem of the motherland's reunification* . . . Amidst the celebrations of Hong Kong's return, *we realize more deeply* that, *without* the leadership of the Chinese Communist Party, *without* the motherland's thriving and consolidation, *without* the great achievements of reform and opening up, *without* the persevering of New China's thirdgeneration leadership, especially without the guidance of Deng Xiao Ping's theory of building-socialism-with-Chinese-characteristics, Hong Kong's return today *would not have been possible. This is the solemn conclusion inscribed by a century's Chinese history.*
>
> (Editorial, A century's exhilarating event of the Chinese nation', *People's Daily*, 1 July 1997)

To start with, a little (con)textual information round this text will be handy. A passage preceding this fragment provides an account of the persistent but fruitless efforts of the previous Chinese generations and governments. That is, in the old, weak and poor China, generations of combatants tried but failed to regain HK. This narrative lends a 'contrastive' support to the central, historical thesis of the discourse under discussion (note the last sentence): namely, history proves that HK's return would not have been possible without the leadership of the Chinese Communist Party and the consequential greatly increased economic vitality.

The text under study refers to a number of events and actions leading up to the return of HK to China at the time it occurs and defines the nature of these events and actions in relation to HK's return. These can be distinguished into three general types. The formal distinctions between these are made apparent partly by the three phrasal repetitions (為了這一天, for this day) which introduce a new topic each, and partially by the temporal demarcations (新中國成立後, after the founding of New China; 黨的十一屆三中全會以後, after the 3rd plenary session of the Party's Eleventh Committee) which similarly contribute to the introduction of a new topic. The nature of the three general types of causes themselves is indicated by (1) the explicit, separate *definitions* of the different situations (為香港的順利回歸創造了必要性條件, these created the necessary condition for the smooth return of HK; 提供了一條現實可行的途徑, provided a practical and feasible solution) on the one side and (2) the thematic coherence amongst the three clusters of sentences (see, for example, the topical coherence on the increased productivity) on the other side.

Consequently, we see here that the first cause of HK's return has to do with New China's insistence that HK has historically been an inseparable part of China and its rejection of 三個不平等條約 (the three unequal treaties). Note that this effectively counters and undermines the implicit or explicit discourse in the western media that Britain 'hands over' HK to China according to an international agreement. The second type of cause, signalled in particular by and defined as 必要性條件 (necessary condition), is the strengthened economic power and elevated international standing. The construction of this necessary condition reclaims the basis for the return of HK and therefore effectively repudiates the implicit Western notion that the British government 'hands over' HK according to a historical treaty. The third, signalled especially by and defined as 可行的途徑 (a practical and feasible solution), finally, is the construct of 'one country, two systems' in the interest of national reunification and HK's stability and prosperity. This projection in terms of the feasibility of the just-mentioned condition or basis that the Chinese government creates serves to confirm the effectiveness of the Chinese government's efforts behind the return of HK.

It may be noted, too, that the nature of these causes is respecified and 'solidified', as it were, in the last part of the example. It is respecified in that these causes are traced back to the Chinese Communist Party's leadership and especially to the top level (鄧小平建設有中國特色社會主義理論的指引, the guidance of Deng Xiao Ping's theory of building-socialism-with-Chinese-characteristics). The solidification is done through three sorts of devices: (1) the construction of in-depth consciousness or understanding of these causes (更加深刻地体會到, realize more deeply), which in turn strengthens the truthfulness of the construction of the causes; (2) the conditional conjunction (沒有…就不可能有, without . . . it would not have been possible), which renders the causal link factual and absolute; and (3) the construction of a conclusion that is based on history (這就是一百多年歷史寫下的庄重結論, This is the solemn conclusion inscribed by a century's Chinese history), which conclusively determines the truthfulness of the assertions about the three causes. As a whole, the discourse that it is the Chinese continuous political struggle and economic efforts that have made the return of HK possible highlights China's anti-colonial struggle, especially in the context of the British refusal made during Sino-British negotiations in the late 1970s and early 1980s. The resounding silence of the British/Western media on the historical events leading up to HK's return bears witness to this cultural struggle.

The discourse of cultural and global interconnections

In the Chinese media, there is a third prominent discourse that is worth special attention from the western discourse community. Namely, this is the discourse on the cultural links between HK and China and between these and the rest of the world. This discourse, it should be noted, not just describes the historical and cultural connections between HK and China, but also, through such a description and other means, recreates and maintains relations between the two and between them and the world. Thus, one recurring pattern found in the data is the account of various sorts of links between China and HK.

For example, it is frequently asserted that HK had been under China's control since antiquity. HK became separated from China only because of British imperialist aggression as well as other countries' repression, hence also the weakness and corruption of the Qing government. At the same time, it is suggested, generations of the Chinese government and people have never accepted the unfair treaties signed between the then British and Qing governments, nor did they stop trying to reclaim HK from the colonizer. Moreover, different kinds of cultural psychological bond are invoked in the discourse: that is, the emotions and memories amongst Chinese and HK compatriots. In addition, historical connections between China and HK are made in terms of shared social, moral and psychological experience. Last but not least, future interrelations are rendered through expressions of intentions of political and institutional support and cooperation. One eminent such expression is the elaboration of the judicial policy of 'one country, two systems'.

What deserves special mention here is the use of a large variety of metaphors that reconstruct and reestablish the close bondage between China and HK and that between these and the rest of the world. These include the mother–child relationship, a bridge between China and the rest of the world, a window for exchange between the two and so on. This discourse of interrelations is particularly noteworthy and significant: it aspires to connection and bondage in an increasingly alienated world and responds and resists to the recurring Western (neo)colonialist discourse of 'HK must remain HK'. Let us look at the following for concrete ways of rebuilding relationships:

Example 5.3

> Mainland China, the vast economic hinterland, provides *a huge space for Hong Kong's economic expansion*. The mainland's healthy economic growth brings *enormous profits to Hong Kong's economy*. The mainland's increasing investment in Hong Kong has become *an important force in the stabilization and development of Hong Kong's economy*. At the same time, Hong Kong is *a centre of trade, finance, transport, tourism and information in the Asia-Pacific region as well as the world*; it is *China's window, bridge and conduit to the world economy*. These capacities have played *an irreplaceable part in the mainland's drive for modernization*.
>
> (Su Bei (commentary), 'Tomorrow will be more beautiful',
> *Bi-Monthly*, 97 (13))

In this passage, the interconnections between China, HK and the rest of the world can be seen as being created through verbal structures at different levels and consequently also of various kinds. First, it may be noted that a particular semantics in terms of economic benefits of one community for the other, hence an economic relationship, is created through descriptions of the economic advantages that China brings to HK. Similarly, another semantics in terms of the usefulness and benefits of HK to China, hence a functional relationship, is rendered available by descriptions of the benefits that HK brings to China and of the needed links that HK provides for China with the rest of the world. Second, it is worth noting that in this relation-building process certain preferred metaphorical–lexical choices play an important part. They are effective in the construction of interrelations because they are everyday metaphors of close relationship in the Chinese language (for example, 中國通向世界經濟的窗口、橋樑和管道, China's window, bridge and conduit to the world economy). Third, a supra-sentential, rhetorical structure in the form of a reversing of the subject–object order of the proposition helps produce a reciprocal, mutual relationship. Note here that not only does China provide links with HK, but also vice versa. In addition, it may be noticed that the first set of interconnections (China and Hong Kong) is linked with the second one (Hong Kong and China), through the temporal marker 同時 (at the same time), creating still another simultaneous relationship. Thus, the textually linking devices such as these produce and reproduce multilevel interrelations between China, HK and the rest of the world.

The discourse of anti-colonial agency

Within the Chinese media, there is an unequivocal and prominent discourse of the role of HK people, as well as China's support for HK, especially in terms of recent economic growth, in addition to other local conditions, in its accounts of HK's success. It may be added in this regard that the construction of China's continuous and consistent cultural relationship with HK as seen above is interwoven with this discourse in that the relationship between China and HK is also a form of agency behind HK's success. This discourse of the agency of success is worthy of special attention for the western readership in particular for two reasons.

First, as I described earlier, there has been a general perception and discourse within the western community that HK's economic success is the result of British colonial administration. The Chinese discourse is then a rebuttal. Here it is important to point out that this is not merely parochial nationalism; we must see it historically and link it to the colonial occupation and injustice. In this sense, this discourse signifies an anti-colonial, oppositional gesture. But it is not merely a gesture: second, it is general knowledge, at least to the local people in HK and China, that HK's economic rise did not occur until the final three decades of a century and a half of British rule. Further, democratic reform in HK happened even later, at the final stage of this colonial history, when the negotiation on the return of HK had begun. So, there is a deeper sense in which this discourse reclaims local identity and agency from British colonial rule.

As an illustration of this discourse, I want to show an extract from the speech by China's president, Jiang Zemin. I choose this also because of the wide impact that his speech could have on China's discourse community. It provides the fullest account amongst all the data investigated.

Example 5.4

> Hong Kong's success today is, *in the final analysis, the work of the Hong Kong compatriots. . . .* Hong Kong's success today is *inseparable from China's development and the support of the people from the mainland . . .* Hong Kong's success today is *also attributable to a number of other factors. Its advantageous geographical location, its free port policy of complete openness, its well-developed legal system and highly efficient team of civil servants, and its effective economic management and civic administration, have all facilitated* Hong Kong's economic development.
>
> ('A shining page in the annals of the Chinese nation' (speech by Jiang Zemin), *South China Morning Post*, 2 July 1997)

Here a variety of causes of HK's economic development and success is presented, in sharp contrast to the exclusive, colonialist, attributions made in the British/Western media discourse. Recall Patten's argumentative explanation (quoted above), which singularly exalts British rule. But here the attributions are made to not only the role of the people of HK and the Chinese people as well as their economic progress, but also other circumstantial factors which range from the geographical location to the social, political economic system. What is particularly noteworthy is that here the most credit is given to HK people as the main agent of success. This is signalled by not only the positioning of the reference to HK people at the beginning of the list of causes, but also, more importantly, the emphatic expression 'in the final analysis' which defines HK people's role as the root cause. This rejects the colonialist explanation and reclaims the agency of the colonized.

It may also be noted that the construction of China's connection with and support for HK (note 'inseparable from') renders the account of HK's success a similar, further anti-colonial gesture and post-colonial realignment. Given that this account is almost completely unseen in the British/Western media, and given the British and Western discourse of HK's success as the result of colonial rule, this new account contributes to the anti-colonial reclaim suggested above.

The third place, as it were, is given to a number of other factors in the Chinese media. This may be seen from (1) the positioning of these factors in the last part of the accounting discourse, (2) the 'supplementary' expressions as in '*also* attributable to a number of *other* factors' (emphasis mine) and (3) the lexical choice 'facilitated', which suggests an auxiliary character. From this part, it may be seen that the British influence is not dismissed but implicated in the account: note 'its free port policy of complete openness, its well-developed legal system and highly efficient team of civil servants, and its effective economic management and civic administration'. From this point of view, the Chinese accounting discourse, in addition to its oppositional and anti-colonial account of agency, is also far more comprehensive than the British and western media's account.

The Hong Kong media

The discourse of the significance of Hong Kong's return

I have earlier commented that the western media portrays the event of HK's decolonization as a *handover* of sovereignty. Here it may be added that if the handover has meant anything special other than 'itself' for the British, then it is often interpreted as the loss of the last crown colony in Asia – the 'handover' is often explicated as such. On the part of the HK media, in contrast, the return means first and foremost national reunification and removal of colonial rule, as reflected directly by the Chinese terms 回歸 (return) or less frequently 收回 (take back), both of which are likewise used in the Chinese media. (As we shall see in the next section, this discourse is also consistent with the notion that HK should (be re)turn(ed) to China.) In this connection, it may be mentioned that the return is held as important to all the Chinese people in the world because HK is connected with them all. Second, in contrast to the Western discourse which routinely expresses concerns and scepticism over China's role in the future HK, the return of HK is often hailed as a joyful and happy moment in HK's history, though this is sometimes mixed with trepidation regarding the Chinese government. For example, news actors are quoted as congratulating themselves as lucky to be able to witness and experience this historical event and change. Furthermore, it is notable that the return of HK to China is sometimes acknowledged as marking, paradoxically, HK's self-government for the first time in its entire history. As is generally known, before the Opium War, HK had been under China's control; after the war, it came under British colonial rule, in which the local HK people had absolutely no say. So there are sometimes rejections of the notion that British rule is democratic at all and expression of hope and expectation that for the first time in their history HK people will be their own 'master'. If we see these new meanings of what the West has portrayed as 'handover' in light of the long and brutal colonial history behind the event, then they are not mere 'different interpretations'. Effectively they accomplish post-colonial resistance and recuperation. The meanings and forms of realization of this discourse are partially reflected in the following example:

Example 5.5

Today is the beginning of *a new era* for Hong Kong. The founding of the PRC Hong Kong Special Administrative Region *marks* the *decolonization* of the most modernized Chinese community in the world and her *return to the motherland*. Further, it *injects new vitality* into the modernization drive by *the motherland* with a population of 1.2 billion people and *opens up new ground for East–West exchange.*

(Editorial, 'Two-systems should feature both separation and integration, Hong Kong people should be neither humble nor arrogant', *Ming Bao*, 1 July 1997)

The Western, British notion of 'handover', together with its presuppositions and implications, is alien here. The passage from *Ming Bao* here assigns a variety of far-reaching significance to the return of HK. To begin with, it may be observed that the article from which the text is extracted attempts to take a neutral stance in relation to China. This stance is visible from the title of the article and as such can be seen as tone-setting for the whole of the article. In the fragment itself, different sorts of symbolic meanings of HK's return are projected. Thus, 今天 (today) and 中華人民共和國香港特別行政區的誕生 (The founding of the PRC HK Special Administrative Region) are broached as the topic of discourse. The former refers to the same fact as the latter, because the day is 1 July 1997 on which the PRC HK Special Administrative Region is formally established. To this subject matter, *other, new* significance, of several different kinds, is assigned: (1) the beginning of a new era, (2) the most modernized Chinese society freed from colonial rule, (3) HK returning to the mother's embrace, (4) injecting new vitality into the modernization drive of the mother country, and (5) opening up new ground for East–West exchange.

The construction of new, symbolic meanings here is signalled by two sorts of devices. One is the 'symbolizing' verb, 標誌著 (mark, symbolize or signal); it assigns a meaning to a topic other than what it normally has. The other is the epithet 新 (new); it helps to assign a new meaning to a topical object by qualifying its property or effect as new. The term is used three times in the fragment. The new meanings assigned to the return of HK are not mere representations or constructions of new images. If we take into account the historical cultural context of the long centuries of colonial repression and exploitation, and if in particular we take into account the local perspective and agency, then these new identifications cannot be understood as merely fitting in Chinese, nationalist ideologies. They celebrate the breaking free from colonial rule (see points 1 and 2 above); they achieve and assume a new sense of belonging and mastery (see points 1, 2 and 3); they play an active part in shaping China (point 4); and they establish links with China and the rest of the world (point 5). All these meanings are overshadowed more or less in the western media.

The discourse of anti-colonial struggle

There is a sizeable consensus, even amongst HK's discourses that are suspicious and critical of China, that HK should be decolonized from British rule and that HK should (be) return(ed) to China. There are expressions of fear over the return of HK to China, which is also sometimes offered as the reason for favouring a 'smooth' transfer. But, regarding the question of whether and why HK *should* break free from colonialism and whether and why it *should* return to China, there is a general agreement. Namely, colonial society is a backward form of society and must be left behind. Further, many people do want to shake off the humiliation from the colonial history. In addition, it is also frequently suggested, as the rationale for the return to China, that HK people are basically *Chinese*.

Thus, there is a fair amount of argumentative discourse in the media which deliberates the reasons such as these that lead to the conclusion indicated above. It offers various explanations of HK's past and present, assesses the influence, including benefits, from China, traces the cultural roots to China and compares different political economic systems of society in the world. These arguments all favour the decolonization from the British and reunification with China. This discourse functions, of course, to argue against the separatist discourse present in HK as in the Western media, but from another perspective it also reflects the existence of discussion, debate and dialogue on the issue of HK's future. In this sense, the HK media discourse of anti-colonial struggle undermines the Western notion that HK has no input to its return to China but is entirely resigned to China's absolutist, ideological decision. In an article analysing the elements and forces in HK that oppose the reunification, the author has the following counter-argument to offer:

Example 5.6

> *Imperialism and colonialism have reconstructed many societies; anti-imperialism, anti-colonialism and decolonization then are a rather natural result* . . . Hong Kong's colonial history *has not been completely separated from her mother's body, so the mother's blood and emotional bond have long been implanted in her own body* . . . In the second half of the 1980s, with China's reforms and opening door, Hong Kong's economic forces spread to South China and *gradually Hong Kong has become merged into the mother's body. Such historical processes are not something that any Hong Kong politician or political party can resist or reorientate.*
>
> (Guo Shaotang, 'Subjective consciousness cannot block
the march of history', *Ming Bao*, 30 June 1997)

First of all, it should be made clear that this part of the article provides an account for HK's reunification with China, indirectly as well as explicitly. It is an explicit account because of the textual expressions of causal relations, 是相當自然的後果 (is a rather natural result) and 因此 (so), as well as 決非…所能改變或左右 (cannot change or reorientate). At an implicit level, it may be seen that the text is embedded in an article that answers the questions of how HK's return comes about and why the opposition did not succeed.

Having determined the causal explanation in the account, second, let us note that the causal relation to HK's reunification with China can be identified at two levels of immediacy, indirect ones and direct ones. Take the first complex sentence for example. The former part describes a cause (many societies created by imperialism and colonialism) and the latter part the result (anti-imperialism, anti-colonialism and decolonization); and yet, implicitly, the latter is presupposed to be a direct cause of HK's return, as the rest of the text would inform us. The same is true of the other ensuing accounts.

Third, and more importantly, three strands of immediate causes of HK's return can be identified here. These are formulated in the latter part of three pairs of cause–effect descriptions, respectively. One is 反帝、反殖和非殖 (anti-imperialism, anti-colonialism and decolonization). Another is 母體的血液和情意結 (the mother's blood and emotional bond). And still another is 香港逐步被吸納入母體 (gradually HK has become merged into the mother's body). These explanations only partially overlap with those offered in the Chinese media, but go directly counter to the corresponding Western media discourse.

Finally, it may be pointed out that these causal accounts of HK's return are (also) argumentatively oriented. That is, on the one hand, the causal relations produced in the accounts are redefined in the last sentence as 這種歷史變化 (Such historical processes or changes). Conceived of as historical processes, they carry with them the quality of inevitability and not being subject to human desires, as would the title of the article from which the text is chosen also suggest, hence the certainty of the causal relations described. On the other hand, other alternative possible outcomes to those historical processes are denied. In this way, the discourse opposing the reunification with China is undermined.

The discourse of cultural and global interconnections

I indicated earlier that the recent Western discourse regarding HK, both popular and scholarly, has tended to emphasize the uniqueness of HK and hence of its identity, through either a general hybridism or a specific colonial blend. By 'hybridism', I mean that the notion of hybridity is used to define the uniqueness of HK; by 'colonial blend' I mean the argument that the mixture of Eastern and Western elements makes HK unique. Such discourse projects a bounded identity of HK in order, effectively, to reduce possible links and relations between HK and China, to separate HK from China, and, arguably, to claim a particular position for HK in the world arena. Consistent with this discourse, as may be pointed out here, is the notion that China is another 'colonizer', like the British, taking over HK, and opposition is therefore expressed through dismissals of China's politics and of the local politicians in favour of reunification with China.

What seems usually ignored, however, is the fact that there is a recurring discourse in the HK media that works precisely to forge and maintain relations between HK and China. It is not the case, as the Western discourse of HK has claimed, that, to its people, HK is entirely unique and self-contained and therefore there is no basis to relate HK to China – other than perhaps to reshape or change China. There is a variety of ways in which the HK media discourse does this relation-building work. Various arguments for linkages that range from historical, cultural, economic and geographical to future-oriented standpoints may be found in the data. Thus, it may be observed that the bond between HK and China is rendered through such notions as returning to the 'motherland', 'compatriots', interrelations in trade and commerce, 'blood', language, culture and geography.

From here it may be noticed that metaphors of various sorts play an important part in establishing and defining the bond between HK and China. For example, HK is regularly portrayed as a 'bridge' between China and the rest of the world, a 'window' on to the world. Similarly, close 'neighbours', 'frontier and hinterland', the 'origin/root and further growth', 'mother and child', 'blood' and so on are used not only to invoke historical and cultural links, but also to draw attention to present, material and especially economic relations between HK and China. Let us look at an example in some detail.

Example 5.7

> Hong Kong *has become not only the capitalist world's pioneer* into mainland China's market, *but also* mainland China's *guide for joining tracks with the international community* . . . Since more than ten years ago, Hong Kong's interests have begun to *merge with* those of Mainland China. After 1997, Hong Kong's prospects will become *even more inseparable from* the broader background and the greater cause of China . . . In the new millennium, the world will *need* China more and China will *also need* the rest of the world more. Hong Kong, as China's most important *meeting point* with the world, will become not only *more Chinese*, but also *more international and more pluralistic.*
> (Bi Feng, 'Hong Kong is the meeting point between China and the world', *Asia Weekly*, 2–8 June 1997)

In this text, it may be seen that connections and interconnections between HK, China and the rest of the world are being constructed through textual devices of various kinds and at multiple levels. One obvious form that directly produces linkages is the lexical and lexico-grammatical expression of connection: 接軌 (joining tracks), 交匯點 (meeting point), 同…融合在一起了 (merge with) and 離不開 (be insepara-ble from). A second 'connecting' device is the compound syntactic structure of what might be called 'mutual connection': 'X 需要 (needs) Y, Y 也…需要 (also needs) X' as in 'the world will *need* China more and China will *also need* the rest of the world more'. Still another is a metaphoric construction of functional relationship. Thus, for example, HK is portrayed as serving the functions of 資本主義世界進軍中國大陸市場 的先驅 (the capitalist world's pioneer into mainland China's market) and of 中國大陸與國際社會 "接軌" 的引導者 (mainland China's guide for joining tracks with the international community), respectively, for China. Finally, the transfer of a property of one entity into another provides a link as well. For example, a future link is created between HK, China and the rest of the world through predicting that HK will assume characteristics of China and of the rest of the world: 變得更加中國化 (become more Chinese) and 變得國際化和多元化 (become more international and diversified).

As a result, a variety of interconnections between HK, China and the rest of the world emerge. A most noteworthy one here is perhaps the notion of HK as a 'meeting point' between China and the rest of the world, so that the three entities converge in HK (note the last sentence). Related to that, a second notable interconnection is the 'mutual need' between China and the rest of the world, for which HK plays the part of a meeting point (note the sentence before the last). A third important form of interconnection is 利益 (interest, profit) that is shared between HK and China (note the second sentence).

Particularly noteworthy in these interconnections is the notion that HK occupies a leading, dominant and central position in relation to China. Note that HK is portrayed here not merely as one of the two halves or components of a connection, but as 先驅 (pioneer), 引導者 (guide) and 中國與世界最重要的交匯點 (the most important meeting point between China and the world). These constructions project a much stronger, assertive and constructive agency of HK vis-à-vis China and the world than the Western media discourse has suggested of HK (for example, as either fitting in with China's ideology or being under the threat of China). At the same time, HK's functional relation with China is acknowledged and maintained where HK's future development is described as inseparable from China's 大事業、大背景 (greater cause and broader background). All these crucial meanings of links, interconnections and, arguably, controlling positions of HK in relation to China are suppressed in the Western media through an implicit notion that HK is a unique society, created by British colonial rule, that is separable, and ought to be separated, from China.

The discourse of the agency of the colonized

Related to the issue of relations of HK is yet another discourse that deserves special, particular attention. This is the discourse regarding the agency of HK's success. As has been said earlier, the British, Western media have it, at least tacitly, that HK's success is the result of British colonial administration, or explicitly as is the case of the last British governor of HK, Patten's, public statement (shown above). This dominant discourse has overshadowed and overridden other sorts of explanation, potential and real. In this case, the HK media discourse of the agency of its success is all the more significant, because, as we shall see, it is not merely 'different' in representation, but, in a post-colonial gesture, it challenges the British and Western version, thereby reclaiming the agency of the colonized.

More specifically, this discourse makes it clear, through a reflexive account of HK history, that HK's economic rise did not begin until the final decades of Britain's one and half centuries' rule (since the 1970s). It recounts that HK was more backward than Shanghai until 50 years ago and its economic ascendancy parallels the economic reform and open-door policy in China in the 1970s. This historical comparative discourse throws into question the role of British colonial administration in HK's transformation. Further, this discourse sometimes asks the rhetorical question why the British political economical system fails to generate the same sort of success in the home country as in HK. This move, from a different angle, undermines the Western, British narcissistic glorification of colonialism. In greater measure, however, this discourse gives credit to the HK people's capacity to fully exploit their own situation in its account of HK's success.[3] For example, in the following extract, the success of HK is attributed argumentatively to the local HK people, instead of the British.

Example 5.8

> *Some people say* that the reason for [Hong Kong's] success lies in the efficient management by the British, *but that cannot explain* why the British have not done so well in the country of 'origin'. *Some other people think* that the people of Hong Kong are particularly capable. *But* Hong Kong people are *merely* Chinese who happen to live in that place. *Why* do they become so different as soon as they emigrate to Hong Kong? . . . *The real reason* why Hong Kong people are successful *is that they can integrate the civilizations of the East and West with commercial interests, creating a unique management milieu and culture that are 'neither a donkey nor a horse'. Consequently, they are able to seize every new opportunity and trend for development in the world.*
>
> (Bi Feng, 'Hong Kong is the meeting point between China and the world', *Asia Weekly*, 2–8 June 1997)

The text may be analysed into a thematic structure of argumentatively organized explanations. It may be noted thus that the text first rejects two kinds of explanation of HK's success. Then it asserts an alternative explanation. This new explanation contains three different kinds of attributions.

The rejection of the opposing explanations is done through a set of rhetorical devices. One is a pair of contrastive sentences (note the disjunctive conjunctions) that undermine certain opinions by pointing at what those explanations fail to account for: 有人説⋯，卻無法解釋⋯ (some people say... but cannot explain...); 也有人認為⋯，但⋯不過⋯ (some other people think... , but *x* is/does merely *y*). Another is the rhetorical question: 為何⋯不⋯呢 (Why... not...), which assumes an answer that is contrary to the negative proposition in question. These textual strategies refute the notions that HK's success is owing to British rule. Implicitly, they draw attention to a notion that it is due to the special ability of the people from HK and China, respectively.

Against these explanatory opinions, three opposing, interrelated attributions are proffered. The first is that HK people are good at combining eastern and western civilizations as well as their commercial interests. The second is that they have been able to create an in-between, 'third' kind of business environment and culture. The third reason for HK's success is that HK has been able to grasp every new trend and opportunity for development in the past half-century. These new explanations contrast with the British, Western version and reclaim the agency and hence identity of the HK people as the central force of HK's transformation.

Conclusion

Finally, let me reflect briefly on what I have done here and how this work may be pursued further. The present study has been intended as a plea for more scholarly attention to non-Western discourses in the field of language and (intercultural) communication. Here I first tried to theorize non-Western discourse as a marginalized topic of interest, considered why the west should study it and how it can study non-Western discourse. The central, critical point here was that, beyond national boundaries and cultural differences, relations and practices of domination, subordination and resistance between the East and West should be an important focus of attention. Then, to take this general proposition seriously, I embarked on an empirical research on the concrete case of China's and HK's media discourses on HK's historic transition.

Based on qualitatively selected data against the backdrop of dominant Western media discourses, I identified and characterized a set of patterns or sub-discourses within the Chinese media discourse and HK's media discourse. In illustrating and detailing such patterns of discourses, I also highlighted some textual properties and their contextual functions of some specific sample texts. Thus, although apparently about the same situation or reality, China's and HK's media discourses are different from the Western counterpart not only in their perspectives but also in topics of interest and certainly in degrees of emphasis. Moreover, even though the negative or oppositional discourses from HK vis-à-vis China (which are already prominently represented in the western media) are not reproduced here, complex differences do appear between HK and China.

The present study shows, for instance, that both China and HK's discourses are predominantly concerned with the symbolic significance of HK's return: that is, its meanings in terms of national reunification, anti-imperialism in human history and a new era for HK and China. Another topic that these discourses pay tremendous attention to is why the return of HK to China becomes possible in the first place. Still another important, shared discourse is that of relations and interconnections between HK and China. These topics are hardly treated in the western media.

Learning about such unfamiliar topics can be enlightening and useful. In this study, I have identified and highlighted the discourse of relations – for example, relations with other places, other peoples, other systems, other histories, other cultures – in China's and HK's media discourses. Amidst the perennial but continuously popular western discourse of self and identity (including the variations of 'hybridity' and 'diaspora') in the social and human sciences, the discourse of relationship would seem hardly interesting. But especially the present-day, interdependent and antagonistic world needs not less but more explorations in relationship and relation-building, hence the human bond and cultural coexistence. The discourses of the causes of HK's return as revealed here would also immediately throw the taken-for-granted notion of HK's 'handover' as well as its other implications into question.

Equally interesting and significant is the fact that China's and HK's media discourses can have very different accounts of HK's success from that of the Western media. As opposed to the Western implicit or explicit attribution of HK's success to the colonial, British administration, these discourses reclaim the agency of the HK people, in addition to other wide-ranging explanations. In the case of the Chinese discourse, for example, the HK people are seen as ultimately responsible for its success and at the same time China's role is pointed out as well as a range of other factors, including the British administration.

Furthermore, differences between the Chinese and HK media discourses can also be seen. For example, whilst the Chinese media, in the explanation of HK's return, emphasizes the role of the strengthened economic power of China and, behind it, the role of the Chinese leadership, the HK discourse tends to give prominence to the 'natural' cultural bond and economic interdependency. In the accounts of the connections between HK, China and the world, the Chinese discourse tends to emphasize the economically complementary relationship between the two, in addition to the notion of HK as a bridge between China and the world. But the HK discourse seems to be more assertive and presents HK as occupying a leading/guiding position in such a relationship.

Study of non-western discourses is an unfinished business. The present attempt is only partial and limited; non-western discourse is varied and continues to change. More and continuous endeavours need to be dedicated to non-western discourses, be they from Asia, Africa or Latin America. The globalized yet divided world can ill afford to ignore them any longer.

6
Fanning the Sparks of Hope from History

Introduction

Northern Ireland is one of those few places on earth that are known the world over for all the wrong reasons. Consequently much social scientific research has been done to account for its problems. This work, involving political, historical, cultural, sociological and psychological sciences, often seems to conclude that it is some external, residual forces in Northern Ireland that have recurrently given rise to its communal strife (see, for example, Boyle and Hadden 1985; Porter 1998). Thus, an image of fixity is presented. So, for example, the most frequently proffered kinds of explanation are 'atavism' and 'tribalism', as McGarry and O'Leary (1995) call them. That is, the atavist discourse, on the one side, attributes Northern Ireland's troubles to its ancestral conditions, as opposed to (post)modern ones; the tribalist discourse, on the other side, to its insular myths, as different from broad and diverse perspectives.

However, it seems to me that the agency of Northern Ireland as a community, particularly the intrinsic power to break away from the tradition and to create new discourses of reality and experience, has been neglected as a result. Is there any change from within the conscious community itself, for example from within its self-understanding? If there is at all, then how is it accomplished? From the viewpoint of the present project, in what way can social (discourse) research help with a tumultuous part of the world such as Northern Ireland?

In this chapter, accordingly, I want to draw attention to the dynamic of Northern Ireland by examining it as a community of *discourses* and hence a community of *speaking agents*. Specifically, I shall be focusing on the discursive construction of collective identity in the mainstream print media over the past hundred years or so. In this shift of topic of enquiry, I have two particular aims. First, I want to determine if and how the group identity discourse has changed through time. For this task, my analytical question will be, 'Given a chosen body of discourse data of a particular historical period, what is the nature of the group identity and through what textual form is it achieved?' Second, using a chosen criterion (the degree of intergroup antagonism), I want to find out if there is any moral progress, that is, from conflict to cohesion, through the history of the identity discourses. For this task, my analytical question will be, 'Is there any increase, or decrease, of animosity with regard to the other, traditionally opposing community through the historically differentiated identity discourses?'

To anticipate the research somewhat, my overall claim will be that, in the course of the past hundred or so years, the identity discourses of the two opposing communities in Northern Ireland, the 'Irish/nationalist/Catholic' and the 'British/unionist/Protestant', have become progressively less acrimonious and more accommodating in relation to the other community. Specifically, during the War of Independence in the early twentieth century, the predominant discourse of identity was that of militant nationalism. Then, during the Civil Rights Movement between the late 1960s and early 1970s, the prevailing identity discourse became one of the minority versus the majority. In the years round the Anglo-Irish Agreement of 1985, the mainstream identity discourse turned into one of neighbours. Finally, in the present period of the Good Friday Agreement since 1998, the common identity discourse seems to be one of equal partnership.

More importantly for the present project, when these discourses are compared with each other in terms of the degree of intergroup animosity, it emerges that each of the subsequent discourses becomes successively less confrontational and more conciliatory towards the other community. Thus, contrary to the common notion that Northern Ireland is determined by the habit of religion or nationalism or tribalism (and contrary to the wider assumption that identity is bound up by the logic of difference and dominance), I demonstrate here that the public discourses of identity in Northern Ireland (henceforth NI) have generally speaking moved, step by step, from hatred towards harmony. If discourse such as these partakes of social cultural reality and if it has impact on the future cultural development, then these historically differentiated discourses constitute a cultural transformation of NI and, more significantly, beckon more hope than has hitherto been realized.

It should be made clear at the outset that the present research is not meant to describe or explain anything in the traditional sense of social science. Rather it is motivated by a specific cultural politics: to rediscover signs of hope from the history of the discourses of a 'troubled' community, group or culture. If we were able to identify new discourses from within, beyond the 'doomed' discourses, for example, we might gain insights into the relevant community's future and perhaps inspire the community to redescribe and revision itself. Thus, the present work is 'to replace knowledge with hope', as Rorty (1998) has advocated (see also Bennett 1998). Barker and Galasinski (2001: 56) also argue for such redescriptions when they say, 'Social change becomes possible through rethinking and re-describing the social order and the possibilities for the future. Rethinking ourselves, which emerges through social practice . . . brings new political subjects and practices into being'. A society like Northern Ireland, which has traditionally been 'beset' by ways of speaking of identity, would be a particularly interesting object for 'cultural therapy' then. And what we learn from this case study may even be instructive for researching other 'troubled' communities in other parts of the world.

Identity: a historical-comparative approach

In this section I shall try to sketch out a discursive, historical and moral perspective on identity. Further, proceeding from this view, I shall suggest what relevant questions should be asked and answered regarding the discursive transformation of identity and its ethical evaluation, as are the central concerns of this study.

Identity as discourse

'Identity' has traditionally been understood as the experience or consciousness of the self and considered as primordial, individual, objective, centralized and stable across time and space. As such, it is thought to influence people's perception and behaviour. This notion of identity has not only tremendous influence in traditional forms of western social science, but also wide currency in everyday western culture.

Critical approaches to subjectivity, language and culture, especially cultural studies, discursive psychology, critical discourse analysis and cultural psychology, have argued that identities, whether individual or collective, cannot be isolated from the cultural context and social practice in and through which they are formed, displayed, mobilized and so constituted (for example, Barker and Galasinski 2001; Butler 1993; Chouliaraki and Fairclough 1999; Grossberg 1996; Hall 1996a, 1999; Sampson 1989; Shweder 1990; van Dijk 1993a). Social constructionism and postmodernism have similarly suggested that identity, self, the person and the like should best be seen as products of historical and cultural discourses as well as agents of new discourses (for example, Anderson 1991; Derrida 1976; Foucault 1985, 1986; Gergen 1999; Shotter and Gergen 1989). They all converge on the point that language (use) is central to identity.

In the present study, accordingly, identity does not refer to individual, given or decontextualized consciousness of the self. Rather, I take it to be a situated construction of the self, in relation to social others, through symbolic – especially discursive – practice in a concrete social cultural context (see also Antaki and Widdicombe 1998). Thus, familiar entities such as 'personality', 'cultural identity', 'social identity' and 'national identity' will not be seen as independent objects already out there, but will be understood as (re)produced through symbolic social practice in specific situations. Here it may be noted that identity can be constructed through different symbolic modes that range from the verbal to the visual. But the discursive one, embodied in text and talk, including those appearing in the conventional and new media as well as interpersonal interaction, constitutes a prevailing part of cultural life. As my focus here will be on the discursive mode of constructing identity, I shall call the present object of enquiry the discourse of identity or identity discourse. This notion makes it possible, among other things, to focus on texts and utterances through which identity, self and others are brought into being and the circumstances under which this is done.

With regard to the discursive notion, it may be stressed that identity discourse is a unity of form and meaning. That is, whilst identity can be of different categories, say personal, collective or professional, with different properties, such as being kind, clever or domineering, and used to achieve a variety of purposes such as to identify oneself with others, or to impress or intimidate them, it must be realized through some specific textual and contextual means. Such textual and contextual forms of constructing identity can be of a great many kinds and in different combinations: vocabulary, accent, grammar, narrative, genre, conversational interaction control and background information. They can also be in different degrees of explicitness: identity may be described, referred to, implied, presupposed or otherwise indirectly produced. It should also be noted that identity may be only one dimension or element of a discourse, as speakers may not be exclusively concerned with identity when engaged in interaction. Other meanings may be present as well. In addition, identity discourse is a culture-specific process. Identity may not be every culture's concern. In some Asian cultures, 'identity' is understood and used differently than in western European culture, for example.

A number of implications follow. First, discourse research on identity should, as a minimum, characterize not only the nature of the identity being constructed, but also the textual and contextual properties that go to constitute them. Second, analysis of identity discourse should not be restricted to a singular, fixed prescription of categories, nor to merely textual categories (later I shall advocate analysis beginning with social, cultural or political issues and not with such analytical categories). Third, local, cultural forms of analysis should be mobilized wherever possible. The present research, consequently, will make use of whatever tools and methods are available in the traditions of language and discourse studies germane to the present research questions (for example, Billig 1995; Chilton 2002; Fairclough 1992; van Dijk 1993b; Wodak *et al.* 1999).

Moreover, identity, as a form of discourse, may not be stable but will shift across situations (Antaki and Widdicombe 1998; Reicher and Hopkins 2001). This also means that identity should be seen as an active, creative process, in response to different circumstances (Foucault 1985, 1986; Giddens 1991; Gergen 1999; Hall 1992, 1996b, 1999). In this process, identity is also a tool, as it were, which serves the interests and purposes of the speaking individuals, groups or institutions. The discursive and creative notion of identity adopted here makes it possible to examine the historical transformations of the discourses of identity, as my subsequent analysis will attempt to do.

Further, identity, as a constituent element of discourse, should also be recognized as a possible instrument of power and so a site of power struggle (Chilton 2002; Wodak *et al.* 1999). In social and cultural life, identities are often created, claimed, denied, redescribed or monopolized for control, dominance or resistance. Giddens (1991: 6) suggests that '[I]ndeed, class divisions and other fundamental lines of inequality, such as those connected with gender or ethnicity, can be partly *defined* in terms of differential access to forms of self-actualisation and empowerment' (emphasis original). In the present case of researching into the moral development of identity discourse, we can usefully study when, in the construction of identity, power interests are sought after and when they disappear, as a way of evaluating the transformation of collective identity and intergroup relations.

Last but not least, if identity is a form of self-consciousness in relation to social others, then it should not be defined as merely bounded entities, be they individual, collective or hybridized, but as relational as well (Gergen 1994). In this way, we can research identity as a way of understanding and assessing the building of relationships – an aspect of human, cultural and international affairs which has been very much repressed or ignored and, given the changing and increasingly divided world, needs urgent attention. With regard to the current identity discourses at hand, although the two broad conflicting communities in NI may each apparently have a 'separate' and 'unique' identity discourse, my interest here will be to take up both in order to register if, when and how they relate to each other's communities.

The moral rationality of discourse community

In the above, I have drawn upon critical insights in cultural and discourse studies, including social constructionism and postmodernism, and outlined a view of identity as a sort of reality that people construct for a variety of purposes and consequently as something that people produce dynamically and creatively. Further, I have argued that it should be seen also as part of a power struggle. However, I want to suggest that there has been a rarely asked but significant question. Is there no principled direction in which identity discourse will move or change, or, apart from the apparent ever-lasting logic of difference, dominance and resistance, will there be no ethical progress to be expected? It seems to me that a longitudinal and consequently *ethical* perspective is needed in current research, especially with reference to identity discourse.

Here I want to argue that the concept of identity should not be understood merely in terms of the logic of difference and consequently of opposition (as Self/Other, us/them, here/there), nor merely in terms of the dynamic of diversity or hybridity. Rather, it can be seen in a broader network of discourse community in which even greater agency is recognized. Namely, the discourse of identity, as an integral part of discourse more generally, is guided, though not determined, by a historical, critical consciousness of the relevant discourse community to continuously construct and transform its discourse into something better according to culture-specific moral ideals, be they 'freedom', 'justice', 'peace', 'the good', 'the true', 'the right' or whatever. The discursive critical consciousness itself may be thought of, more specifically, as a sort of self-reflexive principle to abandon old or existing ways of speaking and to create better and more helpful ones according to culture-specific norms and values. I term this agency of discourse community 'moral rationality'. Discourse community is rational because it is guided by normative rules; it is moral because such rules are culturally defined; that is, they are negotiated and contested within and between discourse communities. If this is true of discourse, then the discourse of identity can be expected to follow the same path.

Such a moral-rational stance on discourse proceeds, of course, from an optimistic view of human cultural development. That is, human culture and hence its discourse are neither predetermined, nor completely unpredictable. Just as the habitus has 'transformative capacity' (Bourdieu and Wacquant 1992; May 1996: 127), so human culture and its discourse in particular have the power to free themselves from the past and strive for a better future. As Benjamin (1968: 246) tells us, 'As flowers turn toward the sun, by dint of a secret heliotropism the past strives to turn toward that sun which is rising in the sky of history'. The moral achievements made in the ways of thinking and speaking of women and non-white peoples in the western world, or indeed the feminist and anti-racism movements, for example, are cases in point.

The notion of the moral rationality of discourse and culture can also be understood by drawing an analogy with the concepts of rationality and social principles underlying language and communication as developed in linguistic philosophy and communication theory (Austin 1962; Brown and Levinson 1987; Grice 1975; Habermas 1976: ch. 2, 1984, 1987). Authors here have argued that human language and communication are rational in that they are governed by and responsive to normative and universal context. Thus, speech acts meet 'felicity conditions', conversation observes 'the cooperative principle' as well as the norm of 'politeness', and human communication models an 'ideal situation'.

The moral-rational agency envisaged here is, emphatically, not meant as a real, essentialistic or universal mechanism behind discourse behaviour. Rather, it can best be taken in metaphorical terms. By 'metaphorical', I mean two specific things. First, moral rationality does not come from outside historically and culturally specific discourse context and practice. What is 'good', 'right' or 'true' to say in one culture may not necessarily be the same in another. Arguing and thinking are oriented towards culturally and historically specific norms and values (Maier 1989; Taylor 1999). Relevant here also is the fact that cultural members continuously engage with each other in a dialogical process of (re)producing norms, values and ideals. This means that cultural morality will itself evolve and change.

Second, a metaphorical understanding of moral rationality means that the way discourse reinvents itself ethically should be seen retrospectively, thus as historical discourse. By historical discourse, I refer to discourse across time, especially over long periods. Studying historical discourse where identity discourse is a constituent part makes it possible to identify and compare transformations of identity, not because historical discourse is organized by some underlying law, but because it is a series of reality constructions that consist in various forms of intertextuality (Fairclough 1992) and ruptures or discontinuities (Foucault 1972; White 1973). When studying the history of knowledge, Foucault (1972: 4–5) suggests thus:

> Beneath the great continuities of thought, beneath the solid, homogeneous manifestations of a single mind or of a collective mentality, beneath the stubborn development of a science striving to exist and to reach completion at the very outset, beneath the persistence of a particular genre, form, discipline, or theoretical activity, one is now trying to detect the incidence of interruptions. Interruptions whose status and nature vary considerably . . . the problem is no longer one of tradition, of tracing a line, but one of division, of limits; it is no longer one of lasting foundations, but one of transformations that serve as new foundations, the rebuilding of foundations.

Foucault (1986, 1987) has analysed the shifting of subject positions in particular as a form of discursive agency. In the present case of NI, when we put the discourse of identity in a moral-rational, and so historical, perspective, we shall see the creativity of collective identity and the ethical progress in self-understanding and self-production in a variety of symbolic forms that, through time, mould and transform identity. But how do we reconstitute historical discourse and how do we assess its moral progress?

History for the future

Historical discourse is not an objectively given body of texts and talk. For one thing, '[H]istory is the subject of a structure whose site is not homogeneous, empty time, but time filled by the presence of the now [*Jetztzeit*]', according to Benjamin (1999: 252–3). For another, what counts as historical discourse is something not unaffected by the interests of the historian (Benjamin 1999: 247).[1]

The historical identity discourse in the present study, by the same token, cannot be neutral. Its reconstruction has the motivation of 'fanning the sparks of hope of the past' (Benjamin 1999: 247) and, specifically, to see if there has been movement towards inclusiveness and partnership in the collective self-understanding in public, mainstream, media discourse in NI, hence hope in its future cultural development. For this reason, I have chosen to concentrate on discourses of identity, mainly those more prevalent ones in the public media, in particular the more moderate versions of identity and so on. I shall come to the principles of selection of historical data shortly.

The criterion of evaluation

Just as historical discourse is not dispassionate, so its comparison and judgement are not impersonal. The moral rationality of discursive practice through time is not a self-evident fact. This means consequently that the evaluating discourse historian has to decide upon and use a yardstick of their own for this purpose, consciously or inadvertently. So, valued 'progress', 'development' or 'evolution' of historical discourse being sought after here will be a positive valuation only from a particular chosen and contemporary perspective. As Nietzsche (1967: 148) once remarked, 'moral evaluation is an *exegesis*, a way of interpreting' (emphasis original).

In the present comparative analysis, the starting point for judgement of the historical identity discourses originates in the concern of this very research, the concern with NI intergroup relationship and consequently to raise the peace prospects of NI. This is therefore a project in the cultural politics aiming at transforming reality. As Barker and Galasinski (2001) have suggested, 'Cultural politics concerns the writing of new stories with "new languages" (or to be more exact, new configurations of old languages or new usages of old words) that embody values with which we concur and that we wish to be taken as true in the sense of a social agreement or commendation'. Here, in looking at some historical identity discourses of the two communities in NI, I shall use the notion of confrontation as a criterion to compare the identity discourses from different historical periods successively in a chronological order. Confrontation here is seen as a continuum ranging from the threat of destruction to the practice of cooperation. Thus, in comparing identity discourses, I shall categorize any identity discourse that is less threatening towards the other community as 'moral-rational progress'.

The reconstitution of historical data

In this section, I shall try to contextualize the present research in terms of data collection, categorization and interpretation. Some methodological considerations about the historical discourse under study are in order:

1. How are historical conditions to be chronologically distinguished?
2. What kind of data is to be chosen that would be relevant and appropriate to the historical periods?
3. What sort of representativeness of the corpus is to be achieved and how?

First, my decision on the segmentation of the historical context from which I extract data is informed by a range of scholarly accounts of NI history (Bardon 1992; Beckett 1966; Moxon-Brown 1991; Boyle and Hadden 1985; McGarry and O'Leary 1995; Mitchell and Wilford 1999; Moody and Martin 1994; Porter 1998; Stringer and Robinson 1992), as well as public information (online) sources (especially http://cain.ulster.ac.uk/). There appear to be no significant discrepancies between them in terms of major historical events. From these authorities, I have attempted a synthesis of my own, which will be presented piecemeal and in tandem with the appropriate discourses I analyse.

Second, as is obvious, study of collective identity discourse from a historical-comparative perspective will have to depend on documentary evidence, that is, accounts or records from the past. Retrospective narratives would not be suitable in this instance; nor would private documents have a comparable social relevance in respect of public communication. Accordingly, I have chosen to base the present research on public media discourse from major, mainstream or official media outlets available in NI since early last century to 2000.[2] Such general public media discourse has been an important mode and means of constructing and acting upon collective identity in the particular case of recent NI history. That does not mean that such discourse necessarily reflects ordinary people's own versions and actions with regard to identity. However, it is not irrelevant but constitutive of wider cultural transformation. For one thing, media discourse is produced dialogically oriented towards the public in society – its interests and experiences. For another, it has impact on the public and especially its identity and relations. As Giddens (1991: 4) has pointed out, 'Mediated experience, since the first experience of writing, has long influenced both self-identity and the basic organisation of social relations'. It may also be noted that it might be interesting and useful to examine other symbolic modes, say radio or television or, unique to NI, murals as well, but mass-mediated print material can be a good start in the present case. In any case, the choice of public, mainstream media discourse will not greatly restrict the objective of this study, as it is unlikely that what is constructed in one mode (for example, print media) in a given period will be radically different in another (for example, radio or television) in the same period.

Third, a set of principles for determining the relative representativeness of the corpus is adopted in this study. One is that data must come from major and mainstream media sources. This means, however, that dominant voices tend to be represented here and extremist ones excluded. Consequently, it also means that the discourses of influential political individuals and institutions tend to receive more attention. But, as announced at the outset, the present purpose is mainly to reflect public media discourses as a major part and player of a culture. More generally, I have resorted to a random sampling, rather than exhaustive, method and collected texts in reasonable quantity that are germane to the specified historical period.

A further associated yardstick here is that the data must be 'felicitous' in the context of the identified, relevant historical conditions, which include those from the current as well as previous periods. That is, the ways of constructing identities to be chosen must be relevant to the appropriate historical aura and not out of tune with it. It should be cautioned, though, that the discourses I have identified and characterized in this study are not the only discourses there have been; there have been alternative, though less dominant and general, discourses of various kinds and there is no intention to deny them.

Still another standard is that the data must reflect the diversity of NI communities. NI is anything but homogeneous and there has been historical cross-community antagonism. With regard to this complexity, my interest is in the nature of identity discourse in NI as a whole and ultimately its transformation. Therefore I have included discourses from the perspectives of both 'British/Protestant/unionist' and 'Irish/Catholic/nationalist' communities, broadly defined.

Analysing discourses of identity

The analysis below will follow a chronological order in which I first describe the historical context of the relevant period and then analyse the corresponding discourse of identity. Thus, the account of the time frame and social conditions will form the context of the discourse data and so part of the resource for making sense of the data. Then, with reference to the relevant historical period, I identify the dominant group identity discourse and characterize it in terms of meaning and form. To overcome the apparent difficulty of taking up historical discourse, I have attempted here a duet of 'macro' and 'micro' analysis: that is, a general analysis in tandem with a detailed sample analysis. Finally, I shall compare the identity constructions according to the chosen criteria.

In the following discourse analysis, I shall take a somewhat unconventional tack. It is a standard approach in discourse analysis to begin with an a priori analytical procedure (usually linguistic or textual but not contextual) derived from a particular theoretical perspective. An important assumption underlying such practice is that structures of discourse, such as thus categorized (say word, grammar, conversational turns), are containers of meaning. But using such linguistic or textual categories as starting points may lose sight of the multidimensional, historically variable and interpretative nature of discourse production, distribution and consumption or even 'distort' the situated discourse at hand. The historically and generically diverse data under question evidently require an ethnographically appropriate and eclectic approach. Moreover, as may be stressed, the present project is concerned primarily with specific, local cultural issues. To counter rigid methods then, I shall begin by characterizing the nature of the identity of a particular period in question. (Here the characterization must not be taken as describing the data samples as a whole; it is an interpretive analysis of only one dimension of the meanings involved, namely the collective identity.) Then, I shall point to some specific textual and contextual features that contribute to its construction and its functions in the relevant historical context.

War of independence: militant nationalist identity

It is often said that the oldest problem of Britain is Ireland and vice versa. In an important sense, the problem is one of struggle over identity and its boundaries. This struggle began in the twelfth century when Britain invaded Ireland. Although both islands had had mutual and mixed immigrations for thousands of years, the British and Anglo-Irish came to be the 'rich', 'Protestant' and a dominant force in European and world politics, and the Irish the relatively 'poor', 'Catholic' and committed to neutrality. The differences between the two communities became marked in the latter part of the nineteenth century through the movements of, first, religious freedom, then, Home Rule and, finally, national independence.

The events just mentioned came to a turning point, when, in 1916, Irish activists, including socialist James Connolly, declared the independence of the Republic of Ireland and the Easter Rising erupted. Behind these developments were two historical factors. One was Home

Rule, the idea to have a parliament in Dublin, as opposed to Westminster in London and, for Irish Protestants in the north of Ireland, this meant 'Rome Rule'. Another was the outbreak of the First World War; some Irish nationalists thought it their opportunity to secure independence from Britain when the latter joined the war. But there was an important *textual* background to these as well. Patrick Pearse, the central figure behind the Easter Rising, admonished: 'we may make mistakes in the beginning and shoot the wrong people; but bloodshed is a cleansing and sanctifying thing' (Mitchell and Wilford 1999: 7).

In 1920, as a compromise between the Protestant and Catholic communities and the two countries, Ireland was partitioned, with a small portion – six counties in the north-east – remaining with Britain, called Northern Ireland. In the ensuing half-century or so, the local Protestant majority found a renewed sense of identity ('unionists') and sought to consolidate their political and economical position. The substantial Catholic minority, frustrated by the partition, continued to assert their right to be part of united Ireland ('nationalists').

Now, against this tumultuous background, what is the public identity discourse like? In other words, how did discourses from the conflicting communities portray their identities and relate to each other in the public domain? Relevant public mediated texts during this period are relatively limited. The main sources are found in printed political statements, speeches and other similar documents. From such scattered data, it appears that the predominant notion of group identity is a threatened or injured but unyielding national identity, from both the Irish and British perspective. Thus, implicitly or explicitly there is often an image of the nation of Ireland as invaded, usurped, humiliated and deprived by a foreign nation, namely Great Britain, on the one side. On the other side, there is a notion of an endangered, Protestant community in Ireland as part of the British Empire, about to be severed from the mother country. Thus, there is a sense in which the two strands of identity construction here are dialectically related, such that one strand is shaped by the other. In this sense, it may be asserted, too, that, together, they constitute a discourse of warring nationalism.

This identity discourse can be seen in a variety of distinct textual forms. One is the prevalent reference to 'our' presumed nationhood, British or Irish, and the intrinsic properties thereof. Thus, people are categorized as 'the Irish race' or 'Irishmen and Irishwomen', Ulster as part of 'the unity of the United Kingdom', and aggression to Ireland as 'our national apostasy', for example. Similarly, people are assigned 'the right to national freedom', 'citizenship in the United Kingdom', and so on. Another, in close connection with this, is the use of the speech act of the declaration of national independence. Still another is the use of particular words that, often indirectly, describe the nature of the presumed nationhood. For example, occupation by a foreign country would be described as 'usurpation', 'degradation' and 'humiliating', the possibility of being ruled by a foreign element as 'threatened calamity'. Terms such as these signify the relevant characteristics of the nationhood in question, for example, humiliated, threatened. Similar to this indirect way of rendering nationhood are the recurring calls to arms, and so calls for sacrifice, in defence of nationhood. Thus, in the context of threatened nationhood, there is plenty of 'defence', 'pledge of sacrifice', 'defeating', 'the red tide of war on Irish soil', 'shedding of blood', and so on. Mobilizations in these terms imply the warring state of the national identity at the time (see, for example, 'The ties that bind', *Worker's Republic*, 2 May 1916).

In terms of their links to the historical context or their functions in it, it may be suggested that these belligerent identity discourses not only reinforce nationalist ideologies or myths, notably that of 'blood sacrifice', but also effectively contribute to the violent 'national liberation' (Mitchell and Wilford 1999: 7–8). For they provide justifications and hence preparation for the 'War in Ireland', mobilize the relevant communities into action and militate them further against each other. To illustrate the identity discourse just described, and to highlight some of the details there, let me examine two texts from the conflicting communities. (The bold type in all the following examples highlights the more salient types of textual features that contribute to the construction of collective identity.)

Example 6.1

> IRISHMEN AND IRISHWOMEN: In the name of God and the dead generations from which **she receives her old tradition of nationhood**, Ireland, through us, summons **her children** to **her flag** and strikes for **her freedom** . . . We **declare the right of the people of Ireland** to the ownership of Ireland, and to the unfettered control of the **Irish** destinies, **to be sovereign and indefeasible**. The long **usurpation** of that right by a **foreign** people and government has not **extinguished** the right, **nor can it ever be extinguished except by the destruction of the Irish people**. In every generation the **Irish** people have asserted their right to national freedom and sovereignty: **six times during the past three hundred years they have asserted**

it in arms. Standing on that fundamental right and **again asserting it in arms** in the face of the world, we hereby **proclaim the Irish Republic as a Sovereign Independent State**, and we **pledge our lives and the lives of our comrades-in-arms** to the cause of its freedom, of its welfare, and of its exhaltation among the nations . . . In this supreme hour, the **Irish** nation **must**, by its valour and discipline and by the readiness of its **children to sacrifice themselves** for the common good, prove itself worthy of the august destiny **to which it is called**.

> (The Proclamation of the Provisional Government of the Irish Republic to the People of Ireland, Dublin, 1916)

In this proclamation, it may be seen that, as far as the issue of group identity is concerned, there is a notion of Irish national identity on the part of the Irish people. This identity is, further, presented as being under subjugation by a foreign nation, namely, colonialist Britain, as would be known from the historical context outlined earlier. In addition and more prominently perhaps, this national identity is in a state of open, militant defiance to foreign aggression and occupation.

Now, how is the warring Irish national identity rendered present, or realized, textually and contextually? First, several lexical features may be noteworthy. One is the series of lexical *categorizations* in terms of Irish nationality. Thus, men and women, people more generally, as well as the country, are classified as 'Irish', as opposed to the 'foreign', or the background context, the colonial British ('IRISHMEN', 'IRISHWOMEN', 'the Irish people' and 'the Irish nation'). Another is the group of references to (Irish) national symbols: 'her children', 'her flag' and 'her freedom'. Still another is a number of references to the properties of Irish nationality: 'the right of the people of Ireland' and 'their right to national freedom and sovereignty'. References such as these presuppose referents; these *references to Irish national properties and symbols* then contribute to the construction of Irish national identity. Similar to these lexical forms descriptive of Irish national identity is the use of narratives of Irish national identity, as in 'she receives her old tradition of nationhood' and 'six times during the past three hundred years they have asserted it [national freedom and sovereignty] in arms'. These stories, as representations of the Irish tradition, achieve the effect of maintaining Irish national identity, too.

Apart from the lexical and rhetorical forms *descriptive of* Irish national identity, second, there are also speech acts that *formally declare* it. Thus, there is the speech act on the part of the leading Irish nationalist activists which declares Irish national rights: 'We declare the right of the people of Ireland . . . to be sovereign and indefeasible'. There is also the speech act in the same context that declares the founding of the Irish state: 'we hereby proclaim the Irish Republic as a Sovereign Independent State'. Through these acts of declaration, the nationalist activists may be seen as rendering the Irish national identity public and official, thereby reproducing and reinforcing it.

Third, a set of verbal and nominal structures that reflect the nature of the opposing *other's actions* upon the Irish indirectly contribute to the construction of Irish national identity. For example, the nominalization, 'usurpation' on the part of colonial Britain, indicates the violent and unjustified nature of the opposing other's action upon the Irish people and so indirectly shows the sorry state that the Irish are in. The verbal and nominal structures, 'has not extinguished . . . nor can it ever be extinguished except by the destruction of the Irish people', similarly, suggest that the Irish people are strong and defiant, however. This leads to my final point.

The militant nature of the Irish national identity may be seen as reproduced especially by the *speech acts of calls to arms* and *pledges of lives* by the authors of the proclamation. Thus, for example, defending the Irish nation is made an imperative: 'the Irish nation must . . . by the readiness of its children to sacrifice themselves . . . prove itself worthy of the august destiny to which it is called'. Closely connected with that is the pledge of one's life in defence of the Irish nation: 'we pledge our lives and the lives of our comrades-in-arms'. Such calls and pledges render clear a combative and defiant Irish national identity vis-à-vis the foreign – British – occupiers.

Let us look at an example from the opposing, British community. It is taken from the 'Ulster Solemn League and Covenant' (28 September 1912). The document from which the following sample is taken disapproved of the proposal of Home Rule in Ireland (explained above) and was signed by over 400,000 Ulster Protestants, some using their own blood. Here in the example, an equally militant nationalist identity is constructed. Many of the same types of structures found in the above example are used in this text.

Example 6.2

Being convinced in our consciences that **Home Rule** would be **disastrous** to the whole material well-being of **Ulster as well as the whole of Ireland, subversive** of our civil and religious freedom, **destructive** of **our citizenship**, and **perilous** to **the unity of the**

Empire, we, whose names are under-written, **men of Ulster, loyal subjects of His Gracious Majesty** . . . do hereby **pledge ourselves in solemn covenant** throughout this time of **threatened calamity** to stand by one another in **defending** for ourselves and our children **our cherished position of equal citizenship in the United Kingdom** and **in using all means** that may be found necessary **to defeat the present conspiracy** to set up a Home Rule parliament in Ireland.

('Ulster Solemn League and Covenant', 28 September 1912)

In this document, we may see the construction of a nationalist identity, loyal to the British Empire, threatened yet threatening, similar to the kind of Irish national identity we saw above. In terms of the conception of collective identity, specifically, there is a notion of Ulster as an inalienable part of the empire–nation of the United Kingdom. Further, it may be seen that this empire–national identity is threatened by destruction through Home Rule. And yet the people in this part of the empire are ready to sacrifice their lives and defend it through armed struggle.

Now this sort of national identity may be seen as realized through a variety of interrelated (con)textual forms. A first noteworthy type is a set of self-descriptions in terms of British national identity: 'our cherished position of equal citizenship in the United Kingdom' and 'men of Ulster, loyal subjects of His Gracious Majesty'. Some references to the elements of British nationhood achieve the same self-descriptive effect: 'our civil and religious freedom . . . our citizenship'. In addition, British national identity is rendered through a contrastive reference to the opposing, foreign entity, through the synecdoche of Home Rule. Thus, similar to the 'nationalist' references of the previous example, these terms implicitly maintain and reinforce (aspects of) British national identity.

Another form contributing to the construction of British identity is the set of epithets signifying the nature of the opposing other's actions to 'us'. They indirectly reflect the character of 'our' identity. So, 'disastrous', 'subversive', 'destructive' and 'perilous' do not merely describe the attributes of the doers or the nature of their actions; they also indicate the state and the nature of the identity of the recipients. At this juncture, it may be mentioned that some nominal structures describing states of affairs and actions do the same identity-constructive work: 'threatened calamity' and 'the present conspiracy'. So, Ulster–British national identity may be seen as being critically threatened and endangered.

With respect to this threatened dimension of identity, it may be observed that a speech act of solemn pledge, as of the document as a whole, is made of armed struggle and sacrifice of one's life to defend the British empire–nation. A pledge of this content and this nature indirectly adds a further dimension to the identity in question: it is a defiant and infeasible British national identity at that. Thus observe 'we . . . do hereby pledge ourselves in solemn covenant . . . in defending . . . and in using all means . . . to defeat the present conspiracy'.

Now, if the overall pattern of group identity discourse in this period of Ireland is one of warring nationality, then the broader question of the present study is: is this kind of belligerent and hostile discourse carried over, modified or replaced by some other discourse in the subsequent period?

Civil Rights Movement: the majority versus the minority

The historical conditions in NI changed considerably between the late 1960s and the mid-1980s. During this time, Catholics had felt more acutely than ever before that Protestants violated their civil rights and discriminated against them in jobs, housing and other areas of social welfare. In the late 1960s, groups of Catholics and liberal Protestants formed the Northern Ireland Civil Rights Association (NICRA) and demanded social reforms, such as 'one man, one vote' and equal opportunity for employment and housing. In alliance with similar other movements internationally, these social developments formed what was known as the Civil Rights Movement in NI. On the other side, the unionist community tended to see a nationalist conspiracy behind this social movement, against their majority's will, for a united Ireland and so also a threat to their position within the UK establishment. In 1969, a series of violent confrontations broke out, which led to the intervention by and deployment of British troops. The latter's action prompted the Irish government and people to align with the nationalist community in the north. Subsequently, there followed a terrorist campaign by the Irish Republican Army (IRA). In 1972, the local NI government was suspended and direct rule from Westminster introduced.

If we pose the same analytical question about the print media during the Civil Rights Movement, what sort of identity discourse do we recognize here? First of all, I would like to observe that there is a qualitative change in terms of the construction of the two opposing communties in NI and therefore a break from the past discourse. Categorically, the earlier predominantly nationalistically and antagonistically defined identity discourse is replaced with one of the majority and the minority. That is, both the Irish/Catholic/nationalist and British/Protestant/unionist discourses would call the former community the 'minority' and the latter the 'majority'. Conceptually, however, the constituent qualities of the categories usually differ according to the perspective of the particular community that is adopted in the discourse. Thus, a text taking a Catholic/nationalist stance would define the minority by social disadvantages, ill treatment, injustices and the like; its opposite, the majority, then would derive its meaning, often implicitly, from those properties of the minority. Conversely, a text taking the perspective of the Protestant/unionist community would normally characterize the majority as representing the larger section of the NI society's population and therefore a broader view and will.

In terms of textual forms, it may be seen that the sort of identity and relationship just described are realized routinely through the categorizations of the 'minority', as for the 'Catholic/nationalist' community, and of the 'majority', as for the 'Protestant/unionist' community. Such a majority/minority discourse may be clearly evidenced, for example, by the title of a *Belfast Telegraph* article (29 September 1982) on the Catholics' opinions about the up-coming Assembly election: 'Which way will the minority vote?'. Moreover, these social-class categories are also rendered present through implicit or explicit descriptions of or references to the conventionally constituent properties of the majority and the minority: for example, social advantages and disadvantages in housing and jobs and rights in voting. Further, the interrelationship between these social categories is often reproduced through explicit and direct expressions of opposition to the other group or its action.

It should be realized that these discourses of the majority and of the minority are politically motivated. The notion of the minority is often used to express dissatisfaction with the social conditions of the Catholic/nationalist community and so demand for change. The idea of the majority, in contrast, is usually deployed as an argument of democracy (that is, general consensus) to reject calls for social and institutional change, thereby maintaining the status quo. In addition, from these identity constructions and associated actions, a particular social relationship emerges between the communal categories in question: one of opposition to each other over social and constitutional change.

Let us now witness two concrete samples of such discourses. They are taken from the Catholic and Protestant media sources, respectively.

Example 6.3

There was great interest also at [*sic*] the wide coverage given to the Derry incidents [of violence] by the British papers, radio and television. Such coverage, it is said, could **force the British Government to open a full inquiry into discrimination in Northern Ireland** ... Fine Gael ['soft' Republicans in the Republic of Ireland] supports a policy of civil and friendly contact with the leaders of **the Northern majority.** But that policy is **not to be taken as acquiescence in the ill-treatment by that Government of the minority in the North.** It would be **disgraceful,** in the interests of a superficial harmony **to ignore the injustices to which people are being subjected in Northern Ireland** ... 'The absence of civil rights in the **North was highlighted by the police in their indiscriminate attack** on the courageous marchers,' a statement said.

('F.G. sends Derry inquiry team', *Irish News*, 5 May 1969)

Example 6.4

[Former British Prime Minister Mr Brian Faulkner:] we have ... responsibility ... – and that is to speak for that body of Ulster people – **the vast majority** ... The Unionist community in Northern Ireland will **not tolerate such a proposition** [of a united Ireland by the minority]. We are more than ready to discuss how the institutions of Northern Ireland may be framed on a renewed basis of **general consent.**

('United Ireland? No chance', *The News Letter*, 2 March 1972)

To start with, it may be pointed out that, conceptually, the Catholic and Protestant communities, as we would know from the context, are now represented as *the minority* and *the majority*, respectively. This is a qualitative difference in identity discourse and self-understanding from the previous period as we just saw. It should be noted, too, that the specific properties of each category are not, however, the same from the viewpoint of the respective texts. Thus, from the 'minority's' perspective, its own community is such that it suffers from various social disadvantages and this dimension of the minority has elaborate details ranging from discrimination, ill-treatment and injustices to absence of civil rights – whereas the notion of its counterpart, the majority, is left implicit in the background. From the 'majority' side, in contrast, its community is such that it represents the larger population of NI, hence there is a broader consensus. This notion has almost equally prominent qualities in the text: it is the vast majority of NI, represents the general opinion and is in opposition to the minority community's proposition for a united Ireland – whereas the meaning of the minority here is left implicit from the former notion. Thus, it may be said that each of the texts 'over-represents' its own community and 'under-represents' the other.

That leads to my next point, namely, that the two subsets of the group identity here may be seen as reflecting mutually opposing objectives. For, on the one hand, the notion of the minority in example 6.3, with all its qualities of social disadvantages just highlighted, serves as part of an argument for achieving the social change that the minority desires. The notion of the majority in example 6.4, on the other hand, with the specified feature as representing the general opinion of the population, may be seen as constituting the reason to maintain the status quo. So, the minority discourse and the majority discourse, while accepting the two communities as the related constituents of the same society, construct each other's communities in essentially oppositional terms.

The textual realization of categories of the minority and the majority, conceptions thereof and the resultant interrelations may be teased out in the following way. First and obviously, new vocabularies may be recognized: the Catholic community is recategorized as the 'minority', the Protestant as the 'majority'. This sort of vocabulary is present in the texts from both the Catholic and Protestant perspectives; it is acceptable or routine then in both sub-discourses of identity. Here it may be added that the redefinition in 'that body of Ulster people – the vast majority' achieves an emphatic categorization in terms of the majority.

Second, it may be noticed that the categorizations of the 'minority' and the 'majority' co-occur with references to conventionally constituent features of these social categories. The categorizations and the references reinforce each other and form networks of identity construction. Thus, in example 6.3 where the category of the minority is taken up as a topic, such typical accompanying features as 'discrimination', 'ill-treatment', 'the injustices' and 'absence of civil rights' are brought in as well in a short textual space. In example 6.4, similarly, the category of the majority is placed in the context of a proposition by the minority that it cannot tolerate and the context of 'general consent' that it enjoys. In this way, the categorizations and the congruent and coherent references co-produce the identities of the majority and the minority, respectively.

Third and more importantly, presuppositions of the existence of identity properties are made which effectively produce the minority and majority identities. These presuppositions are rendered, more specifically, by particular verbal or nominal structures that assume the existence of the object of actions that they describe. Thus, in example 6.3, 'could *force* the British Government to open a full inquiry into discrimination in Northern Ireland' presupposes the existence of discrimination. The nominal structure '*acquiescence in* the ill-treatment' assumes ill-treatment to be true. Similarly, 'disgraceful . . . *to ignore* the injustices' makes it clear that the injustices do exist. 'The absence of civil rights in the North *was highlighted*' takes for granted 'the absence of civil rights'. (Emphasis mine in all cases.)

In sum, the new vocabularies, the networks of categorizations and constitutive references and the presuppositions through verbal and nominal structures combine to produce the reality of the NI minority and majority. Further, such textual properties make the minority/majority identity internally divisive and oppositional.

Anglo-Irish Agreement: neighbours

Following the violent clashes during the Civil Rights Movement, it became clear to the British and Irish governments that peace, stability and reconciliation in Northern Ireland and, ultimately, a devolved government there were the best options for themselves as well as for Northern Ireland (O'Leary and McGarry 1993). To achieve these objectives, a peace accord was signed between the UK and Ireland on 15 November 1985, which has come to be known as the Anglo-Irish Agreement. The agreement formulates among other things an interrelated, overlapped and shared identity for NI society. An intergovernment conference, endorsed by the agreement, was set up as a transition towards an eventual devolved government in Northern Ireland acceptable to both communities. The agreement identified the British and Irish governments as the guardians of NI issues, in the event that NI political parties failed to cooperate. This arrangement met a great deal of opposition from the unionist parties, namely DUP, UUP and PUP, whereas it received general support from the nationalist parties, namely SDLP, FF, FG and Labour. But more generally, with the new deal, it had become clear to both opposing communities that the old ways of the unionists and the nationalists could be held no longer. The opening statement of the agreement reveals the required new identity and relationship quite clearly (emphasis mine):

The Government of Ireland and the Government of the United Kingdom: Wishing further to develop the unique relationship between their peoples and the close co-operation between their countries as *friendly neighbours* and as partners in the European Community.

Whilst the kinds of hostile discourse of British/Irish nationalism and oppositional discourse of majority/minority which we saw earlier have not entirely gone away in the current period, a new discourse of closer relationship between the two otherwise conflicting communities is becoming dominant. This relationship is defined by the notion of 'neighbour'. It is thus essentially a geographical and communal connnection, beyond the historical divisions of nations, classes and opinions. Here the notion of neighbour, which of course can have a variety of properties, is often used in the sense of being entitled to the civil order of a society. It may be added that the related notion of democ racy seems to creep in as well. For, congruent with 'neighbour', notions of peaceful persuasion, social inclusion, coexistence and respect for each other are often used in close connection with the neighbourly relationship, thereby reinforcing it.

The construction of the new relational identity in NI consists formally in a new designation for the communities in NI in public media communication, namely 'neighbours'. In conjunction with this, further, are expressions indicating the close relationship of living close to each other in a geographic space, such as sharing, connection and involvement. Further, the intergroup link or relatedness may be found in a variety of action verbs (for example, 'to live together') as well as the second-person form of addressing ('you') and even the inclusive first-person pronoun ('we'). These help execute dialogue and interrelation between the opposing communities (for example, 'respect for your identity'). Thus, compared with the discourses from the previous periods, the notion and the name of neighbour project a closer relationship between the two communites.

Given the historical past, as both contexts and discourses that I have described, it may be asserted that the present discourse of the NI communities as neighbours is a great leap forward. For the first time in its modern history, a new identity discourse is constructed that acknowledges a dimension and kind of equal social relationship between the two otherwise polarized communities, that is, neighbours. In so doing of course it echoes a new identity and relationship called for by the agreement. More implicitly, it dovetails with the broader political aspiration for an eventual devolved government in NI, as I alluded to above. Further, this discourse relinquishes the social and communal antagonisms seen in the previous periods. Most significantly perhaps, this new identity discourse is often appealed to as an argument for neutralizing existing community conflicts.

To see the concrete manifestations of this discourse of neighbours, let us look at a quotation of the nationalist SDLP leader in a mainstream newspaper in NI though arguably with a larger Protestant readership:

Example 6.5

> [The SDLP leader, Mr John Hume:] It is all right to keep on saying **you** want to live apart and on **your** own and maintain sectarian solidarity as the basis of **your** protection, but **you** can't do that in **a society in which you live cheek by jowl with other people. We** must come to terms with **how we are going to live together** and this doesn't wipe out or crush anybody's identity. The new body will do more than just consult.
>
> (Hume, *Belfast Telegraph*, 16 November 1985)

In terms of the notion of collective identity here, it may be observed that, whilst the idea of NI as composed of two different communities is still implicit (as in 'doesn't wipe out or crush anybody's identity'), these communities are also conceptualized as *living close to each other like neighbours*. Thus, there is yet another kind of collective self-understanding, unseen and perhaps unthinkable in the previous period. This new inclusive construction of the NI communities and people has of course implications for their future life: since they are neighbours, they should no longer live separate lives.

A set of interrelated textual forms that contribute to the construction of this notion of the NI communities as neighbours may be highlighted here. A first one is the dialogical and inclusive uses of pronouns, different from the impersonal references to the opposing community in the previous identity discourses (for example, 'a foreign people' in example 6.1 or 'the Northern majority' in example 6.3). So, on the one hand, a second-person, dialogical form of pronoun 'you/your' is used; so the nationalist SDLP leader is addressing the 'opposing' community directly. On the other hand, a cross-community, first-person, plural pronoun 'we' is used; so the speaker is projecting an inclusive society of NI, as in 'We must come to terms with how we are going to live together'.

Another noteworthy, identity-constitutive form is the metaphor of neighbours in the text. That is, the formerly conflicting or otherwise opposing communities in NI are now compared to neighbours. So, Hume is telling the people of NI that NI is 'a society in which you live cheek by jowl with other people'. Similarly, he describes the relationship of the NI communities as living together: 'We must come to terms with how we are going to live together'. Paradoxically, it should also be noted that the way that such metaphors are used – that is, as the real reason for choosing a new way of life (note 'you can't do that' and 'We must come to terms with . . .) – also implicitly reproduces the new identity of neighbours. This discourse of neighbours is more explicit in the next example from the Catholic media source. The speaker here represents the Irish government, as arranged by the Anglo-Irish Agreement.

Example 6.6

> In a message to the unionists, Mr Barry [co-chairman of the Anglo-Irish conference] said: '**You** have no cause to fear this Agreement, which brings **you**, no less than **your** nationalist **neighbour**, the reassurance of **your** rights, respect for **your** identity and the promise of a society free from insecurity and violence. I want to co-operate with **you** in removing the barriers of suspicion and rivalry which have divided **neighbour from neighbour** in the North, so that **we** can turn the tide and bring peace and prosperity.'
> ('Important day for Ireland', *The Irish News*, 16 November 1985)

A most prominent aspect of the notion of collective identity here is that, despite the intergroup divisions, differences and difficulties, the unionists and nationalists are conceived of as *neighbours*. Further, it may be noticed that the unionist 'neighbours' here are treated as *being on 'speaking' terms* with the nationalist neighbours.

This notion of the identity, or the relationship, of the two otherwise divided communities is realized first of all by a specific lexical categorization, 'neighbour', as in 'your nationalist neighbour' and 'neighbour from neighbour'. And it is noteworthy, too, that this label is used repeatedly in such a short textual space. This practice, of course, creates the impression that the notion of the two communities as neighbours is a taken-for-granted fact. Still another, though more implicit, form that contributes to the construction of 'neighbour' communities is the use of assumptions or presuppositions of the otherwise opposing communities as neighbours. One such assumption is manifested in the formulation of neighbour as the object of action (note 'which have divided neighbour from neighbour'); another in the formulation of neighbour as part of the real reason for a proposed action (note the last sentence of the example). Finally, the dialogical form of speaking to the 'other' community – second person pronouns 'you/your' – and the cross-community – inclusive pronoun 'we' – arguably also contribute to the construction of the 'neighbour' identity. For the speaker here addresses the 'opposing' community *directly*.

Thus, for the first time in the history under study, a cross-community, inclusive, rather than mutually exclusive, form of identity discourse has emerged. For the first time in this history, too, this discourse has become dialogical, that is, on speaking terms with the 'other' community.

Good Friday Agreement: equal partners

The context that we had seen in the previous period changed again when, in 1994, the IRA declared a ceasefire and subsequently a peace process started. Further, in May 1998, the process reached a new landmark when multiple political parties from the unionist and nationalist communities and the British and Irish governments reached the Belfast Agreement or what is better known as the Good Friday Agreement. This was endorsed in a referendum by a 75 per cent majority of the people in NI. Consequently, in December 1999, direct rule from Westminster was ended and a multiparty devolved government formed.

As a result of these political developments, aspirations for a way of life worth having for all citizens seem to have become a new ethos in NI. The vocabulary and the notions of reconciliation, democracy, equality and the like appear to have become the key elements of public and political argumentation and persuasion. Witness:

> the power of the sovereign government with jurisdiction there shall be exercised with rigorous impartiality on behalf of all the people in the *diversity* of their identities and traditions and shall be founded on the principles of full respect for, and *equality* of civil, political, social and cultural rights, of freedom from discrimination for *all citizens*, and of parity of esteem and of *just and equal* treatment for the identity, ethos and aspirations of *both communities*.
>
> (Belfast Agreement, p. 2; emphasis mine)

Porter (1998: viii) sums up the significance of the agreement thus: 'a fresh political future beckons: a future promising an end to constitutional gridlock and undemocratic practices; a future heralding an era of political partnership and equality between the North's divided people'. Indeed, it may be argued that the official document of the agreement, through a constitutional endorsement and so institutionalization of the principles of diversity, inclusiveness, equality and unity, has created a textual and institutional context and, to a great extent, set the norm of public communication, for a new discourse.

Thus, against this new historic background, yet another kind of identity discourse may be seen in the public, mediated communication. This discourse consists in a concept of community identity and relationship which has previously been unseen or, rather, would be next to unthinkable: namely, *equal parternship* with the communal Other. This sense of identity and relationship is clearly evidenced, for a start, in the routine use of such unambiguous terms as diversity, inclusiveness, sharing, mutual respect and so on. Further, it may be noted that, in conjunction with the use of such terms and notions, being equal with the communal Other may also be confirmed with the use of closely associated terms and notions such as democracy, fairness and justice. In this connection, it may be mentioned, too, that this battery of notions of equality is sometimes used to construct an aspiration for a shared future identity and relationship of equal partnership. Thus, the unionist UUP leader David Trimble speaks of the beginning of a new Northern Ireland as 'Where common problems are tackled together . . . Where unionists are respected – where nationalists are respected' (Speech by Trimble to the Annual Conference of the UUP, 9 October 1999, www.uup.org/dtspeech.html). On the side of the nationalist community, similarly, the Sinn Fein minister the of NI Assembly, Martin McGuinness, says, 'It [the devolved government in NI] is the beginning of a new era of equality, justice, freedom and peace for all our people. ('SF Ministers pledge to work for peace and equality', *Irish Times*, 3 December 1999). At this juncture, it may be stressed that this new quality of the identity discourse in NI is significant in that it would be out of place in any of the previous historical contexts and that, from the general body of data observed, it has itself become a sort of public normative basis for speaking of communal identities and relationships.

The newly emerging meaning of identity and relationship in the public, mediated discourse in NI is realized through a variety of linguistic and interactive forms, and not simply a set of vocabularies. First, there is a dramatic *increase of talk of equality, respect and cooperation*, and, in that connection, also fairness, democracy, justice, and so on. At the same time, this is coupled by a marked decrease of talk of nationalist/Catholitic and unionist/Protestant group identity. Consistent with this topic shift, it should be noted, too, that the question of the decommissioning of weapons has become one of the central topics of debate.

Thus, there is a general shift in the nature of public construction of communal self and others towards unity. Second, there is also a hitherto *unseen set of actions* with specific objects: namely, to express regret for the past, to acknowledge common destiny, to recognize equal rights, to call for joint action, to promise to follow the principles of diversity, equality and cooperation, to imagine a shared better future, and so on and so forth. Third, it is interesting to observe that such actions are carried out, not unilaterally, not merely amongst smaller factions of the society, but *reciprocally* in the sphere of public media between the traditionally political opponents at the highest level: the Ulster Unionist Party and Sinn Fein ('Ourselves Alone', SF hereafter).

Very importantly, it should be pointed out that these discursive, dialogical moves not only form part of the new and fast-changing landscape of political partnership sketched above, but constitute the very foundations of the political process and progress under way in the first place. Dialogue and hence dialogical relationship are thereby maintained between the two broad oppositional political leaderships. Mutual inclusion and hence equal relationship are thereby accomplished, which pave the way for a devolved government in NI that admits of all political parties, including SF.

Now, let us examine in some detail how the equal and cooperative relationship between the two communities is established dialogically (McPhail 1994, 1998), or through 'choreography' in the local parlance. Let me stress at this juncture that such public, print media discourses coming from the 'opposing' communities need to be seen in a framework of intercommunity discourse space where the parties interact with each other, in one way or another. For this reason it will be particularly useful to read the following two texts closely against each other. These are taken from the speeches by two leaders of the main 'opposing' parties and their related communities in NI, David Trimble, from the Ulster Unionist Party, on the one side, and Jerry Adams, from Sinn Fein, the political wing of the IRA.

Example 6.7

> The UUP **recognises and accepts that it is legitimate for nationalists** to pursue their political objective of a united Ireland by consent through exclusively peaceful and democratic methods. The UUP **is committed to the principles of inclusivity** [*sic*], **equality and mutual respect** on which the institutions are to be based. **It is our intention that** these principles will **extend in practice to all areas of public life,** and **be endorsed by society as a whole.** The UUP

sees a new opportunity for all our traditions in Northern Ireland to enter a new era of respect and tolerance of cultural differences and expressions. For too long, much of the unrest in our community has been caused by a failure to accept the differing expressions of cultural identity . . . The UUP is committed to securing equality and mutual respect for all elements of our diverse culture . . . Both of our traditions have suffered as a result of our conflict and division. This is a matter of deep regret and makes it all the more important that we now put the past behind us . . . Unionist, loyalist, nationalist and republican must take these steps together to secure a new era of co-operation, reconciliation and mutual respect.

> ('It is legitimate for nationalists to pursue the political objective of a united Ireland', *The Mirror*, 17 November 1999. This statement was widely carried and explicated in the papers throughout Britain and Ireland, for example, 'UUP looks towards new beginning' in the *Belfast Telegraph*, 15 November 1999)

Example 6.8

We want to work with unionists in sorting out those vexed and difficult issues that continue to divide, and confuse, and separate us. Our immediate goal is to forge a partnership with unionism that will see us labour together within the new institutions and govern in fairness and in honesty, with justice and equality. Unionists have nothing to fear from sharing power with republicans. The fact is that we live on a small island. It is too small for us to stand alone and aloof from each other. Our destiny is intertwined. Our freedoms are inextricably bound up together. We cannot move forward into a new century separately, isolated and alone. We can only move forward together. I believe that all our traditions should enjoy equality of treatment and respect. I have consistently defended the rights of Protestants and have advocated the merit of celebrating our diversity. Anti-sectarianism is a fundamental tenet of Irish republicanism. We believe in the unity of Catholic, Protestant and Dissenter. I look forward to the day when all our people, nationalist and unionist, Protestant and Catholic, can live side by side as equals in mutual trust and tolerance.

> ('A moment in history' (Gerry Adams MP, speaking to the party's Ard Chomhairle and regional leadership in Dublin), *An Phoblacht/Republican News*, 25 November 1999)

From these two texts, it may be seen that both leaders seem to share basically the same kind of notion of one's community in relation to the other community. Namely, each community, nationalist or unionist, is constructed as in equal partnership with the other, despite other differences between them. In comparison with the discourse of neighbours of the immediately preceding period, the present one is explicit about the equality of one's community in relation to the other's and moreover is proactive in terms of cooperation or partnership.

This identity of equal partnership may be seen as enacted out of two major textual forms. A first one is a series of particular speech acts performed on some particular objects, which creates or maintains a relationship as equal partners with the other 'opposing' community. These speech acts may be said to combine to form a higher-level action (Mey 2001; van Dijk 1997: 5–6) that achieves equal partnership between the two otherwise conflicting communities. A second, more important, form is, from the viewpoint of the public, print media discourse space, the reciprocal exchange structure, as it were, of speech acts of 'good will' that exists between the two media texts. Table 6.1 schematizes the kinds of acts and the mutuality of these acts.

The speech acts in Table 6.1 may be seen as falling into two broad types: some acts (1–5) contribute to the construction of equality with regard to the 'other' community; some (6–7) contribute to the construction of partnership in relation to the 'other' community. On the other hand, acceptance of the legitimacy of the other community's aspiration (act 1), committing oneself to the principles of equality and diversity (act 2), pronouncement of one's intention to implement these principles (act 3), welcoming the prospects of equality and mutual respect between the two communities (act 4) and attributing conflict/suffering to failure to accept the other community (act 5) can all be seen as showing respect and appreciation of the 'other' 'different' community as equal to one's own. On the other hand, advocating unity and cooperation (act 6) and expressing regret for divisive action (act 7) may be seen as effectively building up a partnership with the otherwise 'opposing' community.

More importantly, these speech acts are not unilateral, but produced from two sides of the media discourse interaction (though limited and probably negligible lack of reciprocality at a lower level of speech acts may be observed). Since the acts as just described treat the other community as equal partner, they can be seen as broadly an expression of 'good will'. Just as a loving relationship needs 'you' *and* 'I' to say 'I love you', so when good will is expressed dialogically and mutually,

Table 6.1 Schema of mutual acts

Acts	Trimble/UUP leader	Adams/Sinn Fein President
Act 1. Accepting the legitimacy of the other's objective/rights	The UUP recognises and accepts that it is legitimate for nationalists to pursue their political objective	I believe that all our traditions should enjoy equality of treatment and respect
Act 2. Committing oneself to principles of inclusiveness and equality	The UUP is committed to the principles of inclusivity, equality and mutual respect. The UUP is committed to securing equality and mutual respect for all elements of our diverse culture	We want to work with unionists in sorting out . . . issues that continue to divide, and confuse, and separate us. Anti-sectarianism is a fundamental tenet of Irish republicanism. We believe in the unity of Catholic, Protestant and Dissenter
Act 3. Announcing one's intention/goal to implement the principles of equality and partnership	It is our intention that these principles will extend in practice to all areas of public life, and be endorsed by society as a whole	Our immediate goal is to forge a partnership with unionism that will see us labour together . . . and govern in fairness and in honesty, with justice and equality
Act 4. Welcoming the prospects of equality and inclusiveness	The UUP sees a new opportunity for all our traditions in NI to enter a new era of respect and tolerance of cultural differences and expressions	I look forward to the day when all our people, nationalist and unionist, Protestant and Catholic, can live side by side as equals in mutual trust and tolerance
Act 5. Attributing conflict/suffering to failure to accept the other community	For too long, much of the unrest in our community has been caused by a failure to accept the differing expressions of cultural identity. Both of our traditions have suffered as a result of . . . division	
Act 6. Advocating unity and cooperation	Unionist, loyalist, nationalist and republican must take . . . steps together to secure a new era of co-operation, reconciliation and mutual respect	It [NI] is too small for us to stand alone and aloof from each other. Our destiny is intertwined . . . We cannot move forward into a new century separately, isolated and alone. We can only move forward together
Act 7. Expressing regret for one's divisive action	This [suffering as a result of division] is a matter of deep regret	

especially against the backdrop of traditional hostility, rivalry, suspicion in NI, equal partnership is thereby being forged. Needless to say, these interactively and dialogically produced actions of 'good will' have important implications for NI society: they signify and constitute cultural transformation.

Conclusion

Having identified and characterized, at both general and concrete levels, the mediated identity discourses in the different historical periods of NI, let me finally proceed to offer a comparative evaluation. Recall that I had argued earlier that speakers, individual or collective, hence their discourse, including identity discourse, are guided by a culturally defined historical, critical consciousness, which I have called moral rationality. Consequently, they continuously create and adopt new discourses that are better and more useful to them than their past and present ones. I had also indicated that the present work had been motivated to rediscover and so to redescribe the cultural development of a 'troubled' society. It may be remembered as well that my judgement in the present research case is based on the chosen criterion of whether the identity discourse of the subsequent period is less, or more, removed away from group conflict seen in the previous period(s).

So, to begin with, it may be observed that there have been formal and notional ruptures in the recent history of the NI identity discourse in the public media. Thus, the militant nationalist discourse in the period of the War of Independence is subsequently replaced by a class-based, minority/majority discourse during the Civil Rights Movement. In turn, the latter minority/majority discourse is replaced by a discourse of neighbours during the Anglo-Irish Agreement period. Finally, in the present Good Friday Agreement period, the previous 'neighbour' discourse is replaced by a discourse of equal partners. Thus, the identity discourse in Ireland and NI has not continued through time. Rather, at different historical times, qualitative changes have taken place in the ways of speaking of self and the (group) other and to/with the other. It is such discursive discontinuities that constitute cultural change(s).

Second, from these historically differentiated discourses, a steady, linear transformation that moves from conflict towards cooperation, hence cultural progress, may be observed. For although each identity discourse is subsequently replaced by one of a different form and meaning, every replacement carries with it a lesser degree of antagonism between the two group categories than the previous discourse. Put another way, the level of animosity in the constructions of the two tra-ditionally divided communities is decreasing successively. Especially the last identity discourse reflects in fact a measure of active intergroup cooperation and partnership. So, for example, the militantly national-ist discourse in the War of Independence period, with its divisive and exclusionary notion of the nation, call to arms and threat of war, is as belligerent as possibly any intergroup discourse can be. This disappears, however, during the Civil Rights Movement and in its stead there comes to the fore a discourse of the majority versus the minority. This subse-quent discourse shows a considerably smaller degree of confrontation because, as may be argued, it does not exclude the other community in a shared society, despite the contradictory social and institutional objectives between the respective communities. The new discourse of neighbours during the Anglo-Irish Agreement period, especially with its emphasis on geographical coexistence, beyond the religious and constitutional divide, does not contain any of the levels of intergroup animosity previously seen. In fact, the construction of neighbourly com-munities has often been used as a justification for calling for intergroup solidarity. Finally, the discourse of equal partners comes into view in the present Good Friday Agreement era. No more is there the earlier notion of various sorts of difference even as neighbour; instead, there is a sense of equality in the self and other community construction and more importantly perhaps a sense of partnership through the recipro-cal expressions of respect, commitment and cooperation.

Finally, it may be concluded that the construction of identity in the public media in NI has not been simply a matter of constant, so per-manent, struggle for dominance or resistance. Nor is it merely a simple matter of persistent drawing of boundaries between 'us' and 'them'. Over and beyond these, there has been, through time, a culturally reflex-ive struggle for intergroup, cross-community interconnection, relation-ship and partnership. Thus, the discursive transformations of identity here may be seen as at least partial consequences of the intrinsic moral-rational force of cultural speakers and discourse. This also means that the agency of cultural change lies, not outside, but within discourse itself. Such critical consciousness of discourse can only be understood from a historical perspective. Furthermore, the present case study shows that historical-comparative analysis cannot follow any fixed procedure of analytical levels and categories. Historically and generically diverse discourses may consist in not only different forms but also different con-tents or concepts as the present case shows. Received fixed method-ology as practised in current discourse analysis may only leave out ethnographically relevant phenomena as would occur in the present case. Finally, it may be pointed out that the succession of increasingly peaceful discourses achieved so far will doubtless form an important context or speech condition that will impact upon what can be constructed in the future in NI. There is, therefore, greater hope in the future of NI than might have been realized. Perhaps it may be suggested that more hope may perhaps be found, in this part of the world as elsewhere, if we go on to research into other forms of discourse, other issues and topics and other kinds of data.

7
Promoting New Discourses of the Other

Introduction

So far, in the practical part of discourse studies, I have been re-describing *past* and *present* discourses – deconstructing the Western discourse of contradictions (Chapter 4), highlighting marginalized non-Western Other's discourses (Chapter 5) and reconstituting historical discourses of 'troubled' communities (Chapter 6). Now, in this final chapter, I want to take a step further as part of the CAD project and engage in a more proactive mode of discourse research by advocating *future* discourses. Specifically, I shall illustrate this new kind of discourse research by trying to formulate and justify some new and alternative discourses of cultural others in favour of cultural solidarity and prosperity. Thus, the present undertaking harks back to the 'transformative' strategies of discourse research I alluded to in the Introduction and outlined in Chapters 2 and 3, respectively.

Critical studies of language, discourse and communication have identified important issues and problems of capitalism, racism and sexism, particularly in western societies. They have offered models of social, linguistic analysis (or, what some would call, description and explanation) that are sometimes emulated in other parts of the world whereby new issues are raised and criticised. However, I think, as I have argued in Chapters 1 and 2, that critical discourse studies can and should become more creative, or, in other words, practitioners in the field should act like artists or activists in social movements (such as feminism and anti-racism). By this I mean that they should, based on existing studies of discourses of domination, exploitation and exclusion, try to come up with new and alternative ways of speaking and convincing arguments for them. As a result, hopefully, other academic colleagues and students will begin to change their own discourses as part of a broader cultural transformation.

According to the present cultural approach to discourse, the object and objective of discourse studies are dictated by the cultural political priorities of the moment. In Chapter 2, I proposed that, given increasing contemporary cultural division, antagonism as well as interdependence, cultural harmony and progress be adopted as the priorities of CAD. So in this chapter, I shall try my hand at drawing up some discourses round these motifs. In particular I want to focus on discourses about cultural others.

While the discourses I shall formulate may be of interest to the general scholarly community, I have here a particular group in mind, namely, experts (scholars, researchers, pedagogues, trainers and consultants) in intercultural studies, broadly defined, including cross-cultural psychology and communication. There are two reasons for this. First, they have a professional authority on the matter and therefore can exert great influence on the shape of the discourse of cultural others in society. Second, paradoxically, they often seem to be part of the problem rather than part of the solution. Put bluntly, there is a tendency to overlook the historically specific power saturation of the process of intercultural relation and communication; consequently, cultural domination becomes legitimated, cultural repression colluded with and exclusion perpetuated.

In what follows, I shall first offer a critique of the problem just mentioned and my own view of intercultural communication. Then, using these critical analyses as a background and basis, I shall tentatively and provisionally articulate a set of discourses about cultural others and some supporting arguments for them. In conclusion I shall discuss the ways that such creative, transformative practices may be assessed.

Intercultural studies

Within intercultural studies (research, pedagogy, training and consultancy) there seems to circulate a general discourse that sets great store by cross-linguistic and cross-cultural knowledge and skills and the ability to 'translate' linguistic and cultural differences, hence 'intercultural competence'. Underlying this discourse is the assumption that members of different cultures have different sets of cultural and linguistic knowledge and skills. Consequently, this discourse is often used to explain 'misunderstandings' or 'communication breakdown' – in terms of individual deficiencies in the relevant linguistic or cultural knowledge and skills and, ultimately, the linguistic and cultural differences outside the individuals and their practices.[1]

The central problem with this sort of discourse, I think, is that it obscures the power-saturated nature of intercultural contact and communication. That is, it presumes that different cultures are in equal relation to one another. Let us call it the cultural relativist view or the discourse of cultural relativism. But through the entire modern world history, the West has never seen, spoken of, or dealt with, the non-Western Other as equal, or as merely or simply 'different'. Rather, it has often treated the Other as deviant, inferior and so to be controlled and controllable. In other words, the contact and communication between the West and the non-Western, non-White and Third World communities have always been a matter of power struggle. I described this colonial and post-colonial condition at length in Chapters 2 and 4, so here I shall not dwell on it any longer.

In spite of theoretical inadequacy, there is political expediency in the discourse. For, under the auspices of this discourse, institutions of knowledge and skills – research, education, training and consultation – in intercultural contact and communication become the provider of 'intercultural competence', which students, trainees or other people concerned would have to bank on.[2] It may be reflected here that such institutional arrangements of intercultural teaching, training and advising may have to do with the elite group which formulates and advocates such theoretical discourse in the first place.

Nevertheless, the veil cast over the power of intercultural communication may have a series of cultural political consequences. For one thing, since culture is seen as static and fixed in such a discourse, members' capacity to create cultural knowledge and experience through communication may be overlooked. For another, their potential to transform transcultural experience and relations through the very act of intercultural communication could be neglected. In addition, a 'powerless' notion of intercultural contact and communication fails to account for cultural exclusion through non-intercultural communication. But worst of all, when differences in cultural power are reduced to mere semantics or cognition or individual differences, the basic cultural inequality, domination and discrimination that lie at the heart of contemporary intercultural (including international) communication may be smoothed over or explained away. Here I am thinking especially of the Western colonialist and imperialist discourses of its Other that permeates present-day intercultural communication in politics, popular culture, businesses, educational institutions, everyday conversation and so on and so forth.

Power in intercultural communication

In this section, I shall explore the power nature of intercultural contact and communication as I sketch out a cultural, power-minded theory thereof. My central thesis here is that contemporary social life everywhere is transcultural and intercultural through and through and that such cultural life is shot through with power, hence domination, prejudice and exclusion. Whilst such an account stands as a critical, oppositional discourse *vis-à-vis* the cultural–relativist view, it will also pave the way for developing new discourses of cultural others as I shall do subsequently because it will serve as the context to which the new discourses are supposed to be appropriate.

There is recently already a fair amount of critical, discourse-oriented work on intercultural relation and communication (for example, Blommaert and Verschueren 1991, 1998; Koole and ten Thije 1994; Sarangi 1994; Tomic 2000) and I draw on this in the present account. However, my main focus and emphasis will be on the CAD perspective.

Contemporary intercultural communication cannot be detached from the global contest, competition as well as interdependence, where domination and resistance are the order of the day. A very important dimension of intercultural communication is power. Power is conceived of here as the effect of human social practice whereby things get done or people are put under control (cf. Giddens 1984; see also Chapter 1). It may be enacted through instruments or resources of action or symbolic capital (Bourdieu 1991), for example language, knowledge and institutional status. Such hegemonic relations and practices are embodied in the existing relations of domination, exploitation and prejudice of the West with the Rest, the legacy of European colonialism and American neo-expansionism (Said 1978, 1993; Young 2001). Thus, the social conditions under which we live should be analysed in terms of differential power relations and practices, where one group is dominated by another, through differential power resources available to some groups or individuals but not to others.

Power is not absolute, however. It has its antithesis (Chapter 1). Just as conversations are governed by immanent but evolving rules of engagement, so discourse has the intrinsic moral rationality to reflect upon itself and evolve accordingly. It seems to me that, without this moral rationality, the anti-racism discourse or the feminist discourse would not have appeared. It will be useful then for pedagogues to try and awaken, illuminate, advocate and enhance this moral rationality in society. Freire (1972) has called this kind of potential 'critical consciousness'. It is important to emphasize that moral rationality is not universal but culture-specific and continuously evolving. Discourse communities generate their own systems of thoughts, truths, justice, freedom, goodness or, for that matter, 'negative forces'. These culture-specific features may in turn become the conditions of subsequent creative transformations. It should be noted, too, that moral rationality, like discourse itself, may be discontinued, due to a change of conditions of life or the emergence of new discourses.

I now turn to the situation of intercultural communication. 'Intercultural' is used to refer to the fact that the meaning of a difference between two groups of people is present and furthermore that that difference is rendered through a dialogue between members of the two groups, either in the background context or foreground text. It is important to emphasize here that the intercultural dimension is not an external mechanism that dictates communicative behaviour. Rather it is an integral part of communicative practice (that is, what people do); it is, in other words, a meaning(ful element) embedded in the relevant discourse, including discourse context. It is a type of social human meaning that is created, reproduced, sustained, utilized and changed in and through linguistic interaction. As such the (inter)cultural can be either the background ('context') or foreground ('figure') of the ongoing communication.

On the one hand, intercultural communication is not merely a matter of exchange of information but should be considered as a form of social action: not as sentence speech acts, but in terms of people acting with each other and so upon their worlds. In their interaction, people are not simply 'understanding' each other; rather, they are acting with and upon each other. This implies that their actions are not individual but interactively, and thus socially, related to each other. Moreover, such discursive actions are not just 'understood' but also interpreted and appropriated all at the same time. Understanding operates against the background of power differences, power practices and power interests. Consequently, communication cannot be analysed merely in terms of 'understandings' or 'misunderstandings': throughout the process of intercultural, or indeed any human, communication as they are interacting, so they are (re)interpreting and (re)applying their understandings in one and the same hermeneutic act (Gadamer 1989). It is not that the understanding of words and sentences and so on is not relevant for communication, but my point is that the dimension of social action deserves critical attention.

On the other hand, intercultural communication does not take place in a power vacuum but should be understood as situated in the context of power imbalance and inequality. This refers to resources and relations between the West and the continents of Asia, Africa and Latin America, the North and the South, men and women, the majority and the minority, and so on. The global, international and regional order is not one of equilibrium and peace, but essentially one of power and dominance. It is in and against this global context of power – a context in which, as may be pointed out, the poverty-stricken population is growing faster than the world's wealth – that any 'intercultural communication' is conducted. To pretend that these power relations are not there, or to reduce them to domains outside of discourse and communication, is to render intercultural communication research and training ineffectual or, worse still, complicit with problems domination and repression. All this means that acts of domination over and prejudice against the cultural Other, or other repressive cultural consequences, need urgent, critical attention. It is crucial for any serious intercultural communication theorists and educators to pay attention to the power relations in which intercultural communication takes place. There is a serious sense, then, in which intergroup/cultural conflicts are enabled not simply by 'the knowing or understanding of the language and culture of the Other', but, far more importantly, by cultural power (Keesing 1991: 50).

Formulating and warranting new discourses of cultural others

Let me begin by suggesting how an appropriate alternative and critical form of pedagogy in intercultural contact and communication should proceed. This will determine the form and character of the new discourses to be formulated and warranted.

To start with, consistent with the political goals of CAD, the present approach aims ultimately to make the teaching and research process itself part of intercultural communication change in favour of cultural solidarity and prosperity. Thus, the present approach sees itself as what Giroux (1992: 204) calls 'both an oppositional and affirmative force'. Further, obviously, this project is guided by explicit, chosen values. In this respect, intercultural theory, research and training emulate, I would urge, feminist studies (for example, Farganis 1986,

Harding 1987; Richards 1982; Stanley and Wise 1983; Tong 1995). This leads to my next point.

To transform existing intercultural communication and its pedagogy is not to tighten up a linguistic screw here and loosen a cultural bolt there. Rather, the entire attitude towards the cultural 'Other' needs to be changed. This means, from a discursive perspective, that different discourses about the cultural Other, other than the dominant and repressive ones in society, as will be formulated in the next section, must be initiated, promoted and warranted in the pedagogical process. To change the entire attitude, the most challenging question for the new critical intercultural pedagogy is how it can accomplish this change. This question may be seen and tackled at three levels of pedagogical practice, which are dialectically related, that is, mutually requiring each other.

First, at a textual level, we as professionals should help formulate and elaborate new themes – for example, themes of diversity, equality, common goals and rational moral motivation on the one hand and convincing and acceptable arguments for those themes on the other. This means that, because diversity, equality, human cultural common destiny and rational moral motivation are far from being well-elaborated or well-established, and because there is an infinite possibility of creating new and alternative discourses, intercultural teachers, trainers and consultants should play an active, stimulating role in formulating such discourses.

Second, at an interactional level, we teachers, trainers and consultants should try to establish and follow new and alternative rules of pedagogical practice. That is, we must abandon the traditional individual knowledge-minded and authoritarian methodology and act out new roles such as coordinators, partners, collaborators and learners as well as experts whilst stimulating, formulating, elaborating and modifying those discourses (see also Freire 1972).

Third, our discourses need to be brought into society as a whole and not merely within the academic circle. Intercultural communication has commonly been thought of and treated as the province of trade, commerce, diplomacy or such other fields of institutional interests. But unless society, including its youngest members, begins to incorporate these new discourses as the starting point of their everyday thinking and speaking, we can hardly succeed in the specialist areas of trade, commerce, or other business. In this way, we can hope to impact on not just pedagogical practice but also, more importantly, human cultural development itself. We educators, trainers and consultants stimulate, help formulate and elaborate, and encourage the use and development of new and alternative discourses. We must try to change the entire cultural attitude and the practice of society at large regarding the cultural Other and to do so starting with young children.

Following the culturalist rethinking about intercultural communication and its pedagogy, I shall in the remainder of the chapter make some tentative and provisional suggestions as to what discourses may be needed and how such discourses may be supported, that is, with what possible arguments. Such discourses have to do with the central issues of contemporary societies, East and West, as their topics of concerns: intercultural and international contact and communication (in the broad sense). Specifically, I shall suggest as the main objective of this chapter why and how we discourse researchers initiate, formulate and justify new and alternative discourses. As 'experimental' examples, I shall formulate the gist of and rationale for the discourses of plurality, equality, common goals and moral rationality, respectively. Thus, guided by a cultural, power-minded view, I shall propose that intercultural teachers, trainers, consultants and mediators begin to adopt new discourses that will directly challenge existing discourses of domination, exclusion and prejudice and embrace instead themes of diversity, equality, common goals and, above all, rational moral motivation. In addition to this change of pedagogical discourse, I suggest that such a discursive transformation be accomplished, not by some external decree, but through an imaginative, teacher–student, theorist–practitioner dialogue which initiates, questions, (re)formulates and warrants those discourses.

It should be cautioned that the discourses suggested below are not the only discourses that are needed, nor that their meanings are determined once and for all. Rather they are presented as part of an evolving dialogical process. Here I shall focus only on the general kinds of discourse without paying detailed attention to particular pedagogical and practical contexts, as these would involve far more particularizations and elaborations than can be handled in a chapter like this. But in doing so I do have in mind various tasks and settings such as intercultural and intergroup management, negotiation, conflict resolution, reconciliation, consulting, counselling and training. Further, what is suggested here might also be relevant to other kinds of intergroup relations and interaction: for example, between different genders and between different generations. It might be objected that the discourses that I spell out below may already be found at certain stages of human cultural history or in particular quarters of social life, for example feminism and anti-racism. But my point here is that these discourses are rather marginal and marginalized or even suppressed voices, in the face of the discourse of the non-western Other as deviant, inferior and having to be disciplined. Moreover, because of this domination there is an urgent need to rekindle, elaborate and advocate these discourses.

Plurality as contemporary global condition

One of the badly needed discourses is that of diversity and plurality. That is, we need to point out that there are different cultural traditions and circumstances, different cultural experiences and practices, different worldviews and perspectives, and different moral (internally diversified) systems. This means that there is not just one world, one reality, one truth, one theory, one system of moral values, one correct way of doing things. It may be suggested, too, that diversity exists not just between cultures but also within cultures. Indeed, 'universality' of anything is merely a wilful universalization of historical and geographic particulars, usually to the detriment of underprivileged or disadvantaged groups of people, who are then seen as deviant from the norm or standard. Thus, no culture can be compared as intrinsically superior or inferior than the other. In this way, tolerance of difference can also develop to become part of the broader discourse of diversity. Further, the discourse of diversity means that when different cultures meet and interact, they are not merely 'understanding' each other, or 'translating' (or 'representing') respective linguistic and cultural meanings, but also jointly produce new meanings, new realities, new futures – a third culture as it were.

As part of the argument for the new theme of cultural plurality, we may draw attention to the changed conditions of globalization/localization, mass (hyper)media, mass migration and international travel. These new conditions will only make the diversity and plurality of different ways of thinking, feeling, seeing the world and conducting oneself, for example, a more, not less, salient fact of life. Moreover, plurality is necessary: human problems cannot be solved from singularly cultural perspectives, or by singularly cultural efforts. We only have to think of diseases, poverty, civil war, national and religious conflicts. Furthermore, diversity is desirable: the diversity of human thoughts, feelings, imaginations, habits, skills, inventions and so on broaden our horizon and enrich our life. In addition, we can highlight the constructed and moral nature of such notions and boundaries as 'nation', 'culture', 'group', or 'company', so that plurality and diversity can be understood as not just between different such categories but within them as well.

Equality as the basis of intercultural interaction

Given the power saturation of social and cultural life, the discourse of cultural plurality and diversity is not sufficient. Without equality, diversity is merely a difference in power – between ethnicities, genders and classes – which, unfortunately, has continued to characterize contemporary human communities and particularly intercultural communication. Thus, what we need in conjunction with that is a discourse of equality. So it may be suggested that this discourse contain the notion that human cultures are diversified and hitherto such different ways of thinking, feeling, seeing the world and conducting oneself have been hierarchical rather than merely relative to one another. Therefore, this discourse should also promote the idea that we begin to help generate a new way of thinking and speaking that represents the different cultural Other, no longer as less human, less civilized, or less entitled to the world's resources, but as basically equal.

As a way of underpinning the theme of equality, we can encourage people to reflect critically on one's own traditional discourse regarding the cultural Other (see also Tomic 2000). That is, instead of concentrating on the 'relevant' language and culture and the 'translation' of these, we draw active attention to one's own historical discursive practice in and through which the Other has been represented and repressed (see, for example, Said 1978). Thus, for instance, students may examine the power-oriented representations of other cultures, communities and groups of people, and the discursive complexities, dynamics and ideologies leading to unequal power relations or consequences. Here study of the colonial and post-colonial discourse will highlight the deeply rooted ethnocentrism. In addition, it will also reveal that domination and repression cannot be total and absolute but will always encounter resistance (see also Said 1993). Similarly, we can help students and practitioners become alert as to how '(mis-)communication' and '(mis)understanding' are related to power relations, power interests and power effects, where intercultural communication becomes disjointed or breaks down or simply does not happen.

Mutual benefit as common goals

Still another closely related discourse that should be initiated, developed and promoted may be the discourse of common human cultural goals. That is, other than speaking of intercultural contact and communication as a matter of individual knowledge and skills, we should emphasize the need, possibility and usefulness for constructing a common future and therefore a common course of action. More specifically, we should help create a new and alternative discourse of mutually beneficial and maximally possible goals. If cultures differ in power they can, however, be brought together through the construction of mutual benefit. As part of that theme, perhaps, we need also to highlight the social-relational, truly *inter*cultural and hence shared fate of humanity.

The reasons are many. The construction of commonly acceptable and maximally beneficial goals is necessary because we are all inextricably bound together by a common destination. At the very 'micro' level of intercultural communication, for example, a 'misunderstanding', communication breakdown and, indeed, success of conversation, business or cultural relationship is a coordinated and mutually consequential effect; it is a joint responsibility. No individual person, group, nation, culture, region and such like can alone be responsible for anything or achieve maximally possible success or profit. Unfortunately, this is still not well understood, and far from being practised in intercultural and international contact and communication. The theme of common goals is necessary, also and especially because we are now faced with increasing nuclear armament, environmental disaster, financial crisis, regional, ethnic, religious and territorial conflicts – both globalized repression and globalized resistance. It may be noted that practitioners will of course have to rely on or resort to their individual cultural traditions, but we should encourage them to make use of historical discourses imaginatively and inventively in order to construct shared objectives.

Moral rationality as hope for cultural survival

It will be realized that the discourses sketched above might be seen by many as contrary to the familiar and comfortable discourses of individual knowledge, self-interest and cultural superiority that are popular in many societies. Thus, the proposed discourses, despite the compelling arguments, may not initially appear convincing enough for educationalists and students to endorse and so put into practice. The latter may even feel that to take up the proposed new discourses would be detrimental to their own truths, standards, privileges and advantages. To make matters worse, they may become frustrated in intercultural communication practice even if they have engaged in such new discourses.

To overcome fears of, or even resistance to, the discourses suggested above, it might be useful to appeal to cultural members' capacity of critical reflection or moral rationality. As may be recalled from the previous theoretical discussion on intercultural communication, I argued that cultural members are implicitly guided by the culture-specific critical consciousness to find new arguments in order to achieve freedom and progress for all. For the present purposes, this means that researchers and teachers should try to initiate and engage in a discourse that stimulates and mobilizes this moral rationality or cultural consciousness. Such a discourse may contain, on the one hand, a thesis that, for example, there is a need and benefit to rethink and to transform existing assumptions in order to accomplish culturally shared freedom. On the other hand, the discourse of moral rationality may include a set of supporting arguments for such a thesis. Accordingly, it may be reflected, for example, that human cultures are active, creative and dynamic rather than passively conservative. Further, in the future humanity, 'our' own well-being and its betterment rest on culturally shared freedom and progress rather than the powers of individual communities, groups, nations or regions (Freire 1972, 1976, 1985; Giroux 1992). In this way, cultural members may become prepared and motivated to consciously try continuously to engage in dialogue with cultural others.

Conclusion

Once these new discourses are adopted as commonly accepted ways of speaking of cultural 'others' and intercultural affairs more generally, then they may help with preventing failure or breakdown in intercultural contact and communication, even though they cannot guarantee (immediate) success. For the basic understandings of plurality, equality, common goals and moral rational consciousness will keep practitioners on their dialogical process of intercultural communication and interaction. Finally, let me briefly reflect on what I have done here and its implications for future dialogue on intercultural research and pedagogy.

First, I have taken issue with Western intercultural communication theory and pedagogy and highlighted some of the theoretical inadequacies and cultural political consequences. Here it may be suggested that, although deconstruction of western truths, knowledge and power on the issue of intercultural contact and communication is urgent and necessary, it can be useful, too, to engage dialogically with non-Western intellectual traditions in the field.

Second, I have dealt with the problem of intercultural contact and communication mainly from the point of view of discourse. Surely, a discursive change to intercultural studies and pedagogy is much needed, but other broader semiotic approaches to intercultural encounters could also yield complementary insights. In this respect, the media, both conventional and digital, films, art and literature can all come in handy.

Third, I have canvassed only in broad lines the kinds of discourses for a critical societal and international pedagogy on intercultural contact and communication. Moreover, they are subject to cultural contexts and historical moments. Thus, finer details can be added, modifications made and other, or more convincing, arguments found. So it is obvious that much more research is called for.

Notes

Introduction

1. Here let me mention that CAD draws in particular on cultural studies (for example, Ang 2001; Bhabha 1994; Hall 1992, 1996a, 1996b; Said 1978, 1993; Spivak 1988a; Young 2001), communication theory (for example, Carey 1992; McQuail 2000), critical linguistics (for example, Fowler 1985; Fowler *et al.* 1979; Hodge and Kress 1993), critical discourse analysis (for example, Barker and Galasinski 2001; Chouliaraki and Fairclough 1999; Fairclough 1992, 1995; van Dijk 1993a, 1993b; Wodak 1996), discursive psychology (Billig 1991; Edwards and Potter 1992; Wetherell and Potter 1992) and the work of Laclau and Mouffe (1985).

2. The Third World as used here is similar in reference and meaning to 'tricontinent' and hence 'tricontinentalism' as adopted by Young (2001), who follows the lead by Abdel-Malek (1981).

1 Discourse and Reality

1. A parallel view of identity can be expressed in Bakhtin's (1981: 313–14) account of the authorial discourse in the novel, but I think it has general validity regarding discourse as a whole:

> The author manifests himself and his point of view not only in his effect on the narrator, on his speech and his language (which are to one or another extent objectivized, objects of display) but also in his effect on the subject of the story – as a point of view that differs from the point of view of the narrator. Behind the narrator's story we read a second story, the author's story; he is the one who tells us how the narrator tells stories, and also tells us about the narrator himself . . . Every moment of the story has a conscious relationship with this normal [literary] language and its belief system, is in fact set against them, and set against them *dialogically*: one point of view opposed to another, one evaluation opposed to another, one accent opposed to another (i.e., they are not contrasted as two abstractly linguistic phenomena).

2 Discourse and Culture

1. This universalist notion of (scientific) discourse is often even held in certain culture-oriented approaches to language, as in studies of intercultural communication, cross-cultural linguistics and foreign languages teaching (Shi-xu 2001).

2. A different variation here, though, is the notion of culture as a higher form of aesthetic achievement.

3. Drawing on the later Wittgenstein's notion of meaning, Geertz (1973: 17) defines the notion of culture as social practice in this way: 'it is through the flow of behavior – or, social action – that cultural forms find articulation. They find it as well, of course, in various sorts of artifacts, and various states of consciousness; but these draw their meaning from the role they play (Wittgenstein would say their "use") in an ongoing pattern of life, not from any intrinsic relationships they bear to one another'.

4. Similarly, Harrison (2003: 9) suggests: 'postcolonial studies in general may be characterised broadly and simply in terms of an attention to the history of colonialism/imperialism and its aftermath, and may in many instances be distinguished from traditional historical or political writing on the colonial or post-independence era by the particular attention that is paid to the role within that history of "representation" or "discourse"'.

5. It may be stressed here that, in this sense, discourse will be endlessly ideo-logical: any further descriptive discourse of a discourse will be yet another construction, hence an ideological product.

6. Fairclough (1992: 200) also suggests that discourse analysis has not paid much attention to the issue of change. In his own approach he registers discursive changes, such as 'democratization', 'commodification' and 'technologiza-tion', by identifying abstract patterns of discourse and analysing the interac-tion between these patterns.

3   Political Ethnography

1. Here I shall mainly focus on those strategies for data construction, discourse interpretation and new discourse promotion. For those on other aspects of discourse research such as sampling procedures, measuring instruments, statistical treatment of data, see, for example, Titscher *et al.* 2000; Wetherell *et al.* 2001.

2. There are other, slightly different versions of 'social constructionism'; but because it is not a concern of the present work to tease them out, I shall stick to the version outlined here. Here in particular, I would like to highlight two dimensions of this social constructionist perspective on knowledge. On the one hand, knowledge is *cultural* in character. That is, every society has its own concepts, desires, values and outlooks, which render knowledge gender-, ethnicity- and class-oriented, for example. Especially in the late modern conditions of mass hypermedia and migration, factual and evaluative knowl-edge becomes more dynamic and contested, both globally and locally. It is essential then for intellectual work to be critically reflexive on the cultural dimension of knowledge production and to construct multicultural, pluralist perspectives that enhance the justice and freedom of humanity. Similarly, theoretical diversity is to be embraced: thus, discourse as the object of inquiry cannot be simply encapsulated in linguistics, communication studies, psychology, sociology, history, politics, cultural studies, or any other single or combined disciplines.

3. It is common but mistaken to think that social constructionism denies the materiality of the world, as if it were saying that the objects in front of our eyes do not exist or the holocaust did not occur. Nothing is further from the

truth. It merely says that the world of objects cannot exist independently of people's experience and practice in particular time and space, such that both social structure and human action are *interpretative* in nature (Gadamer 1989). This notion of the relationship between the person and world can be traced back at least to Husserl's (1931) concept of *intentionality*, that is, the world is not separable from human consciousness and vice versa. Or as Sartre (1949) has expressed it, 'La conscience et le monde sont donnés d'un même coup'. It is easy and common to confuse social constructionism with relativism. Social constructionism is not relativism. For one thing, it does not subscribe to the infinite notion of variability of versions of reality, because it is not what real social life is like: there is no context-free version. Rather, the present version of social constructionism takes it that although knowledge is always subject to further interpretation and argumentation (which are encouraged here anyway), some version is always more justified in particular time and space than others. For another, more importantly, the present version takes up an explicit political stance, that is, to side with particular groups of people – oppressed and marginalized.

4. In cultural studies Hall (1996a: 337) has called for study of 'the central, urgent, and disturbing questions of a society'. Indeed, racism, sexism, capitalism, ageism, sectarianism and so on and so forth can be recognized across many cultures as most urgent and pressing problems and have been important topics in discourse and cultural studies. But the present work is mainly concerned with cultural imperialism as one of the most prominent and pressing problems endangering world peace and future generations (Bhabha 1994; Hall 1996a, 1999; Said 1993; Wodak 1996).

4 Deconstructing the Other Place

1. There has been a number of other western social, cultural and political analyses of Singapore. Some of these can be found in: I. Buruma (1989) *God's Dust, A Modern Asian Journey*, London: Vintage; P. Biddlecome (1995) *Around the World: On Expenses*, London: Abacus; C. Levine (ed.) (1978) *Singapore*, Singapore: Apa Productions.
2. There has been over a dozen recent Dutch travel books on China.
3. Metaphor, according to Goatly (1997:108), 'occurs when a unit of discourse is used to refer to an object, concept, process, quality, relationship or world to which it does not conventionally refer to. This unconventional act of reference is understood on the basis of similarity or analogy'. I use the notion broadly to include not only such classic metaphors, but also metonymies, similes. Further, I take it that metaphor can be realized through words, phrases and propositions as well as larger units such as narrative.

5 Reading Non-Western Discourses

1. Primary sources include《人民日報》*People's Daily*,《文匯報》*Wen Hui Bao*,《半月談》*Bi-Monthly*, *China Today*, *South China Morning Post*, www.english. peopledaily.com.cn, www.info.gov.hk/press,《明報》*Ming Bao*, *Asiaweek*,

《亞洲周刊》 *Asia Weekly*, 《文匯報》 *Wen Hui Bao* Hong Kong (to distinguish from Mainland China's paper of the same name).

2. Vološinov (1986) has called such symbols, or signs or discourse, 'ideological'.

3. It is noteworthy, too, especially in discourses undermining China's claims, that there is a good measure of acknowledgement of western, especially British, influence in administration and law.

6 Fanning the Sparks of Hope from History

1. Foucault (1972: 6–7) characterizes the interested nature of historical discourse in this way: 'history now organizes the document, divides it up, distributes it, orders it, arranges it in levels, establishes series, distinguishes between what is relevant and what is not, discovers elements, defines unities, describes relations. The document, then, is no longer for history an inert material through which it tries to reconstitute what men have done or said, the events of which only the trace remains; history is now trying to define within the documentary material itself unities, totalities, series, relations'.

2. These include especially the *Belfast Telegraph*, *The Irish News*, *News Letter*, the *Sunday Mirror*, *The Mirror*, the *Daily Mail*, *The Daily Mirror*, the *Independent on Sunday*, the *Independent*, *Sunday World*, *An Phoblacht/Republican News*, *Belfast Agreement*, www.uup.org/dtspeech.html.

7 Promoting New Discourses of the Other

1. The two interrelated foundational concepts of 'intercultural competence' and 'misunderstanding' have guided research and shaped education in intercultural communication. 'Misunderstanding' (or the person who 'misunderstands') is thought to be the cause of all other problems in intercultural communication and relations. On the other hand, the more 'intercultural competence' one has, the less 'misunderstanding' one will have during intercultural communication, hence the more smooth and successful contact and relations one will have (Cushner and Brislin 1996; Hofstede 1980; Trompenaars 1993). Thus, Scollon and Scollon (1995: 11–12) state that 'communication works better the more the participants share assumptions and knowledge about the world. Where two people have very similar histories, backgrounds, and experiences, their communication works fairly easily because the inferences each makes about what the other means will be based on common experience and knowledge... Successful communication is based on sharing as much as possible the assumptions we make about what others mean'. Therefore, they propose two principles for solving the intercultural problem (1995: 13): 'The first approach is based on knowing as much as possible about the people with whom one is communicating... The second approach is based on making the assumption that misunderstandings are the only thing certain about interdiscourse [intercultural] professional communication'.

2. For the 'banking' notion of education see Freire 1972.

References

Abdel-Malek, A. (1981) *Social Dialectics*, 2 vols (trans. M. Gonzalez). Albany, NY: State University of New York Press.

Adorno, T.W. (1974) *Minima Moralia: Reflections from Damaged Life*. London: NLB.

Anderson, B. (1991) *Imagined Communities: Reflection on the Origins and Spread of Nationalism*, 2nd edn. London: Verso.

Ang, I. (2001) *On Not Speaking Chinese: Living between Asia and the West*. New York: Routledge.

Antaki, C. and S. Widdicombe (eds) (1998) *Identities in Talk*. London: Sage.

Appadurai, A. (1996) *Modernity at Large: Cultural Dimensions of Globalization*. Minneapolis, MN: University of Minnesota Press.

Appiah, K.A. (1992) *In My Father's House: Africa in the Philosophy of Culture*. London: Methuen.

Ashcroft, B., G. Griffiths and H. Tiffin (1989) *The Empire Writes Back: Theory and Practice in Post-colonial Literatures*. London: Routledge.

Ashcroft, B., G. Griffiths and H. Tiffin (1995) *The Post-colonial Studies Reader*. London: Routledge.

Atkinson, P. (1990) *The Ethnographic Imagination: Textual Construction of Reality*. London: Routledge.

Atkinson, P. (1992) *Understanding Ethnographic Texts*. Newbury Park, CA: Sage.

Austin, J.L. (1962) *How to Do Things with Words*. Oxford: The Clarendon Press.

Back, Les (1996) *New Ethnicities and Urban Culture: Racisms and Multiculture in Young Lives*. London: University College London.

Bakhtin, M.M. (1981) *The Dialogic Imagination: Four Essays* (ed. M. Holquist; trans. C. Emerson and M. Holquist). Austin, TX: University of Texas Press.

Bardon, J. (1992) *A History of Ulster*. Belfast: Blackstaff Press.

Barker, C. and D. Galasinski (2001) *Cultural Studies and Discourse Analysis: A Dialogue on Language and Identity*. London: Sage Publications.

Bauman, Z. (1998) *Globalization: The Human Consequences*. Cambridge: Polity Press.

Bazerman, C. (1998) Emerging perspectives on the many dimensions of scientific discourse. In J.R. Martin and R. Veel (eds), *Reading Science: Critical and Functional Perspectives on Discourses of Science*. London: Routledge, pp. 15–28.

Beckett, J.C. (1966) *The Making of Modern Ireland*. London: Faber & Faber.

Bellah, R.N., R. Madsen, W.M. Swindler and S.M. Tipton (1985) *Habits of the Heart: Individualism and Commitment in American Life*. Berkeley, CA: University of California Press.

Benjamin, W. (1999) *Illuminations* (trans. H. Zorn). London: Pimlico.

Bennett, A. (1998) *Culture: A Reformer's Science*. London: Sage Publications.

Berger, P.L. and T. Luckmann (1967) *The Social Construction of Reality: A Treatise in the Sociology of Knowledge*. London: Penguin Press.

Bhabha, H. (1990) The Third Space. In J. Rutherford (ed.), *Identity, Community, Culture, Difference*. London: Lawrence & Wishart, pp. 207–21.

Bhabha, H.K. (1994) *The Location of Culture*. London: Routledge.

Billig, M. (1991) *Ideology and Opinions*. London: Sage Publications.

Billig, M. (1995) *Banal Nationalism*. London: Sage Publications.

Billig, M. (1999) 'Whose terms? Whose ordinariness?' Rhetoric and ideology in conversation analysis. *Discourse & Society*, 10 (4): 543–58.

Billig, M. *et al.* (1988) *Ideological Dilemmas: a Social Psychology of Everyday Thinking*. London: Sage Publications.

Blommaert, J. (1997) Whose background? *Pragmatics*, 7 (1): 69–81.

Blommaert, J. and J. Verschueren (eds) (1991) *The Pragmatics of Intercultural and International Communication*. Amsterdam: John Benjamins.

Blommaert, J. and J. Verschueren (1998) *Debating Diversity: Analysing the Discourse of Tolerance*. London: Routledge.

Bloor, D. (1976) *Knowledge and Social Imagery*. London: Routledge & Kegan Paul.

Bloor, M. (1978) On the analysis of observational data: a discussion of the worth and uses of inductive techniques and respondent validation. *Sociology*, 12 (3): 545–57.

Boas, F. (1966) *Race, Language and Culture*. New York: The Free Press.

Bourdieu, P. (1991) *Language and Symbolic Power*. Cambridge: Polity Press.

Bourdieu, P. and L. Wacquant (1992) *An Invitation to Reflexive Sociology*. Cambridge: Polity Press.

Boyle, K. and T. Hadden (1985) *Ireland: A Positive Proposal*. Harmondsworth: Penguin Books.

Briggs, A. (1985) The sense of place. In A. Briggs, *The Collected Essays of Asa Briggs, Vol. I: Words, Numbers, Places, People*. New York: Harvester Wheatsheaf, pp. 87–105.

Brown, P. and S.C. Levinson (1987) *Politeness: Some Universals in Language Usage*. Cambridge: Cambridge University Press.

Burr, V. (1995) *An Introduction to Social Constructionism*. London: Routledge.

Butler, J. (1992) Contingent foundations: feminism and the question of 'postmodernism'. In J. Butler and J.W. Scott (eds), *Feminists Theorize the Political*. New York: Routledge, pp. 3–21.

Butler, J. (1993) *Bodies That Matter*. New York: Routledge.

Butler, J. and J.W. Scott (eds) (1992) *Feminists Theorize the Political*. New York: Routledge.

Cameron, D. (1992) *Feminism and Linguistic Theory*, 2nd edn. London: Macmillan.

Cappella, J.N. (1991) Mutual adaptation and relativity of measurement. In B.M. Montgomery and S. Duck (eds), *Studying Interpersonal Interaction*. New York: Wiley, pp. 325–42.

Carbaugh, D. (1993) Communal voices: an ethnographic view of social interaction and conversation. *The Quarterly Journal of Speech*, 79: 99–113.

Carey, J.W. (1992) *Communication as Culture: Essays on Media and Society*. New York: Routledge.

Cassirer, E. (1944) *An Essay on Man: An Introduction to a Philosophy of Human Culture*. New Haven, CT: Princeton University Press.

CCCS (Centre for Contemporary Cultural Studies) (1982) *The Empire Strikes Back: Race and Racism in 70s Britain*. London: Hutchinson.

Césaire, A. (1972) *Discourse on Colonialism*. New York: Monthly Review Press.

Chen, G.-m. (1998) Understanding the Chinese: a harmony theory of Chinese communication. Paper presented at the annual conference of the National Communication Association, New York.

Chen, G.-m. (2002) The impact of harmony on Chinese conflict management. In G.-m. Chen and R. Ma (eds), *Chinese Conflict Management and Resolution*. Westport, CT: Ablex Publishing, pp. 3–17.

Chilton, P. (2002) *Language, Politics and Discourse*. London: Sage.

Chouliaraki, L. and N. Fairclough (1999) *Discourse in Late Modernity: Rethinking Critical Discourse Analysis*. Edinburgh: Edinburgh University Press.

Chow, R. (1992) Between colonizers: Hong Kong's postcolonial self-writing in the 1990s. *Diaspora*, 2 (2): 152–70.

Clark, K. and M. Holquist (1984) *Mikhail Bakhtin*. Cambridge, MA: Harvard University Press.

Clifford, J. (1986) Introduction: partial truths. In J. Clifford and G. Marcus (eds), *Writing Culture: The Poetics and Politics of Ethnography*. Berkeley, CA: University of California Press, pp. 1–26.

Clifford, J. (1988) *The Predicament of Culture: Twentieth-century Ethnography, Literature, and Art*. Cambridge, MA: Harvard University Press.

Clifford, J. (1992) Traveling cultures. In L. Grossberg, C. Nelson and P.A. Treichler (eds), *Cultural Studies*. New York: Routledge, pp. 96–116.

Clifford, J. (1997) *Routes: Travel and Translation in the Late Twentieth Century*. Cambridge, MA: Harvard University Press.

Clifford, J. and G. Marcus (eds) (1986) *Writing Culture*. Berkeley, CA: University of California Press.

Crotty, M. (1998) *The Foundations of Social Research: Meaning and Perspective in the Research*. London: Sage Publications.

Culler, J. (1983) *On Deconstruction: Theory and Criticism after Structuralism*. London: Routledge & Kegan Paul Ltd.

Cushner, K. and R.W. Brislin (1996) *Intercultural Interactions: A Practical Guide*, 2nd edn. Thousand Oaks: Sage Publications.

Derrida, J. (1976) *Of Grammatology* (trans. G.C. Spivak). Baltimore, MD: Johns Hopkins University Press.

Derrida, J. (1981) *Positions*. Chicago, IL: University of Chicago Press.

Dissanayake, W. (ed.) (1988) *Communication Theory: The Asian Perspective*. Singapore: Asian Mass Communication Research and Information Center.

Duncan, D. and D. Ley (eds) (1993) *Place, Culture, Representation*. London: Routledge.

Duranti, A. (1997) *Linguistic Anthropology*. Cambridge: Cambridge University Press.

Duranti, A. and C. Goodwin (1992) *Rethinking Context: Language as an Interactive Phenomenon*. Cambridge: Cambridge University Press.

During, S. (1987) Postmodernism or post-colonialism today. *Textual Practice*, 1 (1): 19–43.

During, S. (1999) *The Cultural Studies Reader*, 2nd edn. London: Routledge.

Eagleton, T. (1983) *Literary Theory: An Introduction*. Oxford: Basil Blackwell.

Eagleton, T. (1991) *Ideology: An Introduction*. London: Verso.

Edelman, M. (1988) *Constructing the Political Spectacle*. Chicago, IL: University of Chicago Press.

Edwards, D. and J. Potter (1992) *Discursive Psychology*. London: Sage Publications.

Fabian, J. (1983) *Time and the Other: How Anthropology Makes its Object*. New York: Columbia University Press.

Fairclough, N. (1989) *Language and Power*. London: Longman.

Fairclough, N. (1992) *Discourse and Social Change.* Cambridge: Polity Press.

Fairclough, N. (1995) *Critical Discourse Analysis: The Critical Study of Language.* London: Longman.

Fanon, F. (1967) *The Wretched of the Earth.* London: Penguin Books.

Fanon, F. (1986) *Black Skin, White Masks* (trans. C.L. Markmann). London: Pluto Press.

Farganis, S. (1986) *Social Reconstruction of the Feminine Character.* Totowa, NJ: Rowman & Littlefield.

Fenton, S., J. Carter and T. Modood (2000) Ethnicity and academia: closure models, racism models and market models. *Sociological Research Online*, 5 (2): http://www.socresonline.org.uk/5/2fenton.html.

Feyerabend, P. (1993) *Against Method*, 3rd edn. London: Verso.

Flowerdew, J. and R. Scollon (1997) Public discourse in Hong Kong and the change of sovereignty. *Journal of Pragmatics*. 28: 417–26.

Foucault, M. (1970) *The Order of Things: An Archaeology of the Human Sciences.* New York: Vintage Books.

Foucault, M. (1972) *The Archaeology of Knowledge and the Discourse on Language* (trans. A.M. Sheridan Smith). New York: Pentheon Books.

Foucault, M. (1980) *Power/Knowledge: Selected Interviews & Other Writings 1972–1977* (ed. Colin Gordon). New York: Pentheon Books.

Foucault, M. (1985) *The Uses of Pleasure: The History of Sexuality*, Vol. 2 (trans. R. Hurley). London: Penguin Books.

Foucault, M. (1986) *The Uses of Pleasure: The History of Sexuality*, Vol. 2. (trans. R. Hurley). London: Penguin Books.

Foucault, M. (1987) *The Care of the Self: The History of Sexuality*, Vol 3. London: Penguin.

Foucault, M. (1999) Space, power and knowledge. In S. During (ed.), *The Cultural Studies Reader.* London: Routledge, pp. 134–41.

Fowler, R. (1985) Power. In T.A. van Dijk (ed.), *Handbook of Discourse Analysis*, Vol. 4. London: Academic Press, pp. 61–82.

Fowler, R., B. Hedge, G. Kress and H. Drew (eds) (1979) *Language and Control.* London: Routledge & Kegan Paul.

Freire, P. (1972) *Pedagogy of the Oppressed.* Harmondsworth: Penguin.

Freire, P. (1976) *Education: The Practice of Freedom.* London: Writers & Readers Publishing Cooperative.

Freire, P. (1985) *The Politics of Education: Culture, Power and Liberation.* London: Macmillan.

Fung Y.-L. (1948) *A Short History of Chinese Philosophy* (ed. D. Bodde). New York: The Free Press.

Gadamer, H.G. (1989) *Truth and Method*, 2nd, rev. edn (trans. revised by J. Weinsheimer and D.G. Marchall). London: Sheed & Ward.

Gee, J.P. (1999) *An Introduction to Discourse Analysis: Theory and Method.* London: Routledge.

Geertz, C. (1973) *The Interpretation of Cultures: Selected Essays.* New York: Basic Books.

Gergen, K. (1994) *Realities and Relationships: Soundings in Social Construction.* Cambridge, MA: Harvard University Press.

Gergen, K. (1999) *An Invitation to Social Construction.* London: Sage Publications.

Giddens, A. (1976) *New Rules of Sociological Method: A Positive Critique of Interpretative Sociologies*. New York: Basic Books.

Giddens, A. (1984) *The Constitution of Society: Outline of the Theory of Structuration*. Cambridge: Polity Press.

Giddens, A. (1991) *Modernity and Self-identity: Self and Society in the Late Modern Age*. Cambridge: Polity Press.

Gilbert, G.N. and M. Mulkay (1984) *Opening Pandora's Box: A Sociological Analysis of Scientists' Discourse*. Cambridge: Cambridge University Press.

Gill, R. (1995) Relativism, reflexivity and politics: interrogating discourse analysis from a feminist perspective. In S. Wilkinson and C. Kitzinger (eds), *Feminism and Discourse: Psychological Perspectives*. London: Sage Publications, pp. 165–86.

Gilroy, P. (1987/2002) *There Ain't No Black in the Union Jack: The Cultural Politics of Race and Nation*. London: Routledge.

Gilroy, P. (1990) It ain't where you're from, it's where you are at . . . : the dialectics of diasporic identification. *Third Text*, 13 (Winter): 3–16.

Gilroy, P. (1992) Cultural Studies and ethnic absolutism. In L. Grossberg, C. Nelson and P.A. Treichler (eds), *Cultural Studies*. New York: Routledge, pp. 187–97.

Giorgi, A. (1970) *Psychology as a Human Science: A Phenomenologically Based Approach*. New York: Harper & Row.

Giroux, H.A. (1992) Resisting difference: cultural studies and the discourse of critical pedagogy. In L. Grossberg, C. Nelson and P.A. Treichler (eds), *Cultural Studies*. New York: Routledge, pp. 199–211.

Goatly, A. (1997) *The Language of Metaphors*. New York: Routledge.

Goffman, E. (1974) *Frame Analysis: An Essay on the Organization of Experience*. New York: Harper & Row.

Grace, G. (1987) *The Linguistic Construction of Reality*. London: Croom Helm.

Greenblatt, S. (1991) *Marvelous Possessions: The Wonder of the New World*. Chicago, IL: University of Chicago Press.

Grice, H.P. (1975) Logic and conversation. In P. Cole and J.L. Morgan (eds), *Syntax and Semantics 3: Speech Acts*. New York: Academic Press, pp. 41–58.

Grossberg, L. (1996) Identity and cultural studies: is that all there is? In S. Hall and P. du Gay (eds), *Questions of Cultural Identity*. London: Sage Publications, pp. 87–107.

Gumperz, J. (1982) *Discourse Strategies*, Cambridge: Cambridge University Press.

Gumperz, J. and S. Levinson (1996) (eds) *Rethinking, Linguistic Relativity*. Cambridge, NY: Cambridge University Press.

Habermas, J. (1972) *Knowledge and Human Interests* (trans. and Introduction T. McCarthy). Cambridge: Polity Press.

Habermas, J. (1976) *Communication and the Evolution of Society* (trans. J. J. Shapiro). London: Heinemann.

Habermas, J. (1984) *The Theory of Communicative Action, Vol. I: Reason and the Rationalization of Society* (trans. T. McCarthy). Boston, MA: Beacon Press.

Habermas, J. (1987) *The Theory of Communicative Action, Vol. II: Lifeword and System: A Critique of Functionalist Reason* (trans. T. McCarthy). Oxford: Polity Press.

Hall, S. (1977) Culture, the media and the 'ideological effect'. In J. Curran, M. Gurevitch and J. Woollacott (eds), *Mass Communication and Society*. London: Edward Arnold.

Hall, S. (1981) Encoding/decoding. In S. Hall, D. Hobson, A. Lowe and P. Willis, *Culture, Media, Language.* London: Hutchinson.

Hall, S. (1990) Cultural identity and diaspora. In J. Rutherford (ed.), *Identity: Community, Culture, Difference.* London: Lawrence & Wishart, pp. 222–37.

Hall, S. (1992) The question of cultural identity. In S. Hall, D. Held and T. McGrew (eds), *Modernity and its Futures.* Cambridge: Polity Press.

Hall, S. (1996a) Cultural studies: two paradigms. In J. Storey (ed.), *What is Cultural Studies? A Reader.* London: Arnold, pp. 31–48.

Hall, S. (1996b) Introduction: who needs 'identity'. In S. Hall and P. du Gay (eds), *Questions of Cultural Identity.* London: Sage Publications, pp. 1–17.

Hall, S. (1996c) Marxism without guarantees. In D. Morley and K.-H. Chen (eds), *Stuart Hall.* London: Routledge.

Hall, S. (ed.) (1997) *Representations: Cultural Representation and Signifying Practices.* London: Open University.

Hall, S. (1999) Cultural studies and its theoretical legacies. In S. During, (ed.), *The Cultural Studies Reader.* London: Routledge, pp. 97–109. (Also in L. Grossberg, *et al.* (eds) 1992, *Cultural Studies.* London: Routledge.)

Hammersley, M. (1992) *What's Wrong with Ethnography? Methodological Explorations.* London: Routledge.

Hammersley, M. and P. Atkinson (1995) *Ethnography: Principles in Practice.* London: Routledge.

Harding, S. (eds.) (1987) *Feminism and Methodology.* Milton Keynes: Open University Press.

Harré, R. and G. Gillett (1994) *Discursive Mind.* London: Sage Publications.

Harrison, N. (2003) *Postcolonial Criticism: History, Theory and the Work of Fiction.* Cambridge: Polity Press.

Hart, R. www.stanford.edu/dept/HPS/RethinkingSciCiv/etexts/Hart/BeyondSciCiv.html.

Heidegger, M. (1962) *Being and Time* (trans. J. Macquarrie and E. Robinson). Oxford: Blackwell.

Heisey, D.R. (ed.) (2000) *Chinese Perspectives in Rhetoric and Communication.* Stamford, CA: Ablex.

Heritage, J. (1984) *Garfinkel and Ethnomethodology.* Cambridge: Polity Press.

Hodge, R. and G. Kress (1988) *Social Semiotics.* Oxford: Polity Press.

Hodge, R. and G. Kress (1993) *Language as Ideology.* London: Routledge.

Hofstede, G. (1980) *Culture's Consequences: International Differences in Work-related Values.* Newbury Park, CA: Sage.

Hoggart, R. (1958) *The Uses of Literacy.* Harmondsworth: Penguin.

Horkheimer, S.P. (1982) *Critical Theory: Selected Essays.* New York: Continuum.

Huntington, S.P. (1998) *The Clash of Civilizations and the Remaking of World Order.* London: Touchstone Books.

Husserl E. (1931) *Ideas: General Introduction to Pure Phenomenology.* London: George Allen and Unwin Ltd.

Hutcheon, L. (1989) Circling the downspout of empire: post-colonialism and postmodernism. *Ariel*, 20 (4).

Hymes, D. (1974) *Foundations in Sociolinguistics: An Ethnographic Approach.* Philadelphia, PA: University of Pennsylvania Press.

Jenks, C. (1993) *Culture.* London: Routledge.

Jessor, R., A. Coby and R.A. Shweder (1996) *Ethnography and Human Development: Context and Meaning in Social Inquiry.* Chicago, IL: University of Chicago Press.

Keesing, R.M. (1991) Asian cultures? *Asian Studies Review,* 15 (2): 43–50.

Kincaid, D.L. (ed.) (1987) *Communication Theory: Eastern and Western Perspectives.* San Diego, CA: Academic Press.

Kluver, R. (2000) Globalization, information and intercultural communication. *American Communication Journal,* 3 (3): 72–95.

Knight, A. and Y. Nakano (eds) (1999) *Reporting Hong Kong: Foreign Media and the Handover.* London: Curzon.

Knorr-Cetina, K.D. (1981) *The Manufacture of Knowledge: An Essay on the Constructivist and Contextual Nature of Science.* Oxford: Pergamon.

Koole, T. and Ten Thije, J. (1994) *The Construction of Intercultural Discourse. Team Discussions of Educational Advisers.* Amsterdam: RODOPI.

Kress, G. (1991) Critical discourse analysis. *Annual Review of Applied Linguistics,* 11: 84–99.

Kress, G. and R. Hodge (1979) *Language as Ideology.* London: Routledge & Kegan Paul.

Kuhn, J.S. (1970) *The Structure of Scientific Revolutions.* Chicago, IL: University of Chicago Press. 2nd ed.

Laclau, E. and C. Mouffe (1985/2001) *Hegemony and Socialist Strategy: Towards a Radical Democratic Politics,* 2nd edn (trans. W. Moore and P. Cammack). London: Verso.

Lee, C.-C. (ed.) (1994) *China's Media, Media's China.* Boulder, CO: Westview Press.

Lee, C.-C. (2000) The paradox of political economy: media structure, press freedom and regime change in Hong Kong. In C. Lee (ed.), *Power, Money and Media: Communication Patterns and Bureaucratic Control in Cultural China.* Evanston, IL: Northwestern University Press.

Lee, C.-C., J.M. Chan, Z.-D. Pan and C.Y.K. So (2002) *Global Media Spectacle: News War over Hong Kong.* Hong Kong: Hong Kong University Press.

Lee, D. (1992) *Competing Discourses: Perspective and Ideology in Language.* London: Longman.

Liu, Y. (1996) To capture the essence of Chinese rhetoric: anatomy of a paradigm in comparative rhetoric. *Rhetoric Review,* 14 (1): 318–34.

Lucy, J. (1992) *Language Diversity and Thought: A Reformulation of the Linguistic Relativity Hypothesis.* Cambridge: Cambridge University Press.

Lutz, C.A. (1988) *Unnatural Emotions: Everyday Sentiments on a Micronesian Atoll and Their Challenge to Western Theory.* Chicago, IL: The University of Chicago Press.

Lyotard, J.-F. (1984) *The Postmodern Condition.* Minneapolis, MA: University of Minnesota Press.

Maier, R. (ed.) (1989) *Norms in Argumentation.* Dordrecht: Foris Publications.

Malinowski, B. (1936) The problem of meaning in primitive languages. Supplement 1 to C.K. Ogden and I.A. Richards, *The Meaning of Meaning.* London: Kegan Paul, pp. 296–336.

Marshall, C. and G.B. Rossman (1995) *Designing Qualitative Research,* 2nd edn. London: Sage Publications.

May, S. (2001) *Language and Minority Rights: Ethnicity, Nationalism and the Politics of Language.* London: Longman.

May, T. (1996) *Situating Social Theory*. Buckingham/Philadelphia, PA: Open University Press.

McGarry, J. and B. O'Leary (1995) *Explaining Northern Ireland: Broken Images*. Oxford: Blackwell.

McPhail, M. (1994) The politics of complicity: second thoughts about the social construction of racial equality. *Quarterly Journal of Speech*, 80: 343–57.

McPhail, M. (1998) From complicity to coherence: rereading the rhetoric of afrocentricity. *Western Journal of Communication*, 62: 114–40.

McQuail, D. (2000) *Mass Communication Theory*, 4th edn. London: Sage Publications.

Merleau-Ponty, M. (1974) *Phenomenology of Perception*. London: Routledge.

Mey, J.L. (1985) *Whose Language? A Study in Linguistic Pragmatics*. Amsterdam: John Benjamins.

Mey, J.L. (2001) *Pragmatics: An Introduction*, 2nd edn. Oxford: Blackwell.

Milhouse, V., M.K. Asante and P. Nwosu (2001) *Transcultural Realities*. London: Sage.

Mishra, V. and R. Hodge (1991) What is post(-)colonialism? *Textual Practice*, 5 (3): 399–414.

Mitchell, P. and R. Wilford (eds) (1999) *Politics in Northern Ireland*. Oxford: Westerview Press.

Montgomery, M. (1995) *An Introduction to Language and Society*. London: Routledge.

Moody, T.W. and F.X. Martin (eds) (1994) *The Course of Irish History*. Dublin: Mercier.

Moxon-Brown, E. (1991) National identity in Northern Ireland. In P. Stringer and G. Robinson (eds), *Social Attitudes in Northern Ireland: The First Report*. Belfast: Blackstaff Press.

Mulkay, M.J. (1979) *Science and the Sociology of Knowledge*. London: George Allen & Unwin.

Munck, R. and D. O'Hearn (1999) *Critical Development Theory: Contributions to a New Paradigm*. London: Zed Books.

Needham, J. (1954–95) *Science and Civilisation in China*. Cambridge: Cambridge University Press.

Newmeyer, F.J. (1986) *The Politics of Linguistics*. Chicago, IL: University of Chicago Press.

Ngũgĩ, w.-T. (1986) *Decolonising the Mind: The Politics of Language in African Literature*. London: James Currey.

Nietzsche, F. (1967) *The Will to Power* (ed. W. Kaufmann). New York: Vintage Books.

O'Leary, B. and J. McGarry (1993) *The Politics of Antagonism: Understanding Northern Ireland*. London: Athlone Press.

Pennycook, A. (1998) *English and the Discourses of Colonialism*. London: Routledge.

Polkinghorne, D. (1983) *Methodology for the Human Sciences: Systems of Inquiry*. Albany, NY: State University of New York Press.

Popper, K.R. (1959) *The Logic of Scientific Discovery*. London: Hutchinson.

Porter, N. (ed.) (1998) *The Republican Ideal: Current Perspectives*, 2nd edn. Belfast: Blackstaff Press.

Potter, J. (1996) *Representing Reality: Discourse, Rhetoric and Social Construction*. London: Sage Publications.

Potter, J. and M. Wetherell (1987) *Discourse and Social Psychology: Beyond Attitudes and Behaviour*. London: Sage Publications.

Pratt, M.L. (1992) *Imperial Eyes: Travel Writing and Transculturation*. London: Routledge.

Reddy, M. (1993) The conduit metaphor: a case of frame conflict in our language about language. In A. Ortony (ed.), *Metaphor and Thought*, 2nd edn. Cambridge: Cambridge University Press, pp. 164–201.

Reicher, S. and Hopkins, N. (2001) *Self and Nation*. London: Sage.

Renkema, J. (1993) *Discourse Studies: An Introductory Textbook*. Amsterdam: John Benjamins.

Richards, J.R. (1982) *The Sceptical Feminist: A Philosophical Enquiry*. Harmondsworth: Penguin.

Robbins, B. (1999) *Feeling Global: Internationalism in Distress*. New York: New York University Press.

Rorty, R. (1991) *Objectivity, Relativity, and Truth: Philosophical Papers*, Vol. 1. Cambridge: Cambridge University Press.

Rorty, R. (1998) *Achieving Our Country: Leftist Thought in Twentieth-century America*. Cambridge, MA: Harvard University Press.

Rushdie, S. (1992) *Imaginary Homeland*. London: Penguin Books.

Said, E. (1978) *Orientalism*. London: Routledge & Kegan Paul.

Said, E.W. (1993) *Culture and Imperialism*. New York: Alfred A. Knopf.

Sampson, E.E. (1989) The deconstruction of the self. In J. Shotter and K.J. Gergen (eds), *Texts of Identity*. London: Sage Publications, pp. 1–19.

Sapir, E. (1949) *Selected Writings in Language, Culture and Personality* (ed. D.G. Mandelbaum). Berkeley, CA: University of California Press.

Sarangi, S. (1994) Intercultural or not? Beyond celebration of cultural differences in miscommunication analysis. *Pragmatics*, 4 (3) 409–27.

Sarangi, S. (1995) Culture. In J. Verschueren, J.-O. Ostman and J. Blommaert (eds), *Handbook of Pragmatics*. Amsterdam: John Benjamins, pp. 1–30.

Sartre, J.-P. (1949) *Situations, I: Essays Critiqued*. Paris: Gallimard.

Sartre, J.-P. (1969) *Being and Nothingness: An Essay on Phenomenological Ontology*. London: Methuen.

Saussure, F. de (1966) *A Course in General Linguistics* (trans. W. Baskin). New York: McGraw-Hill.

Schegloff, E.A. (1981) Discourse as an interactional achievement: some uses of 'uh huh' and other things that come between sentences. In D. Tannen (ed.), *Analyzing Discourse: Text and Talk*. Washington, DC: Georgetown University Press.

Schiffrin, D. (1994) *Approaches to Discourse*. Oxford: Blackwell.

Scollon, R. and S.W. Scollon (1995) *Intercultural Communication: A Discourse Approach*. Oxford: Blackwell.

Searle, J. (1969) *Speech Acts*. Cambridge: Cambridge University Press.

Sesser, S. (1994) *The Lands of Charm and Cruelty: Travels in Southeast Asia*. New York: Alfred A. Knopf. (Including 'Singapore: the prisoner in the theme park', pp. 5–68.)

Shen, X.-L. (1999) *Shen Xiaolong Zi Xuan Ji* (Collected Essays by Shen Xiaolong). Guangxi shi fan da xue chu ban she (Guangxi Normal University Press, China).

Sherzer, J. (1987) A discourse-centred approach to language and culture. *American Anthropology*, 89: 295–309.

Shi-xu (1994) Ideology: strategies of reason and functions of control in accounts of the non-Western Other. *Journal of Pragmatics*, 21 (6): 645–69.

Shi-xu (1995) Cultural perceptions: exploiting the unexpected of the Other. *Culture and Psychology*, 1 (3): 315–42.

Shi-xu (1997) *Cultural Representations: Analyzing the Discourse about the Other*. New York: Peter Lang.

Shi-xu (2000a) Linguistics as metaphor: analysing the discursive ontology of the object of linguistic inquiry. *Language Sciences*, 22 (4): 423–46.

Shi-xu (2000b) Opinion discourse: investigating the paradoxical nature of the text and talk of opinions. *Research on Language and Social Interaction*, 33 (3): 263–89.

Shi-xu (2001) Critical pedagogy and intercultural communication: creating discourses of diversity, equality, common goals and rational-moral motivation. *Journal of Intercultural Studies*, 22 (3): 279–93.

Shi-xu and M. Kienpointner (2001) Culture as arguable: a discourse analytical approach to the international mass communication. *Pragmatics*, 11 (3): 285–307.

Shi-xu and J. Wilson (2001) Will and power: towards radical intercultural communication research and pedagogy. *Journal of Language and Intercultural Communication*, 1 (1): 1–18.

Shi-xu, M. Kienpointner and J. Servaes (eds) (2005) *Read the Cultural Other*. Berlin: Mouton.

Shneider, D.M. (1976) Notes toward a theory of culture. In K. Basso and H. Selby (eds), *Meaning in Anthropology*. Albuquerque, NM: University of New Mexico Press; pp. 197–220.

Shoot, J. (1993) *Conversational Realities: Constructing Life Through Language*. London: Sage Publication.

Shotter, J. (1993) *Conversational Realities: Constructing Life through Language*. London: Sage Publications.

Shotter, J. and K.J. Gergen (eds) (1989) *Texts of Identity*. London: Sage Publications.

Shweder, R.A. (1984) Culture Theory: Essays on Mind, Self and Emotion. Cambridge: Cambridge University Press.

Shweder, R.A. (1990) Cultural psychology – what is it? In J.W. Stigler, R.A. Shweder and G. Herdt (eds), *Cultural Psychology: Essays on Comparative Human Development*. Cambridge: Cambridge University Press, pp. 1–43.

Silverman, D. (1993) *Interpreting Qualitative Data: Methods for Analysing Talk, Text and Interaction*. London: Sage Publications.

Silverstein, M. and G. Urban (eds) (1996) *Natural Histories of Discourse*. Chicago, IL: University of Chicago Press.

Simons, H.W. (1989) *Rhetoric in the Human Sciences*. London: Sage Publications.

Soyland, A.H. (1994) *Psychology as Metaphor*. London: Sage Publications.

Spender, D. (1980) *Man Made Language*. London: Routledge.

Spivak, G.C. (1988a) *In Other Words: Essays in Cultural Politics*. New York: Routledge.

Spivak, G.C. (1988b) Can the subaltern speak? In C. Nelson and L. Grossberg (eds), *Marxism and the Interpretation of Culture*. London: Macmillan.

Stanley, L. and S. Wise (1983) *Breaking Out: Feminist Consciousness and Feminist Research*. London: Routledge & Kegan Paul.

Stratton, J. and I. Ang (1996) On the impossibility of a global cultural studies: 'British' cultural studies in an 'international' frame. In D. Morley and K.-H. Chen (eds), *Stuart Hall*. London: Routledge, pp. 361–91.

Stringer, P. and G. Robinson (eds) (1992) *Social Attitudes in Northern Ireland: The First Report*. Belfast: Blackstaff.

Surra, C.A. and C.A. Ridley (1991) Multiple perspectives on interaction: participants, peers, and observers. In B.M. Montgomery and S. Duck (eds), *Studying Interpersonal Interaction*. New York: Guilford Press, pp. 35–55.

Tannen, D. (1990) *You Just Don't Understand: Women and Men in Conversation*. New York: Ballantine.

Taylor, C. (1999) Two theories of modernity. *Public Culture*, 11 (1): 153–74.

Titscher, S., M. Meyer, R. Wodak and E. Vetter (2000) *Methods of Text and Discourse Analysis*. London: Sage Publications, pp. 5–17.

Tomic, A. (2000) A critical pedagogy for teaching intercultural communications to language learners. Paper presented at the International Conference on Sociolinguistics, Bristol, April 2000.

Tomlinson, J. (1991) *Cultural Imperialism: A Critical Introduction*. Baltimore, MD: Johns Hopkins University Press.

Tong, R. (1995) *Feminist Thought: A Comprehensive Introduction*. London: Routledge.

Tracy, K. (1995) Action-implicative discourse analysis. *Journal of Language and Social Psychology*, 14: 195–215.

Trinh, M.-h. (1991) *When the Moon Waxes Red*. New York: Routledge.

Trompenaars, F. (1993) *Riding the Waves of Culture: Understanding Cultural Diversity in Business*. London: Brealey Publishing.

Tu, W.-m. (1994) *The Living Tree: The Changing Meaning of Being Chinese Today*. Stanford, CA: Stanford University Press.

Urban, G. (1991) *A Discourse-Centered Approach to Culture: Native South American Myths and Rituals*. Austin, TX: University of Texas Press.

Valsiner, J. (1989) *Human Development and Culture: The Social Nature of Personality and its Study*. Lexington, MA: Lexington Books.

van Dijk, T.A. (ed.) (1985) *Handbook of Discourse Analysis*, Vols 1–4. London: Academic Press.

van Dijk, T.A. (1987) *Communicating Racism: Ethnic Prejudice in Thought and Talk*. Newbury Park, CA: Sage Publications.

van Dijk, T.A. (1993a) *Elite Discourse and Racism*. London: Sage Publications.

van Dijk, T.A. (1993b) Principles of Critical Discourse Analysis. *Discourse and Society*, 4 (2): 249–83.

van Dijk, T.A. (ed) (1997) *Discourse Studies: A Multidisciplinary Introduction*, Vols 1 and 2. London: Sage Publications.

van Eemeren, F. and R. Grootendorst (1992) *Argumentation, Communication, and Fallacies: A Pragma-dialectical Perspective*. Hillsdale, NJ: L. Erlbaum Associates Publishers.

van Eemeren, F. and R. Grootendorst (2004) *A Systematic Theory of Argumentation: The Pragma-dialectical Approach*. Cambridge: Cambridge University.

Verschueren, J. (1999) *Understanding Pragmatics*. London: Arnold.

Visser, C. (1982/1991) *Grijs China*. Amsterdam: Meulenhoff.

Visser, C. (1990) *Buigend Bamboe*. Amsterdam: Meulenhoff.

Vološinov, V.N. (1986) *Marxism and the Philosophy of Language*. Cambridge, MA: Harvard University Press.

von Humboldt, W. (1988) *On Language: The Diversity of Human Language-structure and Its Influence on the Mental Development of Mankind* (trans. P. Heath). Cambridge: Cambridge University Press.

West, C. (1993) *Keeping Faith: Philosophy and Race in America*. London: Routledge.

Wetherell, M. and J. Potter (1992) *Mapping the Language Racism: Discourse and Legitimation of Exploitation*. London: Sage Publications.

Wetherell, M., S. Taylor and S. Yates (2001) *Discourse Theory and Practice: A Reader*. London: Sage Publications.

White, H. (1973) *Metahistory: The Historical Imagination in Nineteenth-century Europe*. Baltimore, MD: Johns Hopkins University Press.

White, H. (1990) *The Content of the Form: Narrative Discourse and Historical Representation*. Baltimore, MD: Johns Hopkins University Press.

Whorf, B.L. (1956) *Language, Thought, and Reality: Selected Writings of Benjamin Lee Whorf* (ed. and Introduction J.B. Carroll). Cambridge, MA: MIT Press.

Widdicombe, S. and R. Wooffitt (1995) *The Language of Youth Subcultures*. London: Harvester Wheatsheaf.

Williams, P. and L. Chrisman (1993) *Colonial Discourse and Post-colonial Theory: A Reader*. New York: Harvester Wheatsheaf.

Williams, R. (1976) *Keywords*. London: Fontana (2nd edn 1983).

Williams, R. (1981) *Culture*. London: Fontana.

Willis, P. (1978) *Profane Culture*. London: Routledge & Kegan Paul.

Willis, P. (1980) Notes on method. In S. Hall, D. Hobson, A. Lowe and P. Willis (eds), *Culture, Media, Language*. London: Hutchinson.

Wittgenstein, L. (1968) *Philosophical Investigations*. Oxford: Basil Blackwell.

Wodak, R. (1996) *Disorders of Discourse*. London: Longman.

Wodak, R., R. de Cillia, M. Reisigl and K. Liebhart (1999) *The Discursive Construction of National Identity*. Edinburgh: Edinburgh University Press.

Woolgar, S. (1988) Reflexivity is the ethnographer of the text. In S. Woolgar (ed.), *Knowledge and Reflexivity: New Frontiers in the Sociology of Knowledge*. London: Sage, pp. 14–36.

Wuthnow, R. (1989) *Communities of Discourse*. Cambridge, MA: Harvard University Press.

www.apophaticmysticism.com/tttpractice.html

www.rwor.org/a/v20/970–79/970/luxun.htm

Young, L.W.L. (1994) *Crosstalk and Culture in Sino-American Communication*. New York: Cambridge University Press.

Young, R. (2001) *Postcolonialism: A Historical Introduction*. Oxford: Blackwell.

Zhong, X. (2002) *China, 2002*. Beijing: New Star Publishers.

Author Index

Adorno, T. 76
Ang, I. 48, 55, 64, 99
Antaki, C. and Widdicombe, S. 169
Appadurai, A. 67
Appiah, K. 55
Ashcroft, B. *et al.* 135
Atkinson, P. 89
Austin, J. 17, 171

Back, L. 32
Bakhtin, M. 35, 57, 66, 108
Barker, C. and Galasinski, D. 19, 26, 57, 88, 96, 135
Bauman, Z. 67
Bellah, R. *et al.* 63
Benjamin, W. 17, 171
Bennett, A. 68
Berger, P. and Luckmann, T. 23, 76
Bhabha, H. 55, 68, 99, 105, 109, 135
Billig, M. 17, 95, 169
Billig, M. *et al.* 96
Blommaert, J. 39, 87
Blommaert, J. and Verschueren, J. 57, 95, 202
Bloor, D. 53
Bloor, M. 87
Boas, F. 46
Bourdieu, P. 202
Bourdieu, P. and Wacquant, L. 33, 171
Briggs, A. 108
Brown, P. and Levinson, S. 32, 171
Burr, V. 23, 82
Butler, J. 10, 55, 76, 81, 167
Butler, J. and Scott 81

Cameron, D. 64
Cappella, J. 87

Carbaugh, D. 63
Carey, J. 16, 30, 46, 49, 63
Cassirer, E. 57
Centre for Contemporary Cultural Studies (CCCS) 52
Césaire, A. 134
Chen, G.-M. 30, 63
Chilton, P. 169
Chouliaraki, L. and Fairclough, N. 19, 167
Chow, R. 143
Clark, K. and Holquist, M. 108
Clifford, J. 25, 48, 65, 105, 108, 138
Clifford, J. and Marcus, G. 89
Confucius 85
Crotty, M. 72, 83
Culler, J. 80

Derrida, J. 35, 76, 79–80, 95, 168
Dilthey, W. 76
Duncan, D. and Ley, D. 108
Duranti, A. 57
Duranti, A. and Goodwin, C. 35–7, 57
During, S. 55, 89
Durkheim, E. 79

Eagleton, T. 67, 95
Edelman, M. 142

Fabian, J. 118
Fairclough, N. 35, 63, 66, 67, 95, 96, 169, 171
Fanon, F. 55, 66
Farganis, S. 205
Fenton, S. *et al.* 53
Feyerabend, P. 72, 75, 84
Flowerdew, J. and Scollon, R. 141

Foucault, M. 4, 17, 19, 28, 29, 33, 63, 76, 79–80, 83, 108, 168, 171
Fowler, R. 63
Fowler, R. *et al.* 17, 24
Freire, P. 66, 203, 205
Fung, Y.-L. 85

Gadamer, H. 39, 76, 78–9, 203
Geertz, C. 53, 56, 57, 98
Gergen, K. 16, 25, 29, 50, 76, 82, 168, 169
Giddens, A. 72, 169, 174, 202
Gilbert, G. and Mulkay, M. 79
Gill, R. 81, 100
Gilroy, P. 49, 55, 58, 99
Giorgi, A. 72
Giroux, H. 204
Goffman, E. 36
Gorky, M. 66
Grace, G. 16, 17, 25, 63
Greenblatt, S. 108
Grice, H. 32, 171
Grossberg, L. 167
Gumperz, J. 57, 61
Gumperz, J. and Levinson, S. 57, 62

Habermas, J. 32, 75, 76, 82–3, 171
Hall, S. 10, 17, 49, 52, 53, 55, 58, 92, 99, 109, 135, 167, 169
Hammersley, M. and Atkinson, P. 75, 89
Harding, S. 205
Harré, R. and Gillett, G. 20
Harrison, N. 55, 92
Hart, R. 83
Heidegger, M. 76, 77
Heritage, J. 35
Hodge, R. and Kress, G. 20
Hoggart, R. 52, 67
Horkheimer, S. 76
Huntington, S. 67
Husserl, E. 76, 77
Hutcheon, L. 55
Hymes, D. 36, 61

Jessor, R. *et al.* 89

Kluver, R. 57
Knight, A. and Nakano, Y. 141, 144
Knorr-Cetina, K. 53
Koole, T. and Ten Thije, J. 202
Kress, G. 17, 95
Kress, G. and Hodge, R. 23
Kuhn, J. 75

Laclau, E. and Mouffe, C. 19, 24
Lee, C.-C. 17, 141, 143, 144
Lee, C.-C. *et al.* 125, 141
Liu, Y. 63
Lucy, J. 62
Lutz, C. 57, 62
Lyotard, J.-F. 53, 76

Maier, R. 171
Malinowski, B. 30
Marshall, C. and Rossman, G. 75
May, T. 33, 171
McQuail, D. 57
Merleau-Ponty, M. 77
Mey, J. 17, 20, 36, 95, 194
Mishra, V. and Hodge, R. 55
Mulkay, M. 53
Munck, R. and O'Hearn, D. 137

Ngũgĩ, W.-T. 55, 64

Pennycook, A. 64
Polkinghorne, D. 72, 90, 101
Popper, K. 75
Potter, J. 23, 25
Potter, J. and Wetherell, M. 19, 25
Pratt, M. 92, 108

Reddy, M. 16
Reicher, S. and Hopkins, N. 169
Renkema, J. 19
Richards, J. 205
Robbins, B. 137
Rorty, R. 4, 59, 84, 96
Rushdie, S. 133

Said, E. 25, 55, 58, 64, 92, 105, 109, 134, 202
Sampson, E. 167
Sapir, E. 5
Sarangi, S. 57, 202
Sartre, J.-P. 77
Saussure, F. de 25, 79
Schegloff, E. 35
Schiffrin, D. 19
Searle, J. 17
Sesser, S. 111
Shen, X.-L. 65
Sherzer, J. 57, 62
Shi-xu 49, 95, 99, 108, 119, 135, 137, 140
Shi-xu and Kienpointner, M. 126, 141, 147
Shi-xu and Wilson, J. 49, 99, 137
Shi-xu *et al.* 125
Shneider, D. 56
Shotter, J. 20, 23, 35, 96
Shotter, J. and Gergen, K. 168
Shweder, R. 23, 167
Simons, H. 95
Spender, D. 76, 81
Spivak, G. 64, 105, 132
Stanley, L. and Wise, S. 76, 81, 100, 205
Suura, C. and Ridley, C. 100

Tannen, D. 63
Taylor, C. 48, 66, 171
Tomic, A. 202
Tomlinson, J. 109
Tong, R. 205
Tracy, K. 100
Trinh, M.-H. 99

Urban, G. 57, 62

Valsiner, J. 55
van Dijk, T. 19, 20, 58, 67, 90, 95, 109, 167, 169, 194
van Eemeren, F. and Grootendorst, R. 95
Verschueren, J. 20
Visser, C. 118
Vološinov, V. 24, 57, 60
von Humboldt, W. 5, 46

Weber, M. 79
West, C. 64, 67, 96
Wetherell, M. and Potter, J. 109
White, H. 25, 172
Whorf, B. 5, 25, 46, 62
Widdicombe, S. and Wooffitt, R. 89
Williams, P. and Chrisman, L. 135
Williams, R. 52
Willis, P. 89
Wittgenstein, L. 17, 44, 57, 61
Wodak, R. 19, 95
Wodak, R. *et al.* 169
Woolgar, S. 53
Wuthnow, R. 134

Xu, L. 66, 73

Young, L. 63
Young, R. 55, 92, 202

Zhong, X. 144
Zhuang, Zi 73, 85

Subject Index

agency 60, 172
anti-racist movement 31, 51

categorizations 79
colonialism 22, 50, 55
  neo-colonialism 55
consciousness
  critical 32, 66, 97, 203
  double-cultural 66
context 35–40
  interpersonal 38
  intersubjective 38
  situational 38–9
  symbolic 39
  the researcher's 39
  and understanding 36
contradiction 106–7
  and uncertainty 109–10
contrastive structure 113
conversation analysis 76
critical pedagogy 205
critical theory 76, 81–2
cultural imperialism 92–3, 98
cultural politics 1, 67–8, 71, 90,
  167
cultural studies 51–5
  of discourse 74
culture 2, 45–48, 50, 52–55, 201
  as discourse 56–7
  as history 55–6
  as hybridity 55–6
  interstitial space 59
  language-oriented approaches
    62
  third 207
  marginalization of 43, 48, 95

deconstructive strategies 91–6
definition 124
diasporicism 55–6
differance 35, 79
discourse 1, 19–22, 59–67
  aculturalism 44, 45–8

and reality 13, 22–7, 77
and relation 29–31
anti-imperialist 66
binary model 26
central characteristics 67
colonial 94, 208
community 165
constructing meaning 63
conventional notion 18
diversity of 62
description and action 27–9
evaluation 173
historical 171–2
identity 166
ideological 29, 60
imperialist 94, 201
language 5
linguistic communication 19,
  32; normative principles
  32
meta- 61
nationalist perspective 147
non-Western 132–9
norms and values 32
of objectivity 3
of universality 3
of war 3
pessimistic view 18
pluralist account 59–67, 72
reality-constitutive perspective
  13, 26
scientific 3, 45, 67, 73
self and relation 29–31
speech acts 28, 180
stereotyped sense 46
text and context 20
theoretical 42, 49
tradition and moral rationality
  31
'ways of speaking' 1, 2;
  patterns of speaking or
  writing 21
Western 141–3

discourse research strategies 71,
    89, 90–100
  deconstructive 73
  transformative 73
discourse studies 48–51, 75
  culture-specific origins 48–9
  universalism 44–5, 84
  whiteness 48–51

endangered languages and
    cultures 63
epithets 181
equality 208

feminism 76, 81
  feminist movement 31
form and meaning 168
foundationalism 74–6, 81
  reliability 74
  validity 74

globalization/localization 207

'handover' 154–5
hermeneutics 76, 78–9
history 32, 172–3
  colonial 139
  modern world 201

identity 29
  and subjectivity 167
  as discourse 167–70
  hybridity 56
in-between cultural perspective
    6, 43, 61, 63, 66, 67, 73,
    86–9
  advantages 88–9
intellectual 140
intentionality 77
intercultural communication
    200–4
  and power 202–4
  misunderstanding 203, 208
  understanding 203
intercultural competence 200–1
interpretation 39, 78
interpretivism 76–83

joint responsibility 209

knowledge 6, 75, 82
  and power 79
  and reality 82
  Chinese version 85–6
  constitution of 14
  stereotypical 116

language games 1
linguistic anthropology 62
linguistic relativity 62
linguistics 14
  modern western 75
  universalism and relativism
    14

meaning 1, 60, 74, 78, 80, 137
  and context 33–5
  and language 15
  construction 2, 21
  dialogical construction 33–5
  making 76
media interests 135
metaphor 117–18
method 71, 72–4
  universal form 87
methodology 72–4
  feminist 81
  imperialism 5
  interest 82–3
  non-Western 73
  research system 72
  Western bias 83–6
moral rationality 170–2, 203,
    209
multiculturalism 47

normative standards 82

Other 31, 94, 105, 132, 138,
    201
  attitudes toward 205
  discourse of 105, 205
  otherness 105
  place 108

phenomenology 77–8
plurality 207
political ethnography 89–91
post-colonial perspective 6

post-colonialism 55–6, 63
postmodernism 76, 79–80
post-structuralism 76, 79–80
power 28–9, 63, 65, 84, 201,
    208

re-articulation 80
reflexivity 6, 60, 66, 90
relations 30
    and self 28–31
representationalism 14–8, 72
    anti- 42
    mainstream scholarship 14
research
    cultural political priorities 7
    mode of 6, 7
    nature of 71
    social 82

scholarly community 3
science 16, 78, 83
    critical social 79–80
    Western 4
September 11, 2001 22, 37
social constructionism 76, 82–3
social movements 199
stereotype 109

strategic realism 10
structuralism 17, 25
    post- 17
subaltern 98
symbolic practices 3

transformative strategies 96–100

universal models 106
universalism 14, 72
universality 207
understanding 78

Verstehen 79

West(ern) 10, 92
    and whiteness 51
    as the norm 65
    materials and reality 72
world
    and linguistic communication
        15
    cultural 77
    external 26
    intentional 23, 77
    ordinary 2
    non-Western 132